An Introduction to
John of the Cross

When GODS Die

John Welch, O. Carm.

PAULIST PRESS
New York/Mahwah

Copyright © 1990 by John Welch

Library of Congress Cataloging-in-Publication Data

Welch, John, 1939–
    When gods die: an introduction to St. John of the Cross / by John Welch.
        p.   cm.
    Includes bibliographical references.
    ISBN 0-8091-3183-8
    1. John of the Cross, Saint, 1542–1591.   2. Spiritual life—History of doctrines—16th century.   I. Title.
    BX4700.J7W44   1990
    248.2'2'092—dc20   90-36759
                                                                                                             CIP

Published by Paulist Press
997 Macarthur Blvd.
Mahwah, N.J. 07430

Printed and bound in the
United State of America

CONTENTS

INTRODUCTION   1

CHAPTER ONE
  Who Was John of the Cross?   3

CHAPTER TWO
  The Imagination of John of the Cross   15

CHAPTER THREE
  John, a "Pioneer of Humanity"   30

CHAPTER FOUR
  Humanity Transformed
  The Living Flame of Love   45

CHAPTER FIVE
  Liberation of the Heart
  The Ascent of Mount Carmel, 1   70

CHAPTER SIX
  The Dark Night and Contemplative Prayer
  The Dark Night, 1   89

CHAPTER SEVEN
  Toward a Mature Faith
  The Ascent of Mount Carmel, 2, 3   118

CHAPTER EIGHT
  The Fear of Losing God
  The Dark Night, 2   149

CHAPTER NINE
   A Mystic's Story of Our Humanity
   The Spiritual Canticle   175

CONCLUSION   202

NOTES   207

SELECTED BIBLIOGRAPHY   222

INDEX   224

ACKNOWLEDGMENTS

The Publisher gratefully acknowledges use of the following materials: Excerpt from *The Collected Works of St. John of the Cross*, translated by Kieran Kavanaugh and Otilio Rodriguez. © 1979 by Washington Province of Discalced Carmelites, ICS Publications, 2131 Lincoln Road, N.E., Washington, D.C. 20002; excerpt from "The Mystics and the Development of Consciousness" and "The Imagination of John of the Cross" copyrighted in audio cassette form 1987 by Alba House Communications, Canfield, Ohio, 44406; excerpt from (Jung) *The Collected Works of C.G. Jung*, ed. Herbert Read, Michael Fordham, Gerhard Adler, William McGuire; trans. R.F.C. Hull. Bollingen series XX. Vol. 6: "Psychological Types," © 1971; Vol. 7: "Two Essays on Analytical Psychology, © 1953, 1966, © 1981 renewed; Vol. 8: "The Structure and Dynamics of the Psyche," © 1960, 1969, © 1988 renewed; Vol. 9, I: "The Archetypes and the Collective Unconscious," © 1959, 1969, 1972, © renewed 1987; Vol. 11: "Psychology and Religion: West and East," © 1958, 1969, © renewed 1986; Vol. 12: "Psychology and Alchemy," © 1953, 1968, © renewed 1981; Vol. 14: "Mysterium Coniunctionis," © 1965, 1970, by Princeton University Press. Excerpt from *C.G. Jung Speaking: Interviews and Encounters*, edited by William McGuire and R.F.C. Hull, Bollingen Series XCVII. Copyright © 1975 by Princeton University Press. Excerpts from *C.G. Jung Letters: 1951–1961*, ed. Gerhard Adler and Aniela Jaffe, trans. R.F.C. Hull, Bollingen Series XCV. Copyright © 1953, © 1975 by Princeton University Press. "The Mercy of God," a poem from *Selected Poetry of Jessica Powers*, by Siegfried and Morneau. Used with permission of Sheed and Ward, 115 East Armour Boulevard, Kansas City, Mo. Excerpt from *Religious Education Development*, by Gabriel Moran. Copyright © 1983 by Gabriel Moran. Reprinted by permission of Harper and Row, Publishers, Inc. Excerpt from *Becoming Adult, Becoming Christian: Adult Development and Christian Faith*, by James W. Fowler III. Copyright © 1984 by James W. Fowler III. Reprinted by permission of Harper and Row, Publishers Inc.

To my sisters and brothers of the Carmelite Forum:

Donald Buggert
Kevin Culligan
Keith Egan
Constance FitzGerald
Kieran Kavanaugh
Thomas Kilduff (dec.)
Ernest Larkin
Vilma Seelaus

INTRODUCTION

This work is an introduction to the writings and spirituality of John of the Cross, the sixteenth-century Spanish Carmelite mystic. It summarizes his teachings, and then discusses them in contemporary language.

The writings studied are the four major works of John: *The Ascent of Mount Carmel, The Dark Night, The Spiritual Canticle* and *The Living Flame of Love.* These writings are a combination of three poems and their prose commentaries. Together they communicate the rich spiritual teachings of the saint.

This book uses as an integrating theme the "imagination" of John of the Cross, who wrote poetry as the first expression of his experience of God. John's imagination conjures symbolic images which catch the glint of God in the dark of his experience. His language of image is an archetypal language which often expresses the reader's own desires and journey.

The first chapter provides a brief biography of John of the Cross. It describes a prayerful man who was also reformer, administrator, and writer. A knowledge of John's life often helps in interpreting his writings.

The second chapter specifically focuses on the imagination of John of the Cross and tries to track his psyche's movement from an unwordable experience of God, through its poetic expression, to the meaning expressed in his commentary.

In keeping with the theme of John's imagination, the third chapter relates the experience of God to the evolution of humanity and the coming of consciousness in the psyche. The mystic's psyche is sensitively attuned to Mystery.

John's commentaries, and the spirituality they contain, are the focus of the remaining chapters of the book. These chapters have two parts: the first is a summary of a particular commentary, the second a reflection on aspects of that work.

The summaries of John's writings stay close to the language of the translation. John's language is initially foreign to a contemporary ear, but the reader may eventually find it uniquely expressive.

My reflections on his spirituality use understandings and categories from studies of human and religious development. Carl Jung, Bernard Lonergan, James Fowler and Gabriel Moran are among the authors cited. Their studies and insights illumine the spirituality of John of the Cross, and they are themselves illumined by the Carmelite mystic.

It is a contention of this work that the writings of John of the Cross are particularly apt for adults who are looking for a spirituality with substance. John speaks about the fundamental spiritual journey which grounds and accompanies adult maturation. His spirituality remains ahead of us, challenging us to let go of the known and walk in trust.

CHAPTER ONE

Who Was John of the Cross?

John was born in Fontiveros, Spain, in 1542; he died at Ubeda in 1591.[1] Just fifty years before John's birth, Ferdinand and Isabella had united Spain when they drove the Moors from Granada. Granada was the last Moorish stronghold after an 800-year presence in Spain. In that same year of 1492 Columbus sailed for the Indies.

John lived in a sixteenth-century Spain which exercised great influence in Europe, and which was also vigorously exploring the New World. Among the explorers of South America were the brothers of Teresa of Avila.

John's father, Gonzalo de Yepes, was from a family of silk merchants in Toledo. They were probably "conversos," Jewish converts to Christianity. John's mother was Catalina Alvarez, a weaver, who was also originally from Toledo. Gonzalo and Caterina met and married in Fontiveros and there began a family.

John was the youngest of three brothers. When he was three years old his father died, and the family became destitute. Gonzalo's relatives were not able to help the family so Catalina and her sons attempted to earn a living as weavers. Luis, the middle brother, died when John was eight or nine.

The family moved to Medina del Campo, northwest of Madrid, when John was nine years old. The city bustled with merchants and trade fairs. John learned to read and write in a school for orphans and the poor, the Colegio de la Doctrine. He served mass at the Convento de la Magdalena, home for the Augustinian nuns.

John was asked to work in a local hospital, Nuestra Señora de la Concepción (Las Bubas), by the administrator Don Alonso Alvarez de Toledo. The hospital had 45 to 50 beds and it served the poor who had ulcers and contagious diseases. John worked as a male nurse, feeding,

3

bathing, and changing bandages when necessary. He worked with these
suffering people during his sensitive adolescent years, "telling stories
and singing songs." He collected food and money for the hospital during
the trade fairs.

While he was working in the hospital, John also began to attend a
new Jesuit school. One of the Jesuits, Juan Bonifacio, became his men-
tor. For four years, between the ages of seventeen and twenty-one, he
studied metaphysics, Latin and Spanish classics, among other subjects.
He learned literary technique, and wrote his own compositions and
poems. In these years he "grew" to a height of just under five feet.

The administrator of the hospital, Don Alvarez, wanted John to be
ordained and serve in the hospital as chaplain. For whatever reason this
suggestion did not appeal to John and he left the hospital to enter the
Carmelite Convento de Santa Ana in Medina del Campo in 1563. He
was twenty-one years old. John immediately entered the novitiate.

The Book of the First Monks

In the novitiate John probably studied the *Liber de institutione pri-
morum monachorum*, also known as *The Book of the First Monks*, a work
mandated for all Carmelite novitiates.[2] This work was the first synthesis
of Carmelite spirituality, and is second only to the *Rule of Carmel* in its
importance in formulating the spiritual tradition of Carmel. It purports
to have been written in Greek in 412 by John XLIV, Bishop of Jerusalem. However, it is actually dated at approximately 1370, and is perhaps
a collection of literature that had been developed in the order over the
previous one hundred years. The author is thought to be Philip Ribot
from Catalonia who died in 1391.

The work takes the form of a letter from the Bishop of Jerusalem,
who supposedly had been a hermit on Mount Carmel, to a young Carmelite, Caprasius. It tells the spirit and "history" of Carmel and roots
the foundational charism of Carmel firmly in the prophet Elijah and the
Blessed Virgin Mary.

Central to the account in the *Institutio* (meaning foundation or way
of life), or *The Book of the First Monks*, is the instruction given to Elijah
in 1Kgs 17:3–4: "Depart from hence, go eastward, and hide in the brook
Carith, which is over against the Jordan. There you shall drink of the
torrent, and I have commanded the ravens to feed you there."

In commenting on this text the author shows that Carmelite life
requires a detachment which is a freedom of heart (Depart from hence),
a renunciation of sin and self-will (go eastward), a life of love of God and

neighbor (hide in the brook Carith, which through a Latin pun is related to hide in "caritate," or love). There the Carmelite will experience God (drinking the torrent and being fed by ravens).

The great themes and symbols of the Carmelite tradition are presented in this work, establishing a powerful myth for the order. The ascetical ideal, offering to God a pure and holy heart, opens to the mystical ideal, experiencing in mind and heart the presence of God which is pure gift.

Vows, Ordination, and Teresa's Reform

John had a deep love for silence and solitude, but he was thought to be too devout and too severe by the members of the community. Nevertheless, he took vows in 1564, with Don Alvarez present. His name became Juan de Santo Matía.

In that same year five hundred Carmelites met in Rome at a General Chapter which was to inaugurate the Counter-Reformation in the order. John Baptist Rossi (Rubeo) was elected General by the forty-two Definitors. By this time Teresa of Avila had already begun a renewal among the Carmelite nuns and had founded the first convent of the reform, St. Joseph's of Avila, in 1562.

The Carmelites sent John to study at the University of Salamanca. From 1564 to 1567 he was listed by the university as an Arts student, and from 1567 to 1568 he was listed as a priest and theologian. At the time Salamanca had seven thousand students; seven hundred and fifty were studying theology. The students composed their own songs in the Castilian language, since the vernacular was emphasized.

John resided at the Carmelite College of San Andrés on the banks of the Tormes river. There he was also prefect of studies, which meant he had to conduct some classes, and defend theses. Later, in the university cities of Alcalá and Baeza, he was noted for his knowledge of scripture, the Fathers, and theology. At San Andrés, again, John's severe asceticism disturbed others in the community.

John was ordained in 1567 at the age of twenty-five, but his sense of distance from other community members and his deep contemplative nature led him to consider joining the Carthusians at Monasterio Paular near Segovia. John Rossi, the new General, came to Avila in that same year. He encouraged Teresa to continue her reform of the Carmelite sisters, and authorized the founding of two reformed communities of men.

When John of the Cross went to Medina del Campo for his first

Mass, a companion, Fray Pedro de Orozco, arranged for John to meet
Teresa of Avila. She was in Medina del Campo attempting to begin a
second convent of the reform. Teresa was fifty-two years old. The local
Carmelite prior, Fray Antonio de Heredia, had resolved to join the
Carthusians, but Teresa encouraged him to assist in the reform of the
friars. She was unsure of the next step until she met John. Teresa writes
of their first meeting:

> A little later it happend that a young Father came there who
> was studying at Salamanca. He came along with another, as his
> companion, who told me great things about the life this Father
> was leading. The young Father's name was Fray John of the
> Cross. I praised our Lord. And when I spoke with this young
> friar, he pleased me very much. I learned from him how he also
> wanted to go to the Carthusians. Telling him what I was at-
> tempting to do, I begged him to wait until the Lord would give
> us a monastery and pointed out the great good that would be
> accomplished if in his desire to improve he were to remain in
> his own order and that much greater service would be ren-
> dered to the Lord. He promised me he would remain as long as
> he wouldn't have to wait long. When I saw that I already had
> two friars to begin with, it seemed to me the matter was taken
> care of. . . .[3]

John returned to Salamanca to finish his study of theology, and
await the beginning of the reform of the friars.

In the year following his ordination and the meeting with Teresa,
John, with four others, began a reformed house of friars at Duruelo, not
far from Avila. They renounced the mitigated (modified) Carmelite
Rule, took the "Primitive" Rule which Teresa believed was the original
rule, and John became Fray Juan de la Cruz. Fray Antonio was prior;
John was master of novices. They combined a strict contemplative life-
style with preaching in nearby towns. John's mother, brother, and sis-
ter-in-law joined the community at Duruelo.

The Carmelites

Teresa's reform, and John's community at Duruelo were an attempt to return to the original conditions existing on Mount Carmel
when the Carmelites were founded. The original Carmelites were men
who went into a deserted place, the wadi 'Ain es-Siah on Mount Carmel
in Israel, to be alone with God. They were followers of Jesus Christ.

They lived in his land and identified with his obedient journey to the cross.

These men shared their vision and lives. Fraternity became an integral part of being a Carmelite. The formula of life, written by Albert, the Patriarch of Jerusalem, sometime between 1206 and 1214, was given to a community of men who were to choose their leader, share goods in common, build an oratory where they would celebrate daily eucharist, and have regular community meetings. The description in *Acts* of the church in Jerusalem finds an echo in Albert's words. Present-day Carmelites are the descendents of "Brother B.," who is cryptically addressed in the Rule, and the men gathered with him by the well of Elijah.

These men were, apparently, predominantly lay people who were part of an eleventh to thirteenth century movement to return to the gospels as the first Rule.[4] They were probably in the state or order of "penance" or "conversion," meaning they had made a break with their former lives and had converted to a religious way of living. These men were hermits who "went apart" as part of their conversion. They were also pilgrims, traveling to the periphery of society and the church, living in allegiance to Jesus Christ in the Holy Land, his patrimony.

Albert's formula for life which became Carmel's Rule provides an early vision of Carmel in its long process of maturation. It speaks especially of the original conditions of prayer, solitude, and fraternity. But Carmel's growth continued.

Shortly after the beginnings on Mount Carmel in the Holy Land, Carmelites began foundations in Europe, some as early as the 1230s. Pressure on the original community increased as Moslems and Christians struggled for control of the Holy Land. In the first decades of Carmel's existence, men in Europe engaged in ministry. As they were drawn more and more into the mendicant movement the Rule continued to develop to recognize new realities.

The Rule as mitigated by Innocent IV in 1247 acknowledged Carmel's transformation by allowing foundations "in solitary places, or where you are given a site that is suitable and convenient...." The hermits became friars. They were called to the mobility of the mendicants, and to activities which built up the church. They were with the people, teaching, preaching, counseling, and were noted for institutional poverty. It was to this Rule, already adapted, which Teresa returned, thinking it was the original or "primitive" Rule.

The order argued about life-style in the thirteenth century when Nicholas the Frenchman was Prior General. He feared that Carmelites in the newly emerging cities were too rustic and simple for the struggle in the city. Carmel's salvation was in solitude, he counseled.

But men continued to respond to the Spirit and the church. By the end of the thirteenth century Carmelites were living mendicant life-styles in the cities as well as eremitical life-styles in the desert. After a sometimes tenuous existence in its first century, Carmel was finally and firmly juridically established by Boniface VIII in 1298. By that time all Carmelites had left Mount Carmel. The mature Carmel was no longer only the Carmel of the wadi. Smet captures the perennial paradox within Carmel: "While Carmel launched full sail on the sea of apostolic activity, its spiritual literature remained that of the desert."[5]

After Duruelo: Avila and the Incarnation

After a year in the harsh setting of Duruelo, John and the whole community moved to Mancera de Abajo. John also helped establish a novitiate in another reformed house in Pastrana in 1570, and after approximately a month in Pastrana he was named Rector of the Colegio de San Cyrilo in Alcalá de Henares in 1571. Interestingly, at one point John returned to Pastrana to restore moderate ascetical practices after a superior had introduced extreme exerises.

In 1571 an Apostolic Commissioner appointed Teresa prioress of the Incarnation in Avila. The Commissioner, a Dominican named Pedro Fernández, was one of two Dominicans whom Pius V entrusted with the reform of the Carmelites. Previously King Philip II had obtained a brief from Pius V to have bishops reform the orders, but in the case of the reform of the Carmelites two Dominicans were to assist the bishops.

Later Pius took the reform from the bishops and placed the Generals of the communities in charge of their reform. In the case of the Carmelites, and some other orders, the king encouraged the pope to continue to entrust the reform to two Dominicans for four years. Pedro Fernández was in charge of Castile and the other Dominican, Francisco Vargas, was in charge of Andalusia. Fernández was a sensitive administrator and it was he who placed Teresa as prioress of the Incarnation in an effort to assist that large convent, the place she originally entered and the one she had left ten years earlier to begin the reform.

Teresa then had John of the Cross appointed by Fernández as one of the confessors for the nuns. And so John, along with a Discalced compatriot, Fray German de Santo Matía, began a five-year period in Avila. They lived in a workman's hut on the edge of the property. Among the activities they engaged in were saying mass, hearing confessions, teaching catechism to the children, counseling religious and townspeople, and occasionally traveling to other convents for confessions. During this period John had unusually close contact with towns-people and neighbors because of his unique living situation.

Avila in the Time of Teresa and John

At this time in Avila new movements in the church were being felt.[6] A certain John of Avila, not really of Avila but of La Mancha in southern Spain, attempted to redefine the character and function of the secular clergy. He urged careful formation, and early theological and moral training. He encouraged a vigorous apostolate of preaching the Word to all classes of people. Priests were to live simple and virtuous lives and help alleviate the sufferings of the poor. He especially emphasized the religious education of the poor.

This model of preaching, confession, ministering to the poor and educating the young influenced a group of clerics and lay people in Avila in the 1540s and 1550s. The major figure was Gaspar Daza who formed a "sacerdotal team" which became involved in every reform movement, including Teresa's.

At the same time, the new Society of Jesus began a similar program of clerical reform. Ignatius of Loyola often corresponded with John of Avila. In 1553 the Jesuits founded the College of San Gil in Avila, which provided young men with a moral foundation and humanist ideals of education.

Along with these movements a form of spirituality arose which featured extreme asceticism and acknowledged the direct experience of God on the part of largely autonomous individuals. In Avila, the "beata" or holy woman Mari Díaz was well known for her counsel and media-tion as she served the urban community, and deeply influenced Teresa. She eventually lived in a side-chamber of a church, San Millan. Mari Díaz and Gaspar Daza were among those who proposed the first Tri-dentine seminary in Avila at San Millan. She died in 1572, the year the Seminary of San Millan opened with a rector and six boys.

John's Imprisonment

During the time John was at the Incarnation in Avila, the reform of the Carmelites was proceeding in a manner which guaranteed conflict. Originally it was supported by the leadership in the order who, how-ever, imposed certain restrictions. As the reform progressed members of the order thought that it was being stubbornly carried too far.

The reform was forbidden to found houses in Andalusia, Spain. But

Vargas, the Apostolic Commissioner, authorised the foundation of houses in Seville, Granada and La Peñuela. He also took a house from the friars of the ancient observance and gave it to the reformers.

Even within the Discalced reform disagreements were arising regarding the extent of the contemplative life-style they were attempting to establish. John defended the more strictly contemplative life-style, but the group chose to incorporate more of the apostolic life.

Apparently John became a focal point for the members of the observance in their disputes with the reformers, although he was not directly involved in particular issues. As a founding member of the first house of the primitive rule among the friars, he was a natural target for their anger. And as confessor at the Incarnation he was in a role formerly occupied by the friars of the observance. They had been salaried chaplains there for many years.

The friars of the observance first publicly arrested John in 1576 but the Papal Legate, Nicolás Ormaneto, ordered him released. By then the Pope had ended the Dominican visitation of the Carmelites and entrusted further reform to the General. But Philip II had the Pope reaffirm that the Papal nuncio still had power to visit and reform the orders.

After Ormaneto died John was arrested a second time on December 2, 1577 and imprisoned in the Carmelite monastery in Toledo. He would not escape this confinement until late in the summer of the following year. Teresa, worried about John and not knowing where he had been taken, wrote to King Philip II and said she would rather he were a prisoner of the Moors than a prisoner of the friars, because he would have better treatment.

These months in Toledo were physically harsh and spiritually difficult. If any period in John's life could be identified with the "dark night" it was this period in prison. Here he wrote the first thirty-one stanzas of *The Spiritual Canticle*, along with some lesser poems.

His escape was accomplished through a combination of good fortune, planning, and some mystery. He eventually managed to find the Discalced sisters in Toledo. They disguised John and located him safely in the hospital of Santa Cruz.

Administration and Writing

The Discalced were operating independently by now, and in 1578 they named John superior of their monastery in Andalusia, El Calvario. John was apparently an effective leader of the community whose members were probably initially worried about his severity.

On Saturdays he would walk to the convent in Beas to hear confessions, do spiritual direction, and celebrate the eucharist. His talks with the nuns provided material for his prose commentaries. He wrote the poem *The Dark Night* while at El Calvario, and he began the commentary, *The Ascent of Mount Carmel,* at this time.

However, in less than a year he was requested to found the first house of studies for the Discalced at Baeza. The school was the College of San Basilio. Here he added stanzas 32–34 to *The Spiritual Canticle.*

In the next two years the Discalced became a separate entity, although not a separate order, and in 1581 had their first legal chapter. Jerónimo Gracián was elected Provincial and John was elected one of the Definitors. He began a ten year period of intense administrative work. During this time John's mother died.

John went with Ana de Jesús to Granada to found another reformed convent, and there he met Señora Ana de Peñalosa who was to be a friend and benefactress. That year, 1582, he was elected prior of the Discalced friars in Granada and began a stay which would last six years.

The Carmelite monastery, Los Martires, was situated on the hill of the Alhambra, just below the complex of Moorish fortifications and palaces. An aqueduct brought water from the Alhambra, with its dazzling fountains, to the monastery.

Less than one hundred years earlier, the Moors had been driven from this last stronghold in Spain. The "reconquest" of Spain took eight hundred years. Ferdinand and Isabella besieged the Alhambra for ten years, until finally Boabdil surrendered and Spain was united. Boabdil's retreat is said to have led through a distant mountain pass which is called "El ultimo Suspiro del Moro" (The Last Sigh of the Moor).

From the monastery John had a striking view of the plain below. The houses of Granada were immediately below, and off in the distance were the Sierra Nevada mountains. The view, the beautiful flowers, the delicate architecture of the Alhambra with its lively fountains, the climate, all appeared to assist John in expressing his thoughts in writing.[7]

In 1582 John added the final stanzas, 35–39, to *The Spiritual Canticle.* In a later second redaction he added an additional stanza 11 bringing the poem to forty stanzas.

In 1583 the Discalced held their second chapter and again John argued against placing the contemplative life in second place to apostolic work. He did agree that some apostolic work was necessary, but he argued against any activity which would undermine contemplative prayer.

In 1584 John completed the first draft of the commentary on *The Spiritual Canticle.* This effort was at the request of Ana de Jesús. He also wrote the poem *The Living Flame of Love* for Ana de Peñalosa whom he was directing. The commentary on that poem, written at her request, was completed in a fifteen-month period between 1585–1587. And John completed the commentaries, *The Ascent of Mount Carmel* and *The Dark Night* by 1585. His time in Granada saw his most intense literary effort.

John's Poetry

John's three major poems, *The Dark Night, The Spiritual Canticle* and *The Living Flame of Love* generally reflect a verse form known as the *lira*. The *lira*, with its longer meter, was introduced from the Italian Renaissance style by the Spanish poet, Garcilaso de la Vega. Through this new meter Garcilaso was said to have refined Castilian Spanish and made it more musical, as well as more expressive of a new introverted consciousness in Spain.

Gerald Brenan in *St. John of the Cross; His Life and Poetry* suggests that John would have read Garcilaso during his time in Medina del Campo where he was also studying Latin poets.[8] It is reported that when making his profession with the Carmelites at Medina del Campo he wrote some poems "in heroic verse and in a pastoral style." Brenan thinks that after John joined the Carmelites he would not have been reading Garcilaso but was perhaps reminded of him by reading a third-rate poet, Sebastián de Córdoba, who turned Garcilaso's love poetry into religious allegory. Córdoba may have suggested to John the possibility of writing about religious experience in lira form. John perhaps also took the pastoral idiom from Garcilaso. Colin Thompson, in *The Poet and the Mystic*, a study of John's *The Spiritual Canticle*, argues that commentators overplay the significance of Garcilaso and Córdoba and miss the most important source for *The Spiritual Canticle*, namely the Bible, and especially the Song of Songs.[9] John uses abundant biblical material but in such a way that it enhances his own creativity.

Thompson makes these points: first, John uses the material from the Bible with various intensities, sometimes only faintly echoing the biblical poetry; second, John weaves the biblical material into patterns which include other poetic traditions; third, he baffles the reader by piling-up symbols which are both biblical and non-biblical; fourth, he uses elements taken from the Song of Songs with complete freedom to adapt them to his own poetry.[10]

Thompson writes that John's poetry, particularly the *Canticle*, "is light and color, beauty and love: a world shot through with joy and delight, in which flowers, birds, animals, rivers, mountains, forests, breezes, and flames all join to celebrate an affirmation of life lived in union with its source."[11]

Final Years

John continued in various administrative posts. In the first General Chapter of the Discalced in 1588, Nicholás Doria was elected Vicar-General. John became First Definitor and assumed the role of prior in Segovia. The Carmelites had begun a foundation there two years earlier with the financial assistance of Ana de Peñalosa.

Along with his administrative duties, he continued to counsel numerous people. One man with whom he had long conversations was a Dr. Villegas, a canon-penitentiary. They became good friends. Visits from his brother, Francis, were always most welcome. John called him "my greatest treasure on earth."

John fell upon difficult times because he made an enemy of the Vicar-General, Nicholás Doria. John defended the nuns and Jerónimo Gracián from Doria's unfair treatment. Gracián was Teresa's compatriot in the reform, and a man who wanted an apostolic dimension in the Discalced life-style. When he was Provincial he began missionary activities in Africa and Mexico. Doria believed Gracián was diluting the reform.

When Doria was elected Vicar-General he sought to curtail the laxity he believed had already entered the reform. "Even after my death, my bones, clashing together in the tomb, will cry out: 'Observance, observance!' "

Gracián was eventually brought to trial and dismissed from the Discalced. He made a fruitless appeal in Rome, was captured by Turkish pirates, spent two years in prison, and finally rejoined the Carmelites of the ancient observance.[12]

One of the Definitors elected at the chapter, Fray Diego Evangelista, who was investigating Gracián's case also began to build a case against John. The reports are that the investigator attempted to discredit John and falsified nuns' testimony. He was trying to have John dismissed from the Discalced.

Before the matter could take its course John became seriously ill. He moved from the isolated monstery of La Peñuela to the monastery at Ubeda where the prior initially greeted him with hostility. Matters changed when Antonio de Jesús, John's prior at Duruelo and now provincial of the region, went to Ubeda to attend John.

Crude surgery did not help. John of the Cross died December 14, 1591.

The Carmelite Imagination

The imagination of the Carmelite scans the terrain of Mount Carmel: garden, desert, fountain, cave, chapel, mountain, seacoast. It is a land of paradox and challenge. Carmel carries within it the images of zealous Elijah, contemplative Mary, European missionaries and hermits. In its mythic expression of the demonic, the prophets of Baal are joined by the keepers of Dachau and Auschwitz.[13]

Carmel has attempted throughout its existence to communicate the presence and experience of God. It has contributed a unique language of interiority to the church, a language for soul. Elijah, Mary, Carmel, dark night, interior castle, little way, and all the images these evoke describe a land where the human and God meet.

They tell us that the basic story all humans live is a love story, the story of God pursuing us in love and transforming our lives and our world. The language of Carmel both expresses depth experiences, and shapes them.

John of the Cross immensely enhanced this tradition. The following chapter looks particularly at his major poems. They not only provide a springboard for John's teachings on the spiritual life, but the imagery of these poems, flowing from the imagination of John, is a sensitive attempt to capture the experience of God. The process John used to hear and express this Mystery is at work in all of us.

CHAPTER TWO

The Imagination of John of the Cross

The poetry of John of the Cross, and the imagery woven throughout his writings, is a powerful process of communication. John is addressing us at levels of our being where we simply are mute or only stammer. His language hints at hungers and nourishments which we recognize but cannot express.

These products of the imagination of John of the Cross were not always valued. For three centuries writers generally considered his poems aesthetic addenda to the more important teaching found within his prose commentary on the poems. Today, we have a renewed respect for the power of the human imagination to capture realities which can be expressed in no other way than imaginatively. It is commonly agreed that John's most powerful poems are *The Dark Night, The Spiritual Canticle,* and *The Living Flame of Love.*

The Imagination

Carl Jung was a modern pioneer in the land of the psyche. He concluded that symbolic imagery is the first language of the psyche. The psyche expresses its depth experiences first in imagery and only later in rational concept. For Jung, a dream is not a thought coded, as though one should work through dream imagery to get to the underlying thoughts. No, the dream imagery *is* the thought process of the psyche. We have generally lost our ability to hear this language of the psyche, and to speak it. Jung wrote:

The [imagination] is to be understood here as the real and
literal power to create images—the classical use of the word in
contrast to *phantasia,* which means a mere "conceit" in the
sense of insubstantial thought. . . . [Imagination] is the active
evocation of (inner) images . . . an authentic feat of thought or
ideation, which does not spin aimless and groundless fantasies
"into the blue"—does not, that is to say, just play with its
objects, but tries to grasp the inner facts and portray them in
images true to their nature.[1]

John of the Cross recognized imagination as a faculty or power of
the soul. In his anthropology he described imagination, and the
closely-linked faculty of fantasy, as an inner sense which stored images
coming to it from the five outer senses, or from a "supernatural" source.
He likened imagination to archives, or to a seaport or market where the
intellect comes and shops. Here imagination appears to be a static re-
pository, but he does credit it with the power to create images as well.
And so important is the sense of imagination and fantasy that John calls
it "the gate and entry to the soul."[2]

Contemporary articulations of the role of imagination expand our
understanding. Urban Holmes discusses imagination not as one faculty
or power but as a posture of the whole person toward reality, and it is a
process which involves intuition and wonder.[3] Holmes also understands
imagination, with Owen Barfield, as the capacity to make an image of
the immaterial or spiritual.[4] Phil Keane calls imagination a "basic process by which we draw together the concrete and the universal elements
of our human experience."[5] And Andrew Greeley writes, "The religious experience, symbol, and story come into existence in that dimension of the personality which may . . . be called the imagination. . . .
Religion occurs, at least primordially, in that dimension of ourselves that
produces dreams, poems, stories, myths, and great or lesser works of
art. . . . The poetic and imaginative dimensions of religion come before
its propositional, cognitive and theological dimensions."[6]

John of the Cross says he resorted to poetry, to imagination, because he had no other words for his experience of God. In the prologue
to *The Spiritual Canticle* John writes about his difficulty:

It would be foolish to think that expressions of love arising
from mystical understanding, like these stanzas, are fully ex-
plainable. The Spirit of the Lord, who abides in us and aids our
weakness, as St. Paul says, pleads for us with unspeakable
groanings in order to manifest what we can neither fully understand nor comprehend.

> Who can describe the understanding He gives to loving souls in whom He dwells? And who can express the experience He imparts to them? Who, finally, can explain the desires He gives them? Certainly, no one can! Not even they who receive these communications. As a result these persons let something of their experiences overflow in figures and similies, and from the abundance of their spirit pour out secrets and mysteries rather than rational explanations.[7]

He continues, saying that his prose commentary on the poem is only one possible interpretation. The reader is invited to explore other meanings.

Psyche and Poetry

A true work of art says something about our shared human story. It has escaped the merely personal concerns of the artist. In Jung's view the creative urge in the artist has practically an autonomous existence, and in the creative process the artist cooperates with this inner imperative. It is a process living in the artist, as a tree in the earth, drawing nourishment from the artist. In Jung's paper, "On the Relation of Analytical Psychology to Poetry," he writes, "We would do well, therefore, to think of the creative process as a living thing implanted in the human psyche."[8]

This creative process produces powerful art when it reaches deep down in the psyche and draws on levels present in everyone. "I am assuming," Jung writes, "that the work of art we propose to analyze, as well as being symbolic, has its source not in the personal unconscious of the poet, but in a sphere of unconscious mythology whose primordial images are the common heritage of humankind. I have called this sphere the collective unconscious. . . ."[9]

When art comes solely from personal layers of the psyche it may be more symptom than symbol. The merely personal can be a muddy tributary, but the collective layers are a deep, mighty river. Jung writes: "That is the secret of great art, and of its effect upon us. The creative process, so far as we are able to follow it at all, consists in the unconscious activation of an archetypal image, and in elaborating and shaping this image into the finished work. By giving it shape, the artist translates it into the language of the present, and so makes it possible for us to find our way back to the deepest springs of life."[10]

Because great art is drawing upon such hidden, forgotten sources, it is continually educating the present. Just as a dream may compensate the conscious attitude of the dreamer, the great work of art produces images which compensate for the one-sidedness of the present. It is often just those people who do not seem to "fit," who are open to new and creative sources of life. "Here the artist's relative lack of adaptation turns out to his advantage; it enables him to follow his own yearnings far from the beaten path, and to discover what it is that would meet the unconscious needs of his age."[11]

Primordial Words

Depth psychologist James Hillman holds the view that the poetic process begins when powerful experiences drive the individual inward, into an interiority, a subjectivity. In these depths the psyche then begins to grope for metaphors to capture the experience; "It is like this or that. . . ." Then the psyche begins to relate the metaphors in story form.[12]

The specific events which gave impetus to John's mystical poetry are unknown to us. Unlike Teresa of Avila, John reveals very little about the concrete details of his daily living. It is not that John says nothing about himself. On the contrary, he reveals himself in his most intimate dimensions. He writes of matters which are at the very core of his humanity. Still, we generally do not know how events and experiences in his life are related to particular poems and reflections.

We know about his relatively impoverished childhood, the early loss of his father, his work in a local hospital comforting the dying. We know of his serious, ascetical character which led him to join the Carmelites and later moved him to seek a more contemplative group. Teresa of Avila encouraged him to remain in the community and assist her with the reform of the Carmelites. We know about the difficulties he encountered during the reform, including imprisonment by his brothers in Carmel. We also know that during the time of his imprisonment John began to write his poetry, including most of the verses of *The Spiritual Canticle*. As we have seen, John said that his experiences were basically inexpressible, but that he let something of his experiences "overflow in figures and similes. . . ."

The images that emerge from the imagination of John of the Cross become the basic wording of his experience: a dark night, a still house, a secret ladder, fanning cedar, lilies, an absent lover, shepherds, mountains, watersides, flowers, wild beasts, woods, thickets, meadows, arrows, a wounded heart, crystal, a dove, a wounded stag, silent music, sounding solitude, refreshing supper, north wind and south wind, swift-winged birds, lions, stags, and leaping roes, lowlands and river banks, waters, winds and ardors, watching fears of night, a bride, an apple tree, shields of gold, an inner wine cellar, a lost herd, high caverns, fresh pomegranate juice, a living flame, a wounded soul, gentle hand and delicate touch, lamps of fire, deep caverns, warmth, light, an awakening, a heart swollen with love. These are the images of John of the Cross, the bridges thrown out to the unseen shore of the spirit.

An amazing story of grace and human development is told in these images. Millions of years ago—perhaps only a few thousand years ago—these images were entirely outside the human personality; they were found only in their reality as an actual mountain, waterside, night, flame, thicket, wild beast, silence, island. Slowly, in the course of time, human consciousness arose, spirit unfolded. These realities were given names as language developed, and through their names were brought within the psyche and used as a primordial wording for that which is most deep and interior and sacred. John's images provide an inner landscape, a geography of soul, a topography expressive of the journey of the human spirit.

This journey of the spirit has always been the fundamental journey, but for millenia it was expressed through physical contact, an experience of the senses and an actual traversing of African landscapes and later other landscapes of this earth. And now, in these images, John of the Cross, a "pioneer of humanity" as Evelyn Underhill called the mystic, charts the fundamental journey of the human spirit, taking place in regions of the human where only moanings and primordial words even begin to satisfy. In these images the physical, the concrete, the solid, the sensual, meet with the ethereal, the ungraspable, the atmospheric, the infinitely light. We have all Africa within us.

Wounding and Healing

While the specific experiences that pressured these images into existence are not known to us, there appear to be two basic experiences being expressed in John's imagery: the experience of being wounded, and the experience of being healed.

The experience which John communicates is ultimately a positive experience, but one can see, feel, and read in the imagery experiences of suffering. His major images contain pain: a night in which one is lost (*The Dark Night*), abandonment by a beloved (*The Spiritual Canticle*), a flame which burns (*The Living Flame of Love*). These images speak of times, perhaps years, when John's basic experience was one of feeling lost, alone, and hurt.

Very probably, John's appeal to the popular imagination, and to some extent his forbidding nature, lies in his willing acceptance and clear articulation of the tragic in life. John seems tough to people. His very name, John of the Cross, his ascetical character, and his fundamental image of the dark night speak of realities which one would rather not face.

And yet the spirituality of John of the Cross is no tougher than life itself. People hear in his writings, and feel in his poetry, expressions of their own experience of being lost, alone, hurt. And they ask, with him, where is God in all of this?

Theologian David Tracy has written: ". . . for most of us most of the time, I suspect, the threats to that basic confidence and faith are at least as real and often more powerful than the experience of basic confidence itself. We really do doubt that there exists an inner connection between how we believe we ought to live, and how reality itself is constituted."[13] Tracy quotes Melville's dictum as capturing the dark of human experience: "Say no with thunder, for all who say yes, lie."

And Tracy goes on to conclude, "The presence of the negative is central to most religious experiences and expressions: surely central to any experience available in this contemporary situation."[14]

An appeal of John of the Cross—and it is one which should not be weakened—is his expression of the valleys through which the human journey winds. Here are words for our sorrows. Who has not been lost, alone, hurt?

The second powerful experience expressed in John's imagery is the experience of being healed. The night in which one was lost becomes a truer guide than the light of noon; the experience of abandonment reveals an unsuspecting presence of the beloved; the painful flame cauterizes, heals, enlivens, bringing warmth and light.

This reaffirmation of the graciousness of life, this rekindling of the hope that is constitutive of being human, too, gives words to experiences fundamental to the human journey. The night gives way to dawn and the journey is taken up once again.

Carl Jung writes: "He (the poet) transmutes our personal destiny into the destiny of mankind, and evokes in us all those beneficent forces that ever and anon have enabled humanity to find a refuge from every peril and to outlive the longest night."[15] John of the Cross may be heavy at times, but the ending is happy. His images speak of beneficent forces at the heart of reality.

The Story

As James Hillman reminds us, once the psyche has found images, words for its dark experience, it naturally begins to put these images at the service of a story. The story told in John's three major poems is a love story.

A soul, aching for the love and presence of an absent lover, searches for the beloved. She slips out of the quiet house at night by a ladder and searches unseen. She is undeterred by anyone or anything, stopping only to ask, "Have you seen him? Has he passed by you?" She cries out for a revelation of his presence, to be removed from the death she is experiencing.

The beloved suddenly appears—a wounded stag—on a hill, and calls her. They meet and the lover's senses are filled with the beloved, and all the world speaks of his presence. They rest together in a pastoral setting, putting up around their bower "do not disturb" signs.

They make love, and the bride is quite content to remain in this solitude. She urges that they go apart even farther, "To the high caverns in the rock, which are so well concealed." There her search is ended and her soul fulfilled.

The imagination of John of the Cross presents us with a sensual love story. His communication is more than simply a story line. The wording and patterning of his poetry are all an attempt to capture the ineffable. "Poems are rafts clutched at by men drowning in inadequate minds," writes psychologist Julian Jaynes.[16] All minds are inadequate to express the love story John experienced at the core of his humanity; yet, his poems do say something to us.

The effect of these poems rests in the power of the imagery and movement to express archetypical human themes which speak to the humanity of the reader. The poems speak from collective depths, wellsprings of life which we share with one another. As a matter of fact, we may say that these stories tell themselves through John of the Cross. His experiences have opened him to matters which are more than merely personal, and regions which are inhabited by more than himself. And his imagination has groped toward a telling of what he experienced through primordial words, symbols, which present a continual challenge to the mind and heart of the reader.

The symbolic nature of the poems is quite evident in their ability to evoke an atmosphere while at the same time defying any certainty in grasping specifics or even in logically sequencing events. As with all symbols, John's images may point forward and back, up and down, and contain this and that, all simultaneously. To enter into the story too analytically finds the mind thrown into confusion because the unconscious speaks in a many-layered manner which is foreign speech to consciousness.

The Innerwork of John of the Cross

It is possible to follow the work of John's psyche as it moves from the dark of experience through articulation and understanding to a faithful response. Robert Johnson, a Jungian analyst, has provided a four-step process for working with dreams.[17] If we accept the hypothesis that John's poetry is analogous to a dream, since the poem and the dream both draw on collective depths in the psyche and are the psyche's fundamental expression of its experience, then we may follow John's movement through these four steps.

The four steps are a natural process for reflection upon the psyche's symbols. The first step is to make "associations," personal and collective. What in my personal life relates to the symbols of the dream or poem? And what myths, fairy tales, and ancient religious traditions relate to these symbols? The latter-type association is an archetypal amplification which may situate my experience in a collective context.

Jung warned against ready-made interpretations for symbols from reference books, and Johnson concurs. Johnson believes that the unconscious itself will eventually reveal the relationship of the individual to the symbols. "Nevertheless," he writes, "it is a great aid to know what the symbol has meant to others, and how it has appeared in collective myths and folktales. This knowledge can shorten the process. It can also act as confirmation of the personal associations that spring spontaneously out of you."[18]

The second step is to connect the imagery with "inner dynamics." A dream may be about people and situations outside the dreamer, but to take the dream inward and attend to its subjective connotations can be a fruitful direction. "The overall subject of our dreams," says Johnson, "is, ultimately, the inner process of individuation. Most dreams, in one way or another, are portrayals of our individual journeys toward wholeness. They show us the stages along the way, the adventures, obstacles, conflicts, and reconciliations that lead finally to a sense of the self. Every dream, in some way, either shows our effort to integrate some unconscious part of ourselves into consciousness or our resistance against the inner self, the ways we set up conflict with it rather than learn from it."[19]

The third step involves a process of "interpretation." In effect, it involves asking the meaning of these symbols for my life. What is the significance of this material for me? What ideas, insights, meanings emerge as a result of this process? Actually, all four steps of this process for working with symbols involve a process of interpretation. This third step calls for articulation and comprehension of meanings born in the process.

Finally, the fourth step is to "create ritual." A ritual, or "symbolic behavior consciously performed," keeps one in touch with the depths that have been engaged in the experience. A ritual physically manifests inner realities. "The best rituals are physical, solitary, and silent. These are the ones that register most deeply with the unconscious."[20]

Through ritual a sense of reverence may pervade a life, helping enhance psychological health. "If a person has no sense of reverence, no feeling that there is anyone or anything that inspires awe, it generally indicates an ego inflation that cuts the conscious personality off completely from the nourishing springs of the unconscious."[21]

The process of John of the Cross moves from experience, to primordial wording of the experience in poetry, to prose commentary on the poetry. Once John's imagination produced the poem, it is possible to follow his psyche's continued innerwork as his experience works its way into meaning and behavior. Johnson's four-step guideline will be used to trace this process.

Associations: Scripture As Archetypal Amplification

In his commentary on the poems John certainly made associations with his poetic imagery. When Johnson discusses making associations he refers to personal associations which relate specifically to the individual dreamer (or poet in this case), and collective associations which extend and deepen the meaning by relating the imagery to "myths, fairy tales, and ancient religious traditions."

The personal associations John made between his poetry and the events of his life are difficult for us to determine because of the impersonal nature of his commentaries. His writings contain very little autobiographical material. But, as Jung points out, the importance of great poetry lies in its ability to speak to us from our common source of life, the collective, transpersonal layers of psyche.

John did make collective associations, however, with his poetry. In his commentaries on the poems John presents archetypal amplifications of his imagery. Through his extensive use of scripture, he offers stories which parallel and contextualize his own story. John's use of scripture is not simply for didactic purposes to exemplify a point he is trying to make. Certain scriptural stories are chosen by his imagination because they themselves are symbolic expressions of mysteries which make John mute. These stories, sacred images, themselves have power since they come from the archetypal treasury of religious tradition.

John uses these scriptural stories as he uses his own images—to begin to word what is essentially mystery. His prologue to *The Spiritual Canticle* reveals his understanding. Speaking first of his own images, then of scripture, he writes, "If these similitudes are not read with the simplicity of the spirit of knowledge and love they contain they will seem to be absurdities rather than reasonable utterances, as will those comparisons of the divine Canticle of Solomon and other books of Sacred Scripture where the Holy Spirit, unable to express the fullness of His meaning in ordinary words, utters mysteries in strange figures and likenesses."[22] In other words, John is saying both my poetry and the scripture I refer to in my commentary have to be read the same way, i.e., with an openness to realities which cannot be satisfactorily worded.

If we may assume that scripture contains stories which capture fundamental human themes and which address the psyche at levels where the human story waits to be told, then we may view John's use of these stories as his own amplification of the meaning of his poetry through the archetypal symbolism of scripture. John is not chiefly presenting a teaching or a doctrine, much less a program. He is communicating an experience, a process. He is struggling to find a human language to communicate his experiences of God, which experiences he calls "the language and . . . the words God speaks in souls. . . ."[23]

John calls upon his own imagination as well as the Judeo-Christian imagination of the community expressed in the Bible. He uses biblical imagery and story as so many windows to the transcendent. These archetypal amplifications from scripture, from a particular religious tradition, help bring into focus the hues and hints of John's nonreligious imagery.

Wounding and Healing in Scripture

In his commentary on *The Living Flame of Love*, for example, John expands on the symbols used to express his experience of a wounding and a healing. He draws on the imagery and stories of sacred scripture to amplify his images and story.

John finds his pain shared by the Psalmist: "God tries by fire."[24]; by Jeremiah: "Are not my words perchance, like fire?"[25]; by Job: "You are changed to be cruel toward me."[26]; by the Deuteronomist: "Our Lord is a consuming fire."[27]; and by Isaiah (paraphrased): "The fire of God is on Sion, his furnace in Jerusalem."[28]

In an extensive quote John parallels his experience with the words of the author of Lamentations whom John understands to be Jeremiah:

> I am the man that sees my poverty in the rod of His indignation. He has led me and brought me into darkness and not into light. Only against me He has turned and turned again His hand. He has made my skin and my flesh old, and He has broken my bones. He has surrounded me and compassed me with gall and labor. He has set me in dark places as those who are dead forever. He has built around me that I might not get out. He made my fetters heavy. And besides this when I have cried out and prayed, He has shut out my prayer. He shut up my ways with square rocks and turned my steps and paths upside down.[29]

Here there is no question of a privatized spirituality. Not only does John use poetic images which speak to the common human journey, but he contextualizes his experience in the cries of the people of the Old Testament. He hears in their words expressions of his own transformations and he is able to identify with the ministry of the prophets such as Jeremiah.

Walter Brueggemann has written that the task of prophetic ministry is to bring about a consciousness which is an alternative to the predominant consciousness of the culture. And real criticism begins with the capacity to grieve, because grieving is "a visceral announcement that things are not right."[30] The poetic imagination of the prophets was the last and best chance to challenge and conflict the dominant "royal consciousness," a consciousness wishing to remain numb to the possibility of death.

Brueggemann identified Jeremiah as a model of prophetic imagination. Jeremiah offered a language of grief. He knew the end was near for his people as was the time for indifferent affluence, cynical oppression and presumptive religion. Brueggemann writes that Jeremiah had a "ministry of articulated grief" which could be found throughout his poetry.[31]

The imagination of John of the Cross resonates with the prophetic imaginations. The images of their story amplify his own. He finds their "articulated grief" consonant with his own deepest experience, and in his writings it is evident that he continues this ministry.

John's powerful experience of healing, too, finds age-old expression in scripture. He compares the flame with living waters in the gospel of John,[32] and the gentle breeze experienced by Elijah.[33] But he especially turns to the Song of Songs to find language for his renewed soul:

> Behold what my Spouse is saying to me: rise and make haste, my love, my dove, my beautiful one, and come; for winter is now passed, and the rains are over and gone, and the flowers have appeared in our land; the fig tree has put forth her fruits; the vines in flower have given their fragrance. Arise my love, my fair one, and come; my dove in the clefts of the rock, in the hollow of the wall, show me your face, let your voice sound in my ears, because your voice is sweet and your face beautiful.[34]

Here are images to match John's experience of the flame as sweet, delightful, gentle, delicate. And, again, the experience is not just unique to John, but he sees it as the experience of a people who found words for their journey in the Song of Songs. This story of love between two people had always been understood as the story of a people and their God.

The amplification of John's poetic imagery through parallel expressions from scripture provides a context within which his poems may be heard. While not using explicitly religious language in his poems, John moves the reader into otherwise inaccessible levels of understanding through the scriptural imagery woven throughout his writings.

John's poetry is now seen not only as the account of God's relationship with this Carmelite friar, but also as an expression of God's relationship with humanity, specifically evidenced in the history of a particular people. It is a story of the human heart, not just one person's adventure. The wounding and healing disclose a human yearning and divine faithfulness which intertwine in the story of every man and woman. This presence of God and process of transformation is revealed in the history of the Jews, as well as in the life, death, and resurrection of Jesus of Nazareth. John incorporates New Testament as well as Old Testament passages.

Inner Dynamics

Step two of Johnson's guidelines for working with dream imagery encourages looking at the imagery as referring to the emergence of the self. The point of this step is to focus inward and not on the outward possibilities of the dream.

John's poems refer to a deeply interior process. He is expressing the effects of the impact of God on his personality. For John, the human is psychically healthy only when in relationship with God. John's language in his commentaries is drawn from the faculty psychology of his day. He uses the language of sense, appetite, faculty to describe the transformation of his psychic structure as his relationship with God deepens.

Interpretation

Step three involves making interpretations, articulating what has been learned. Here John has offered entire treatises which interpret his poetic expressions. John's commentaries are an effort to somewhat systematically present the "spirituality" he has learned through his prayer.

Studies of John of the Cross frequently begin and end here, with his conclusions. The commentaries are seen as containing the heart of his teachings. But, as John warned, the commentaries are only one way of interpreting the experiences captured in the poetry. The poetic myth, or symbols-in-narrative, does not point to clear statements. Analyst James Hillman observed, "Instead we hover in puzzlement at the border where the true depths are. Rather than an increase of certainty there is a spread of mystery, which is both the precondition and the consequence of revelation."[35]

Johnson's steps for innerwork help us appreciate John's broader interpretative process beginning with the symbolic expressions of his depth experiences. The "interpretations" of his commentaries, while able to stand alone, are most fully appreciated when read in conjunction with his poetry.

Rituals

The process of innerwork leads naturally to rituals which honor what has been heard in the experience. They are a way of keeping in touch with levels of psyche which are met only in symbol.

Prayer appears to be the ritual John urges in *The Ascent of Mount Carmel*, and he makes some specific recommendations regarding the setting. In accord with Johnson's advice that rituals should be "physical, solitary, and silent," John observes that "a solitary and austere location is beneficial for the sure and direct ascent of the spirit to God."[36]

Along with oratories and churches John identifies three types of natural places: "The first includes those sights that have pleasant variations in arrangement of the land and the trees, and provide solitary quietude, all of which naturally awakens devotion."[37] Throughout his life John was drawn to just such places.

The second type of setting is a place where God has been experienced in a powerful way by an individual. Sometimes a person is drawn back to that place with a desire to once again be in touch with God as before. But there may be no going back, John warns. It is possible to be disappointed because God bestows favors without being bound to place or time, or even by the longing of the person.[38]

The third type of setting refers to places in this world, such as Mt. Sinai, where God has chosen to communicate with humanity. Among these places are the numerous shrines which have been identified through special interventions of the Blessed Virgin.[39]

As for rituals recommended by Jesus, John notes there were only two. By example, Jesus retired to solitary places, often in the quiet of the night, in order to pray. And in his teaching he said, "When you pray enter into your secret chamber, and having closed the door, pray."[40]

In his writings John urged a silent, peaceful attentiveness to God. And when God speaks in the solitude of the heart John says to simply listen in freedom, letting go even of the practice of loving attentiveness.

But John of the Cross emerged from all of this quiet with multitudes of words, beginning with his poetry. Surely, here is a ritual of sorts. He was driven to find words for the primordial Word he was hearing in his contemplative experience.

Perhaps John's rituals relate to phases of his prayer. Falling quiet, being a "watch in the night" interiorly, is his response to the experience of God's love. Writing his poetry, and then using it as a basis for further teaching in his commentaries, is a ritual flowing from the silence and responding to psyche's natural language of symbol.

Being Poets of Our Lives

If we are to read John of the Cross, interpret the writings through a dialogue with our own lives, then it appears important to enter into an imaginative process similar to John's, an innerwork which seems normative as psyche speaks of mystery through symbol. By opening my heart and mind to John's narrative and primordial wording I can be led into my own depths and story, and I can be moved to my own images for these experiences.

The symbols of John's poems, archetypal though they may be, are still "his" images. But they have the power to lead me to my images, to poems I am writing in my life. I may actually be writing poems, or painting pictures, or doing some other creative work, but I may also look to the memories which I carry, the places where I feel centered and renewed, the people who enliven me and lead me into my unlived life. Are not these my images, do they not constitute my poem, as I attend to them and link them in the narrative of my life. It is through them that my wider, deeper self is speaking. With this poem I can then engage the poetry of John of the Cross, letting story speak to story.

And, as John did, I can let scripture carry my story into broader channels. I can amplify my poetry by listening for its resonances in the treasury of biblical imagery and story. John was convinced that Jesus is God's final word, the one Word all our stories are trying to express. Through that story, my symbols for wounding and healing are heard as expressive of the paschal mystery, the death and resurrection of the Lord, which is taking place within the transformations of my psychic structure.

Development of Consciousness

Earlier in the chapter it was said that John's images create an inner landscape, and that there was a time when humans traversed only outer landscapes with no experience of interiority. The next chapter further explores this mystery of human development. Humanity's journey is viewed as a graced journey of the spirit which results in the emergence of psyche and consciousness. In his writings John continues to chart a story which has been humanity's story from the beginning, and which continues in all of us.

CHAPTER THREE

John, a "Pioneer of Humanity"

Evelyn Underhill, in her 1911 study of mysticism, referred to the mystics as "pioneers of humanity."[1] Led by the Spirit, these men and women lived at the front of the human column and reported back to others the possibilities of our common humanity. They lived in the far regions of the human spirit where God's Spirit and our spirits touch. They related what happened to their humanity under the impact of God's love. Their claim was that these experiences were not limited to them alone, but were the potential of all people.

John of the Cross was among the most energetic of the explorers. No maps were available for much of the journey. He charted an unknown land, led ever deeper into it by the Spirit. The maps he drew, the names he gave to the land, the experiences he recounted were every bit as engaging and gripping (and, at times, as tedious) as Charles Darwin's *Voyage of the Beagle*, or John Stephens' *Incidents of Travel in Yucatan*. And yet, writes Underhill, the mystic is "no exploring alien, but a returned exile. . . ."[2]

An initial charting of John's experiences can be found in three major poems, *The Dark Night*, *The Spiritual Canticle*, and *The Living Flame of Love*.[3] John says that his poetry is the best, most complete expression of his religious experience because it tells of the great impact of Mystery on John's personality.

The poems are profound expressions of human yearning. They describe the pilgrimage of the human spirit as it reaches for fulfillment, but they also speak of the ineffable richness of that fulfillment. The imagery reflects a language of the heart, a language of desire.

John does not use overtly religious language. He tells a love story set in a primordial landscape. The setting is "earthy"—night, fire, cave, mountain, valley, breezes and winds. Only such language can give expression to realities taking place deep within human experience.

The landscape provides a language for psyche, as well as for spirit. The images tell of the impact of such love on John's psychic structures. In particular, depth psychology would view John's journey as a journey into ancient, nourishing levels of psyche. These depths were humanity's original home until, in the long course of time, humanity migrated into consciousness. Jung spoke of plumbing those depths in dream analysis: "Together the patient and I address ourselves to the 2-million-year-old man that is in all of us. In the last analysis, most of our difficulties come from losing contact with our instincts, with the age-old unforgotten wisdom stored up in us."[4]

The inner landscape of John's poetry was first traversed by human ancestors as an outer landscape. John's feats rest on the long evolution of humanity and particularly on the development of consciousness. The story he tells is the story that has been expressing itself in humanity's emergence in this world.

The story is one seen from the very beginnings of human appearance on this planet. Tracing the outlines of that development will set the foundations for understanding John's profound mystical development.

Beginnings of the Human

The story of the earliest humans is still unfolding. From time to time new fossils are found and another round of interpretation begins: How old are we? Where did we originate? Where are we heading?

The fossil remains of the first undoubted hominids, distant members of our human family, are approximately 4 million years old. One of them was a young woman named Lucy. She was found near Hadar, Ethiopia, in 1974 by Donald Johanson from the Cleveland Museum of Natural History. Forty percent of Lucy's skeleton was intact. Johanson estimates she was between 25 and 30 years old when she died. Her height was approximately three-and-a-half feet.

The scientists named her Lucy because the Beatles' song "Lucy in the Sky with Diamonds," was playing when they returned to camp following the discovery. Johanson writes: "She is the oldest, most complete, best-preserved skeleton of any erect-walking human ancestor that has ever been found."[5] (Only in anthropology is this statement a compliment!)

Before Lucy's time there is a 3-million-year gap in our fossil record. Seven million years ago our ancestors entered the fossil gap on all fours; 3 million years later Lucy and her contemporaries emerged walking upright. Mary Leakey has possibly even found their footprints. Mary Leakey spent decades with her husband, Louis, searching in Africa for the earliest human remains. At Laetoli, in Tanzania, she discovered striding footprints cast in volcanic ash. The prints are more than 3.6 million years old.

Of the three hominid trails, the prints on the left were the smallest, leading Mary to think they belonged to a child. The small prints caused a kind of poignant time-wrench for Mary Leakey. She writes: "At one point . . . (the child) stops, pauses, turns to the left to glance at some possible threat or irregularity, and then continues to the north. This motion so intensely human, transcends time. 3.6 million years ago, a remote ancestor—just as you or I—experienced a moment of doubt."[6]

A year after Lucy was found in Ethiopia, Johanson discovered remains of thirteen other individuals near the same site; the "first family." Reconstructions showed they may have been five feet tall. Lucy and her friends have been identified as the species *Australopithecus afarensis*.

First True Humans

The first "Homo," or truly human, species of hominids appears about 2 million years ago with *Homo habilis*. The subsequent 2 million years of development takes place against the backdrop of the Ice Age and is termed the Paleolithic Age.

With *Homo habilis* the first tool-making is observed. Archaeological sites are found with deposits of used or altered stone and animal remains. *Homo habilis* lasted for only a few hundred thousand years. The next species, *Homo erectus* was long-lived and widespread, migrating into Europe and Asia.

Homo erectus originated in Africa about 1.6 million years ago, and survived in some parts of the world for well over one million years. These people used more sophisticated tools, and some populations may have used fire, but a striking aspect of *Homo erectus* is the lack of any observable development over a great period of time. This species includes the well-known Java man and Teilhard de Chardin's Peking man. Of course, Lucy was walking "upright" long before these "men."

The next identifiable species is called archaic *Homo sapiens*, and probably included the Neanderthals. Neanderthals evolved in Europe over a period of time between 300,000 and 35,000 years ago. Among these people the first graves have been found. In the graves were food, tools, and possibly flowers.

It is generally agreed that modern humans did not evolve from Neanderthals. They died out within a 5,000 year period; they were, in effect, an evolutionary dead end, although they probably did exist contemporaneously with modern humans.

Modern Humans

An intriguing hypothesis suggests that modern *Homo sapiens* originated in Africa between 100,000 to 200,000 years ago. Some scientists even argue that all present humans can be traced back to one African woman. Others argue that the widespread *Homo erectus* formed the basis for modern *Homo sapiens* to evolve in several places around the world.

What is certain is that, beginning about 35,000 years ago, there was a cultural explosion. People began to paint and carve human and animal figures. For example, the Lascaux Cave in southwest France contains hundreds of animal images painted on a grand scale, many showing remarkable skill. Among the colorful figures are bulls, lions, horses, bison, and deer, including a roaring red stag with striking nine-point antlers. The paintings were done 17,000 years ago.

Also, numerous "Venus" or fertility carvings have been found from this period. Some of the female sculptures show elaborate coiffures and jewelry.

Modern humans reached North America probably between 20,000 and 12,000 years ago, crossing on a land bridge from Asia to Alaska and spreading through the Americas.

Up to 11,000 years ago, so writes Richard Leakey, we humans were gatherer-hunters, living in bands of 25 or 30 people, near water sources, and these bands were related in tribes of about 500 people.[7] With the development of agriculture people began to live in larger groups and the first civilizations began, civilization being defined somewhat facetiously by one psychologist as "the art of living in towns of such size that everyone does not know everyone else." The great dynasties of Ur and Egypt began about 7,000 years ago.

One physical anthropologist made this summary observation: "We've hardly shown any anatomical changes in our bodies for 100,000 years. And I don't think we're suddenly going to start again showing anatomical change. I believe what has happened is that our physical and anatomical evolution has become less and less significant, whilst our cultural, behavioral, linguistic, and spiritual evolution has become more and more important."[8]

The Development of Consciousness

Paralleling this anthropological evolution has been an interiorizing process which we refer to as the development of consciousness. Only in our time has the reality of the psyche been established and have we been able to reflect on the awareness, the consciousness, we bring to this world.

In 1925 Carl Jung was traveling in Africa, and he wrote these reflections:

> From Nairobi we used a small Ford to visit the Athi Plains, a great game preserve. From a low hill in this broad savanna a magnificent prospect opened out to us. To the very brink of the horizon we saw gigantic herds of animals: gazelle, antelope, gnu, zebra, warthog, and so on. Grazing, heads nodding, the herds moved forward like slow rivers. There was scarcely any sound save the melancholy cry of a bird of prey. This was the stillness of the eternal beginning, the world as it had always been, in the state of non-being; for until then no one had been present to know that it was this world. I walked away from my companions until I had put them out of sight, and savored the feeling of being entirely alone. There I was now, the first human being to recognize that this was the world, but who did not know that in this moment he had first really created it. . . .
>
> There the cosmic meaning of consciousness became overwhelmingly clear to me. . . . Man is indispensable for the completion of creation; that, in fact, he himself is the second creator of the world, who alone has given to the world its objective existence—without which, unheard, unseen, silently eating, giving birth, dying, heads nodding through the millions of years, it would have gone on in the profoundest night of non-being down to its unknown end. Human consciousness created objective existence and meaning, and man found his indispensable place in the great process of being.[9]

Psychologists and theologians have attempted to describe the major phases of the development of consciousness. John Cobb and William Thompson provide a basic framework for the following discussion.[10]

Pre-Conventional Consciousness

The first stage of consciousness has been called primitive or pre-conventional. This stage refers to the level of consciousness present in our ancestors prior to about 11,000 years ago when agriculture began and towns emerged.

It was a time when consciousness was basically undifferentiated; in other words, people were unconscious. If consciousness means that psychic substance such as thoughts, memories, feelings were related to an ego and this "I" was aware of this substance, then such was not the case in the state of primitive or pre-conventional consciousness.

These people had no awareness of inner psychic material; there was no "I," no subjectivity, no interiority. There was no within, or without. People just participated in life.

Jung writes that most material in the unconscious finds its way out in projection upon the environment. This inner material is first met "out there." In the pre-conventional stage of consciousness the "within" of the human was entirely projected outside and met in the landscape, the animals, other humans. Their inside was all outside, so to speak. When the pilgrims who left footprints at Laetoli were walking through the African landscape they were also, in effect, walking through their psyche, their soul.

This type of consciousness experiences an immediacy in its participation in life. Levy Bruhl has termed this state a time of "participation mystique." He writes: "For the primitive man, like the very young child, has no definite boundaries to his psyche—everything that happens is both in himself and in the object; he feels with the animals, the trees, and so forth. . . ."[11]

Lucy certainly had an immediate participation with her environment. She lived an unconscious psychic life. No interiority, no sense of the presence of the sacred or its absence. No prayers, no attempt to symbolize a deity. Just a oneness with nature and a potentiality for a conscious awareness of her condition some day in the long process of evolution. Lucy could represent the state of human consciousness for over 3 million years.

Language and Consciousness

One would assume that consciousness was slowly developing in humanity over the millions of years of human existence. But a person who would dispute that theory is Julian Jaynes, a creative and controversial psychologist.[12] He believes that consciousness is a relatively recent arrival on the scene, which awaited the development of language. And language, he theorizes, developed no earlier than 70,000 years ago.

Language started slowly. At first intentional sounds were made to designate, for example, danger. The only difference between sounds would have been the intensity. Then sounds would have been modified, perhaps by changing the endings, to tell whether the danger was near or distant, or to express other needs.

Modifiers may have eventually been detached and become commands in their own right. Jaynes argues that the pressures of controlling a group of people would have led to the emergence of a series of commands. He believes that evidence of this language shift can be seen in the qualitatively advanced tools found between 40,000 and 25,000 years ago. The simple command, "Sharper!," could have spurred advances in tool-making. New forms of speech bring new perceptions and new perceptions impact the culture and can be traced in the archaeological record.

Nouns probably followed modifiers and commands. The approaching danger would eventually be named as "tiger" or "bear." These nouns would have emerged between 25,000 and 15,000 years ago. They would have coincided with the first sculptured figurines and cave paintings. More recent datings might vary somewhat from the datings Jaynes uses, but he would still hold for the sequence of modifier, command, noun; and he would look to the archaeological record for indications of language shifts.

It is Jaynes' theory that consciousness began when language was interiorized. By naming the world, humans could then take that world within. Language allowed an inner space to develop. This inner space contained metaphors, images for the outside world, and it contained an "I" analogous to the self. The "I" linked the images in a narrative form.

However accurate these theories may or may not be, they certainly cause us to think about our language and consciousness. Certainly, there was a time when humans had neither.

Conventional Consciousness

A second state of consciousness, following the pre-conventional state, has been termed conventional or civilized. It is a transitional state leading to our present awareness. Following the advent of agriculture 11,000 years ago, the growth of small towns, and then the rise of the great civilizations of the Near East, people experienced a growing rationality. The new conditions demanded more reflective consciousness and, at the same time, growing rationality allowed for these new conditions.

What had previously been projected upon nature was now partially withdrawn and was now projected upon a state with its leadership and rules. Humans no longer simply participated in the life of the sun and the animals, but were now part of an identifiable people with boundaries and norms. The individual found identity and meaning through membership in the community, in relationship to the leader, through fulfillment of the norms of society, and by living on the land.

Julian Jaynes' name for these civilizations is "bicameral." His very creative hypothesis is that when language had evolved, the next step was the interiorization of commands so that the person always had direction. The person's own voice or the voice of the leader is now heard within the person as a command from "another," someone outside the person. Jaynes points to the differentiation of duties of the two hemispheres of the brain as an explanation of how, possibly, one side's communications were heard by the other side as an external voice. In effect, it was an auditory hallucination.

When communities became too large for direct contact, the internalized voices of authorities provided order and stability. Even when the leader died, the voice was still heard within the individual and the dead leader was placed in the center of the community as one still communicating and leading.

An ancient settlement at Eynan, not far north of the Sea of Galilee in Israel, gives evidence of such a situation. This 11,000-year-old site reveals round, stone houses, and in one house two complete skeletons were elaborately entombed, presumably the leader and his wife.

This tomb, one of the earliest known, speaks of an ongoing relationship between the people and the dead leader. According to Jaynes' theory the people, still under the domination of the unconscious, could nonetheless "think" through the still-heard voice of the leader. Jaynes expands his thought: "This was a paradigm of what was to happen in the next eight millennia. The king dead is a living god. The king's tomb is the god's house, the beginning of the elaborate god-house or temples. . . ."[13] Even today our towns show a similar arrangement, a god-house surrounded by people houses.

Again, whether this theory of bicameral civilizations and dead leaders controlling groups through internalized "voices" has any merit is an open question. But it is an intriguing theory and provokes reflection upon our present consciousness and its origins.

Axial Consciousness

Finally, a third stage of consciousness has been identified as "axial consciousness." Its beginnings are located somewhere between the first

millennium B.C. and 500 A.D. This shift in consciousness is character-
ized by a heightened subjectivity, inwardness, and strengthened reason.
This strengthened rationality began to break the hold of the unconscious and its mythic symbolization. Individuality and freedom
emerged. No longer was the psychic life of the group the only life
available to a person. The axial person experienced a separation from the
group and an independent existence. The emergence of freedom meant
that humans did not have to do and think what had always been done and
thought.

The sacred is no longer simply identified with nature, or experienced only within one's people, but God transcends both and is met
within the individual, providing a basis for further autonomy and freedom. This shift from conventional consciousness to axial consciousness
may be seen in certain prophets who embodied both types in their concern for the covenant, and for the widow, the orphan, the stranger. The
worth and dignity of the individual merited attention; not just the traditions and prescribed rites.

Again, Julian Jaynes illumines this shift in consciousness. He points
to the difference in consciousness found in the *Iliad* compared with the
Odyssey. The *Iliad* was written about 900 B.C., recording events that
purportedly happened about 1230 B.C. when the Greeks from Mycenae
attempted to defeat the Trojans who held Helen in Troy. The story of
the Trojan War had been passed down by bards in a meter form. Jaynes
observes that there is, in general, no subjective consciousness in the
Iliad. He writes,

> Iliadic man did not have subjectivity as do we; he had no aware-
> ness of his awareness of the world, no internal mind-space to
> introspect upon. In distinction to our own subjective con-
> scious minds we can call the mentality of the Mycenean a
> *bicameral mind*. Volition, planning, initiative is organized with
> no consciousness whatever and then "told" to the individual in
> his familiar language, sometimes with the visual aura of a famil-
> iar friend or authority figure or "god", or sometimes a voice
> alone. The individual obeyed these hallucinated voices because
> he could not "see" what to do by himself.[14]

There are two occasions in the poem where characters speak to
themselves, indications of greater consciousness. But Jaynes believes
these are later insertions by bards. Even if authentic to the original story,
they demonstrate the infrequency of this kind of thinking. Each speech
ends with the same thought: "But wherefore does my life say this to

me?" For Jaynes the *Iliad* is a great window back into unsubjective times "when every kingdom was in essence a theocracy and every man the slave of voices heard whenever novel situations occurred."[15]

One wonders what percent of biblical stories evince the same level of consciousness? Biblical men and women converse with one another, with angels, and with God. Very few knowingly speak with themselves. The story of the prodigal son is striking in this context because of the inner dialogue it contains: "How many hired hands at my father's place have more than enough to eat, while here I am starving!" (Lk 15:17)

The *Odyssey* gives evidence of this axial shift. Telling the story of the return of Odysseus from the Trojan Wars, it was written down at least a century after the *Iliad*, sometime around 800 B.C.

The characters in this story are much more conscious. The voices of the gods and goddesses are weakened and the humans are left to their own wiles. This poetry is not just expressing external events, but is now expressive of an internal developing consciousness. There is deceit and guile, a heightened sense of time, a frequency of abstract words.

In the often dangerous journeys of Odysseus, Julian Jaynes sees "a story of identity, of a voyage to the self that is being created in the breakdown of the bicameral mind."[16] He views the work as an epic of developing consciousness written down by non-conscious bards. It was as though something were driving the human into consciousness. It cannot be explained. Jaynes concludes:

> But so it is. And as this series of stories sweeps from its lost hero sobbing on an alien shore in bicameral thrall to his beautiful goddess Calypso, winding through its world of demigods, testings, and deceits, to his defiant war whoops in a rival-routed home, from trance through disguise to recognition, from sea to land, east to west, defeat to prerogative, the whole long song is an odyssey toward subjective identity and its triumphant acknowledgment out of the hallucinatory enslavements of the past. From a will-less gigolo of a divinity to the gore-spattered lion on his own hearth, Odysseus becomes "Odysseus."[17]

Historical Consciousness

Somewhere between the thirteenth and seventeenth centuries A.D., a further shift in axial consciousness takes place which is termed "historical consciousness." For the first time human beings begin to reflect on their own consciousness. We become aware of our own awareness, and consequently of the initiative we have in our lives. Culture is now understood as historically conditioned. Rather than being merely objects of history, we begin to understand ourselves as self-creative, as subjects of our history. Mystical literature of the sixteenth century manifests this historical awareness.

In this emergence of consciousness a story is being told, which for most of human history never found words. Christians believe the Jesus story is a fundamental telling of the human story. And the mystic often finds his or her own expression for that story of God's engagement with humanity. Bernard Lonergan's writing provides some illumination for this eons-old drama of God and psyche.

Bernard Lonergan's "Interiority Analysis"

Theologian Bernard Lonergan locates the experience of God within the emergence of consciousness. Drawing upon psychotherapeutic theories, Lonergan engages in an interiority analysis.[18] Psychic life appears to develop according to certain normative operations which themselves are expressive of the dynamism of the human spirit. Lonergan observes that the human being moves from the dark of basic experience to the light of meaning, and then to choice based on that meaning, through "levels of consciousness."

The movement of the psyche proceeds from simple experience, to an attempt to understand what has been experienced, to a judgment about the accuracy or truthfulness of the understanding, to choices for living based on the meaning derived in the process. Psychic life appears to operate according to certain "transcendental precepts": be attentive, be intelligent, be reasonable, be responsible.

This psychic development, in Lonergan's view, is a graced journey. Through these operations the human spirit is reaching out to truth, and ultimately, to God who is absolute truth. Because all humans may reflect on what they do when they "know," Lonergan believes that this cognitional theory is a fundamental starting point for the discussion of religious experience.

Cognition, however, is not the total outcome of the psychic process charted by Lonergan. When an individual moves to a level of consciousness which involves making a choice, then values are operative. The dynamism of the human spirit is revealed to be a thrust toward not only the true, but also the good.

From a faith perspective the thrust toward knowing and valuing inherent in psychic development is a self-transcending process which is meant, ultimately, to involve a relationship with God. The final precept is: Be in love. Because of this outcome, which is involved in making responsible choices, Lonergan sometimes speaks of a final level of consciousness which he terms "religious consciousness."

Religious experience, at this level, is being in love with God "without limits or qualifications or conditions or reservations."[19] The drive of the human spirit at this point becomes an experience of being seized or grasped by God's love. It is actually this love which initiates the journey and impacts on all the levels of consciousness.

John of the Cross and "Unrestricted Eros"

Lonergan understands the dynamism of the human spirit as an "unrestricted eros" which issues in the knowing and loving of God. The mystical experience occurs when one's categories, formulations, constructs fail to satisfy, and the person simply attends to the yearning itself. He writes: "When finally the mystic withdraws into the *ultima solitudo,* he drops the constructs of culture and the whole complicated mass of mediating operations to return to a new, mediated immediacy of his subjectivity reaching for God."[20]

The writings of John of the Cross are illuminated by Lonergan's analysis. John begins with experience in an effort to be attentive. Enter your depths with trust and patience, he counsels. His poetry is a primordial wording of his wordless experience. In his imagery we see the human need to be intelligent, to name what is known darkly.

John's prose commentaries on his poetry are an attempt to be reasonable. He interprets his poetry in traditional theological categories and finds congruences in scripture. Even his prose, however, often sustains the lyricism of his poetry.

John's work also evinces the imperative within our consciousness to be responsible. His advocacy of contemplative prayer is an effort to encourage an appropriate response to the Mystery addressing us, and as the basis for activity which is cooperative with Mystery.

It is evident that John's poetry and prose express the yearnings of the human spirit. When we read John our response is often at inarticulate levels of human hunger. John writes of a knowledge that is a loving knowledge. He experienced a warming of the heart as well as an illumination of the mind. His entire person was transformed as though by fire. We recognize in his pilgrimage and its account a story which is our story, too.

Conversion and Psyche

To authentically cooperate with this self-transcending process identified by Lonergan and recognized in John of the Cross, is to live a spiritual life; and it involves deep changes in the human, or, in Lonergan's terms, conversions. A conversion is a transformation of horizon, a change of heart. Lonergan explicitly refers to three conversions: intellectual, moral, and religious. The dynamism of the human spirit, driven by God's Spirit, involves transformations in one's understanding, the way one lives and, ultimately, involves a surrender to Mystery.

Lonergan's articulation of the process has been extended by others to include a psychic conversion as well. It is discussed as a discrete conversion but would appear to be a fundamental transformation taking place as cognition, morality, and being in love with God occur.

Vernon Gregson discusses this focus on psychic conversion: "The particular importance of psychic conversion for religious consciousness and hence for foundational theology is twofold: first, religious consciousness as orientation of the subject to the Ultimate, i.e., a moving beyond itself to the Other, intends every other level of self-transcendence which can foster and support this final self-forgetfulness. Therefore psychic healing is intended in religious consciousness so that religious consciousness can move toward full term. Secondly, religious consciousness expresses itself most adequately in the limit language of symbol and myth, whose wellspring is the psyche."[21]

Gregson, therefore, calls for "a recovery of psyche in her imaginal and affective dimensions."[22] Implied in this effort is the investigation of the archetypal symbols of one's tradition, as well as the symbols expressive of one's personal religious consciousness.

It is in this realm of image and affect where the writings of John of the Cross are particularly striking. His images become his psyche's basic vocabulary and language. His commentary has to return to the imagery time and again as meaning explodes the confines of his concepts. Of necessity he falls back on the irreducible psychic language of image. The pure light of Mystery is continually refracted through psyche's prism and emerges in multiple forms and colors.

The imagery of John speaks of transformation. The yearning of the heart can be led astray by disordered affectivity. The story John recounts is the transformation of his affectivity, the healing of disordered passions. His poems tell the story of love purified, healed, and reoriented to be in accord with desire's deepest currents.

In his discussions of affective conversion Walter Conn writes that it refers to both passion and commitment. He describes affective conversion as "the transformation of our deepest life of feeling,"[23] and "the radical reorientation of desire."[24] Here is the essential John of the Cross. He is attempting to communicate, analyze, reflect upon the experience of the liberation of an enslaved heart, the transformation of desire.

Human development is most fully carried forward only in conversion. The mystic reveals that the impetus behind humanity's long journey into consciousness is an imperative to be in love. Axial consciousness now present in humanity allows creation, for the first time, to be aware of the journey that has always been going on. Jung was deeply impressed by the miracle of consciousness, a light in the dark of an unknown world. John of the Cross experienced this consciousness as a means of coming to an awareness of the fundamental human story, a story of humanity being pursued into consciousness by love. And in the experience of this love was an invitation to respond. Or, as Jung said of religion, it is nothing if it is not "obedience to awareness."

The vehicle John used for entering the subjective depths of his humanity in order to listen and to communicate was the image. The image carried the story of a psyche being healed, of affectivity being reoriented. When we speak of the imagination of John of the Cross, we speak of the power of his psyche to create images which are primordial wordings of his depth experiences. He continues to address us, particularly as his images address our own psyche and its power of imagination.

John's Commentaries

The following chapters focus on John's commentaries on his poems, in which he uses a prose language to convey his experience of God and the transformation of his humanity. As with his poetry, John hopes to open the reader to the experience of God.

Each of the three commentaries presents an overview of the spiritual journey according to John, but each has a different emphasis. *The Living Flame of Love* is the first commentary to be presented and discussed because it describes the goal of the mystical journey. With this goal in mind then, the ensuing chapters present John's account of the spiritual journey toward this goal.

THE LIVING FLAME OF LOVE

O Living flame of love
That tenderly wounds my soul
In its deepest center! Since
Now You are not oppressive,
Now Consummate! if it be Your will:
Tear through the veil of this sweet encounter!

O sweet cautery,
O delightful wound!
O gentle hand! O delicate touch
That tastes of eternal life
And pays every debt!
In killing You changed death to life.

O lamps of fire!
In whose splendors
The deep caverns of feeling,
Once obscure and blind,
Now give forth, so rarely, so exquisitely,
Both warmth and light to their Beloved.

How gently and lovingly
You wake in my heart,
Where in secret You dwell alone;
And in Your sweet breathing,
Filled with good and glory,
How tenderly You swell my heart with love.

CHAPTER FOUR

Humanity Transformed

The Living Flame of Love

The commentary on *The Living Flame of Love* describes John's deepest experience of union with God and consequently is a profound and often lyrical description of the goal of contemplative prayer. In particular, John's description of his experience as a divinization process, a sharing in the knowing and loving of God, is an exposition of the core of our Christian faith.

To begin with this commentary is to see the journey's end. John is so identified with the dark night that it is sometimes difficult to perceive the results of that night, the outcome of the soul's pilgrimage. *The Living Flame of Love* describes the results, the experience of one whose humanity has been transformed in union with God. Once this outcome is known it then becomes a guide to understanding the stages of the journey as described by John in his other commentaries.

John alludes to the times when the soul experienced darkness and pain, but shows how it was a prelude to great delight and satisfaction. John here describes contemplative prayer as a "loving knowledge." And he offers a lengthy discussion of the role of the spiritual director, warning the director not to be a hindrance but to follow God's lead in the soul.

The first part of this chapter will be a brief summary of John's commentary. The second part will be a reflection on the commentary, aided by understandings developed from Carl Jung and Bernard Lonergan. The discussion focuses in particular on the Mystery experienced at the core of our humanity and the subsequent transformation of that humanity.

A SUMMARY OF *THE LIVING FLAME OF LOVE*

John addresses his commentary to Doña Ana de Peñalosa, for whom he wrote the poem. She has requested this explanation. In the prologue he speaks of the difficulty in explaining the poem. The matters are so deeply interior that words can rarely satisfy. But John has waited until he has experienced a level of recollection which will allow him to begin the task.

Immediately, John points to the core experience which is being expressed in the poem, the experience of the indwelling of God. "He takes up His abode in a man by making him live the life of God and dwell in the Father, the Son, and the Holy Spirit, as the soul points out in these stanzas."[1]

Not only is John speaking about the highest state of transformation in God, he is also describing even more intense moments within this state. The wood has been made one with the fire but the heat is such that flames constantly shoot up from the fire. The soul does not just join with the fire, but produces flames within itself.

> 1. O living flame of love
> That tenderly wounds my soul
> In its deepest center! Since
> Now You are not oppressive,
> Now Consummate! If it be Your will:
> Tear through the veil of this sweet encounter!

Commenting on the first stanza of the poem John lyrically describes a soul "bathed in glory and love."[2] It is so transformed in God that it is almost in heaven. It is as if a thin veil separated it from that perfect union, and it asks for the veil to be removed. The exclamations "O" and "Now" used in the poem are expressions of John's intense desire.

John identifies the flame with the Holy Spirit.[3] The soul is transformed and its will is one with the will of the Holy Spirit. As a flame shoots up, the soul experiences intense acts of love in this state. "One of them is more meritorious and valuable than all the deeds a person may have performed in his whole life without this transformation, however great they may have been."[4]

The will is so united with God that the soul's activity is now God's activity. "Thus in this state the soul cannot make acts because the Holy Spirit makes them all and moves it toward them. As a result all the acts of the soul are divine, since the movement toward these acts and their execution stems from God."[5]

The effect of this intense union with the flame is a wounding of the soul. It melts, as it were, into God. The flames which the soul experiences in its deepest center are the language of God. "For God's speech is the effect He produces in the soul."[6] The effect is the divinization of the soul: "Thus all the movements of this soul are divine. Although they belong to it, they belong to it because God works them in it and with it, for it wills and consents to them."[7]

This intimacy with God takes place in the substance of the soul, a deeply interior and secure realm. John says simply, "The soul's center is God."[8] The soul is in God, and so in its center, but it can always go more deeply into God, to other more interior centers. The strength of its love determines the depth of its center.

John admits that this language may sound exaggerated. He knows some people will not believe that these experiences are possible. But they underestimate the generosity of God who, "always showing himself gladly along the highways and byways—does not hesitate or consider it of little import to find His delights with the children of men at a common table in the world. (Prv. 8:31)"[9]

Previously the Flame Caused Pain

The experience of an inflaming of the soul which John is trying to describe in the poem is a positive experience. But there was a time when the flame was painful. It was an experience of the purgative way. Then, the flame was dark, afflictive, painful, dry, consuming, and contentious. "In the substance of his soul he suffers abandonment, supreme poverty, dryness, cold, and sometimes heat."[10] Nothing is consoling, and it seems that God is displeased with the person.

John explains that this dark experience is the outcome of the brightness of the flame; it illumines the darkness of the soul. Without the illumination the darkness is not seen. The flame is tender and loving, but its presence reveals the will as hard and dry. In this purification process the will does not feel the sweetness of the flame; it is only aware of its own "misery, poverty, and evil."[11]

Fortunately, John says, not many people have to walk such an intense purgative way. It depends upon the degree to which God wishes to raise a person. John reminds the reader that he treats this dark experience more completely in his commentary, *The Dark Night*.

But in the present commentary John is reporting a positive experience, a transformation in love, or the spiritual marriage. And he wants it
to be consummated. Asking for a consummation is like saying "give me
this kingdom, if it be Your will, according to Your will."[12] The encounter with God is so intense that it "seems about to tear through the
veil of mortal life."[13]

John then has an intriguing observation. The death of those in this
state of union is different from the death of other people. Sickness and
old age may be the sole explanation for many deaths; but for those living
in this union of love, death comes from a powerful experience of love
tearing through the veil. It is a peaceful transition. "The death of such
persons is very gentle and very sweet, sweeter and more gentle than was
their whole spiritual life on earth."[14]

A Consonance of Desires

But before this gentle death, the soul has seen life with a great
clarity, "for, since he has God's view of things, he regards them as God
does. . . . All things are nothing to it, and it is nothing in its own eyes;
God alone is its all."[15] With this perspective the soul lives in complete
accord with God. The outcome of this loving union is a consonance of
desires: "What you desire me to ask for, I ask for; and what you do not
desire, I do not desire, nor can I, nor does it even enter my mind to
desire it."[16]

> 2. O sweet cautery,
> O delightful wound!
> O gentle hand! O delicate touch
> That tastes of eternal life
> And pays evey debt!
> In killing You changed death to life.

In the second stanza the soul addresses the Father, Son, and Holy
Spirit through the images of hand, touch, and cautery. All three Persons
transform the soul. The outstanding image is that of the cautery, as-
signed by John to the Holy Spirit. This wounding by the Spirit varies in
intensity depending upon the preparation of the individual and the desire of the Spirit: "He will burn one more, another less. . . ."[17]

The burning is not afflictive but delightful as it divinizes the soul.
This divinization is expressed by John when he says that not only does
the soul experience the wounding of the cautery, but the soul becomes a

cautery itself. "The happy soul that by great fortune reaches this cautery knows all things, tastes all things, does all it wishes, and prospers; no one prevails before it and nothing touches it."[18] John's language challenges a reader to attempt to understand the effects of divinization in a person.

The wounding in the soul by the Spirit is delightful, but there may have been other wounds brought about by "miseries and sins." Still, when these wounds are touched by the cautery of the Spirit they, too, become wounds of love.

No medicine can cure this type of wound. The cautery itself simultaneously wounds and heals. ". . . The very cautery that causes it, cures it, and by curing it, causes it. . . . The more it wounds, the more it cures and heals."[19] This sublime activity takes place in the very center of the substance of the soul. No form or figure accompanies it, whether imaginative or other. But John reports another, less intense, experience of wounding which is accompanied by an intellectual form. It seems as if a seraphim is wounding the soul with an arrow or dart. John's vivid description of this experience locates it "in the substance of the spirit in the heart of the pierced soul."[20]

The result is a tremendously strong and refined love which pervades the soul. "It seems to it that the entire universe is a sea of love in which it is engulfed. . . ."[21] Among the few who have ever experienced such intensities of love John places founders of religious communities. They are so gifted because of the needs of their family.

An example of such a wounding of love is seen in the life of St. Francis, and in this case the wounding becomes physically evident in his stigmata. John comments that usually an interior experience precedes any external manifestation. Nevertheless, experiences of God's love which are solely interior with no external manifestation can result in a more intense and sublime delight.

Mysticism Before Asceticism

John emphasizes the preceding point because people often assume that the spiritual life grows from the outside to the inside. The assumption is that a person will advance through force and activity, and that the movement is from the senses to the spirit. But John says the reverse is true. To reach this peak of union the senses have to be set aside. And then the spirit may overflow into the senses. "I say this in order to make it clear that he who would go to God relying upon natural ability and reasoning will not be very spiritual."[22] The love of God, experienced within, flows out to the senses. Mysticism precedes asceticism.

The favors received by the soul are imaged as a touch by a hand. Here, John says, is the activity of the Son and the Father. This touch of the Son "is a touch of substances, that is, of the substance of God in the substance of the soul"[23] John complains that words make the experience appear to be less than it really is. "The appropriate language for the person receiving these favors is that he understand them, experience them within himself, enjoy them, and be silent."[24]

Someone receiving these favors will have lived a life of faithful service. John says such a person accepts the trials and sufferings that come and does not attempt to run away from them. This combat is necessary for the purification and strengthening of the soul.

The transformation is from death to life, from animal life to spiritual life. The intellect, will, memory, appetites, and all the movements, operations, and inclinations of the soul are now divinized. "Accordingly, the intellect of this soul is God's intellect; its will is God's will; its memory is the memory of God; and its delight is God's delight; and although the substance of this soul is not the substance of God, since it cannot undergo a substantial conversion into Him, it has become God through participation in God, being united to and absorbed in Him, as it is in this state."[25]

John quotes the classic scripture passage for the mystical experience: "I live, now not I, but Christ lives in me. (Gal 2:20)"[26]

> 3. O lamps of fire!
> In whose splendors
> The deep caverns of feeling,
> Once obscure and blind,
> Now give forth, so rarely, so exquisitely,
> Both warmth and light to their Beloved.

In commenting on the third stanza, John identifies the "lamps of fire" as the attributes of God: God's omnipotence, wisdom, goodness, justice, mercy, and other infinite powers. The soul experiences these many attributes in the one act of union. The "lamps" are one lamp, one God, giving the soul a finely differentiated knowledge and love of God.

The fire from these lamps enflames the soul in such a gentle, life-giving manner that John likens them to waters of life, satisfying the spirit's thirst. John speaks of the "spirit of God . . . hidden in the veins of the soul" acting like water which refreshes and flames which enkindle. The transformation of the person is dramatic: "The soul becomes God from God through participation in Him and in His attributes, which it terms 'lamps of fire.' "[27]

The relationship with God in this state is such that one harmonious life is being lived. The movement of the flames is understood to be the work of both the soul and the Spirit now; the air and fire are inseparable.[28]

John then likens the lamps to "overshadowings." Mary was overshadowed by the Holy Spirit, a sign of protection and favor. So, a soul living in the shadow of God is not darkened but made resplendent. "To express it better: it will be the very wisdom and the very beauty, and the very fortitude of God in shadow, because the soul here cannot comprehend God perfectly."[29] The soul takes on the attributes of God.

The "deep caverns of feeling" in the poem refer to intellect, memory, and will. These caverns are the soul's hunger for knowledge and love. When temporarily satisfied with something finite, these caverns are not aware of their vast capacity, the depth of human desire. When emptied and purified the hunger and thirst within their yearning are powerful. "Since they have deep cavities," writes John, "they suffer profoundly, for the food they lack, which as I say is God, is also profound."[30] The nearer to union with God, the more intense the hunger.

John then observes that this very desire for God is itself the possession of God. "The more the soul desires God the more it possesses Him, and the possession of God delights and satisfies it."[31] The awareness of one's infinite hungers at this point is not painful but delightful.

Because the soul has reached a delicate stage in its growing union with God, John warns about detours caused by "three blind men": the soul itself, the devil, and the spiritual director.[32]

The Spiritual Director

At this point in the commentary John unexpectedly offers a small treatise on the role of the spiritual director. He realizes that it is an interruption in his commentary on the poem, but he wants to offer some advice so that people will not fall back, but continue to advance.

He begins by affirming the fact that God is seeking us much more than we are seeking God. Consequently, "God is the principal agent in this matter. . . ."[33] Any other assistance should be careful not to hinder the guidance which God gives.

An accomplished director will be difficult to find. John recommends three qualifications: learning, discretion, and experience. He calls learning and discretion the "foundation," but says there will be no success without experience. Without these qualifications a director may harm a soul. In particular the director may hinder a soul who is being called from meditation to contemplation.

Meditation is the prayer of the beginner. The soul reflects, imagines, makes use of the senses. The director should encourage this intentional activity by suggesting material for meditation. But, in time, God begins to lead the soul into contemplative prayer. "This occurs in some persons after a very short time, especially with religious. . . ."[34]

Dryness indicates the beginning of contemplative prayer. The soul cannot think and meditate as before, nor does it experience sensible satisfaction in prayer. Without this natural ability to be active in prayer, the soul now is in the position of receiving from God in contemplation. John defines contemplation as "loving knowledge."[35]

The spiritual director, then, should not encourage active prayer efforts; a passive, receptive stance is called for. God is working in the soul, and the soul should commune with God through a "simple and loving knowledge or attention. . . ."[36]

John further counsels: "A person should not bear attachment to anything, neither to the practice of meditation, nor to any savor, whether sensory or spiritual, nor to any other apprehensions. He should be very free and annihilated regarding all things, because any thought or discursive reflection or satisfaction upon which he may want to lean would impede and disquiet him and make noise in the profound silence of his senses and his spirit, which he possesses for the sake of this deep and delicate listening."[37] Even this practice of loving attention should be let go when the person is conscious of God's activity in a peaceful, inward absorption.[38]

The soul is not always aware of the good being done in this holy idleness and solitude. "The least that a person can manage to feel," writes John, "is a withdrawal and an estrangement as to all things, sometimes more than at other times, accompanied by an inclination toward solitude and a weariness with all creatures and with the world, in the gentle breathing of love and life in the spirit."[39]

The Director As "Blacksmith"

John observes that it is often at this delicate time that a spiritual director comes along and acts like a "blacksmith," hammering and pounding. The director, not understanding this quiet recollection, recommends more activity for the faculties.

John reminds the director once again that the true guide is the Holy Spirit, not the director. The director should not try to accommodate the individual to the director's method and understanding, but should cooperate with the Spirit's work in that person.

Again, John says that the soul is experiencing contemplation, a supernatural knowledge. "This knowledge is general and dark to the intellect because it is contemplative knowledge, which is a ray of darkness for the intellect, as St. Dionysius teaches."[40] The will, too, is darkened as God communicates both knowledge and love in an indistinct manner.

In John's experience the two faculties of intellect and will are not always equally favored: "sometimes more knowledge is experienced than love, and at other times more love than knowledge, and likewise at times all knowledge is felt without any love, or all love without any knowledge."[41]

Memory and imagination, also, are left with no form or figure. In John's view, they walk more safely this way because God is beyond an imaginative grasp. God is feeding the spirit without the help of the faculties in this experience. However, directors hamper the process when they stress meditation, imaginative reflection, and other interior activity. "These directors do not know what spirit is."[42]

Nor should a director expect to be able to walk the entire journey with someone. A soul will have need for a different doctrine and a change of prayer at different times in life. A director should not presume to know all the stages of the journey.

John writes: "Not everyone capable of hewing the wood knows how to carve the statue, nor does everyone able to carve know how to perfect and polish the work, nor do all who know how to polish know how to paint it, nor do all who can paint it know how to put the finishing touches on it and bring the work to completion. No man can do more with the statue than what he knows how to do, and were he to try to do more than this, he would ruin it."[43]

The Soul Should Have Freedom

John stresses the need for the soul to have freedom in this matter of direction. If the soul is dissatisfied for some reason and finds the director unhelpful, either because God seems to be leading the soul along a different road, or because the director has changed style, then it may be time to change directors. John is particularly concerned about directors who cannot be truly helpful because they are guided by their own self-interests, satisfactions, or fears.

The other "blind men" who may hinder spiritual growth are the devil and the soul itself. In both cases John locates the problem in a regressive movement from spirit back to senses. He maintains that either the devil, or the soul, will undermine the loving attentiveness of this time in prayer by offering to the senses some satisfaction, or particular knowledge, or other acts which will appear more fruitful that the quiet work God is doing in the soul.

Even the desire for God may not be a sure guide because it may not be "supernatural." If the desire for God derives from an attachment to the satisfaction involved in this relationship, then John considers it a natural desire, not truly spiritual. Even in this delicate matter he leaves the soul no place to hide.[44]

John further describes the effects of divinization. Because God is bringing about this transformation the soul is satisfied and happy "to see that it gives to God more than in itself it is worth; and this it does with that very divine light and divine heat and solitude."[45]

The soul is loving God, but with God's love: ". . . the soul here loves God, not through itself but through Him."[46] The soul is absorbed in God: ". . . the soul delights with order in God alone, without any intermingling of creature."[47] And the soul loves God without regard for self: ". . . it enjoys Him only on account of Who he is without any admixture of its own pleasure."[48]

> 4. How gently and lovingly
> You wake in my heart,
> Where in secret You dwell alone;
> And in Your sweet breathing,
> Filled with good and glory,
> How tenderly You swell my heart with love.

The fourth stanza of *The Living Flame of Love* speaks of an awakening in the heart. It is a beautiful image which ostensibly refers to the awakening of the Word in the substance of the soul, but in reality it is the soul that is awakening. The soul awakens to the wisdom of God sustaining and enlivening this world. "For the soul is conscious of how all creatures, earthly and heavenly, have their life, duration, and strength in Him. . . ."[49]

The view of the world from within this state of union allows the soul to see the world differently: "And here lies the remarkable delight of this awakening: the soul knows creatures through God and not God through creatures."[50]

In this awakening of the Bridegroom within the soul, the soul experiences the "sweet breathing" of the Holy Spirit. John protests that he is incapable of further description of this love for God which the Holy Spirit has enkindled. His final lines become a prayer as he explains that "the Holy Spirit, through this breathing, filled the soul with good and glory, in which He enkindled it in love of Himself, indescribably and incomprehensibly, in the depths of God, to Whom be honor and glory forever and ever. Amen."[51]

REFLECTIONS ON *THE LIVING FLAME OF LOVE*

The Living Flame of Love presents the goal of the mystic's journey. It describes a situation in which a human has journeyed to the center of his humanity and there experienced the presence of a loving Spirit. In this meeting the human and divine have entered so deeply into a relationship that John has difficulty knowing what of the experience is his nature and what is God.

During the course of his life, John surrendered that life to the Mystery who is God. He experienced being loved by God and his life was transformed to be more and more in accord with that God. It is evident from his description of the mystical experience that his personality underwent profound changes. He entered into intense psychic conversions. His description of the experience relied upon the psychic categories available to him.

In the following section John's language will be more clearly defined, and then the language of Carl Jung will be introduced to provide a contemporary language for, and understanding of, the psyche. It is the hope that each language helps interpret and challenge the other.

John's Anthropology

John's understanding of the human person, his anthropology, is largely drawn from the Aristotelian psychology of his day. The soul, or person, has a psychological structure which has two major components, the sensory and the spiritual. Each component has specific faculties, or powers.

The sensory part of the soul, sometimes referred to as the lower part and sometimes as the exterior part, consists of the powers of external and internal senses. The external senses are sight, hearing, smell, taste, and touch. The world comes into the person through the external senses. The internal senses are imagination, fantasy, and sense memory. John does not distinguish among them but, in general, they appear to be the recipients of impressions of external images, making the world present within the individual and available to the spiritual faculties. They are capable of conjuring up their own images as well. He refers to the interior sense as an archive or a receptacle for image and forms, and he says it functions as a mirror presenting this material to the spiritual senses.[52]

The Spiritual Part of the Soul

The spiritual part of the soul, sometimes referred to as the upper and sometimes as the interior part, consists of the powers of intellect, will, and memory. These are the faculties which enable a person to know, to love and choose, to envision.

The intellect refers to the ability to understand, to comprehend, to make meaning. It draws its data from the internal senses. John describes the imagination and fantasy as "the gate and entry to the soul." He continues: "Here the intellect comes as though to a seaport or market to buy and sell provisions."[53]

The memory is closely linked with fantasy. It is not only a store-house of the past but a source for envisioning possible futures. Purified, it is the seat of hope.

John generally follows the anthropology of St. Thomas Aquinas who acknowledges only intellect and will as spiritual faculties. In including memory among the spiritual faculties John appears to be following St. Augustine. However, in John's use, at times memory seems to be connected to fantasy, and at times it appears to be a part of intellect. The addition of memory as a distinct spiritual faculty may be quite practical since it allows John to relate the three theological virtues of faith, hope, and love to the three spiritual faculties, intellect, memory, and will.

The will is the final arbiter and governor of the whole personality. It is inclined to the good as the good is comprehended by the intellect. The will has to contend with the appetites and passions, or emotions.

Appetites and Passions

The appetites refer to the drive within each faculty, sensory and spiritual, to obtain its fulfillment. Other terms used by John to express appetites are longing, craving, concupiscence, inclination, seeking, and desire. John speaks of involuntary appetites, such as the desire for food, and the voluntary appetites, which could be the conscious decision to indulge moderately or not.

The passions are related to the will, accompanying and influencing its decisions. When passions are "unruly" the will has difficulty making proper choices. The four passions are hope, joy, fear, sorrow. The soul hopes to have appetites fulfilled, experiences joy at their fulfillment, fears the loss of fulfillment, and sorrows when the object of desire is not attained or is lost. ". . . Keep in mind that wherever one of these passions goes the entire soul (the will and the other faculties) will also go, and they will live as prisoners of this passion."[54] The will, by the light of the soul's memory and intellect, has to govern and direct these passions as it searches for the good.

John uses the verb *sentir* or the noun *sentimientos* to refer to feelings which are also understood as experiences. These experiences, or feelings, may take place in the sensory or spiritual parts of the soul. These feelings may be broadly emotional in response to an experience in life, or subtle and interior in response to the spirit's experience of God.

The Soul's Relationship with God

The spiritual part of the soul is the realm where a relationship with God is established. Here God is known and loved. For John of the Cross, to be human is to be in relationship with God. All the faculties, appetites, and passions are ultimately directed to God. The human spirit is a capacity for this relationship, an openness to the activity of God. God can enter the spirit directly, without going through the door of the senses.

As in *The Living Flame of Love* John sometimes speaks of a point of interiority within the human spirit which he refers to as the substance. In Scholastic thought the substance was the true essence of a thing. John is attempting to name the most interior, most intimate, part of the soul where the substance of God touches the substance of the soul. It is the dynamic point of union of spirit and Spirit. Here it is revealed that God is the center of the soul, and to be human is to have a capacity for divinization.

John speaks a language foreign to people today. But with some patience on the part of the reader his language can be a code which has its own appeal as an expression of the mysteries involved in human and divine interaction. And it is possible that his categories may be further enlivened through dialogue with a more modern developmental language, such as that offered by Carl Jung.

Carl Jung: A Contemporary Model of the Psyche

Carl Jung, Swiss depth-psychologist, was one of the pioneers in the study of the human psyche. He explored this realm of interiority which he defined as "the totality of all psychic processes, conscious as well as unconscious."[55] By consciousness Jung meant the thoughts, memories, feelings which are present in our awareness through the ego. Ego is the center of consciousness. Those psychic contents which are not related to the ego, and therefore not in consciousness, are in the unconscious.

Jung hypothesized a content within this psyche which he termed libido, or energy. For Freud, this energy had a distinctly sexual character. For Jung it was undifferentiated, capable of leading to many forms of development, but essentially it was available for the wholeness of life available to the personality.

Energy in the psyche could be said to operate according to certain laws. Energy appears to be arranged in polarities and the interaction of the polarities generates the development of the personality. Energy also appears to follow a law of equilibrium in that the opposites within the personality seek a balance; for example, a balance between the masculine and the feminine components of the psyche.

The personality which emerges as the opposites interact and balance Jung termed the self. The self is the center of the entire personality, both conscious and unconscious. The task of adult development in Jung's psychology is for ego, the center of consciousness, to learn to relate properly to the wider life of the psyche and its true center, the self.

Personal and Collective Unconscious

Jung viewed the unconscious as having two major components, or two strata, the personal and the collective. The personal unconscious contains material which is the result of the individual's personal development in life. Here reside past experiences which have not been integrated, such as relationships with parents. Here, too, are the results of the inadequate adjustment to our sexual and power needs. The personal unconscious contains the psychic debris, unused or unintegrated, of the development of the individual. Jung at times referred to this realm as the shadow side of the personality.

The second major component of the unconscious, a deeper strata, Jung termed the collective unconscious. It is a layer of psychic life which all humans share. It is, as it were, the underground stream which feeds the wells of individual lives. The psyche is of an immense age. The deeper down the psyche I go, the less I am "I" and the more I am "we." The contents of the collective unconscious are not the result of personal experience, but of millions of years of psychic development. These contents Jung called archetypes. They were being formed in the psyches of Lucy and her ancestors, and found expression on the walls of the Lascaux cave.

Archetypal Symbols

Archetypes are imprints in the psyche, fundamental human patterns, which are available for the growth of the self. While Jung called these seeds of the self "primordial images," they are not actual images but more like negatives needing to be developed. They represent readinesses for the personality to develop in accord with certain typically human themes.

The archetypes are deep in the unconscious and not directly accessible to consciousness. Jung even referred to them as "psychoid"; they are of the psyche but reach out to what is beyond psyche. The archetypes can be known only through symbolic representations, images which confront ego-consciousness and speak of the unknown depths of the personality. When symbols are able to relate the ego to this level of psyche then the energy in the collective unconscious is available for the development of the personality in potentially healthy patterns.

Archetypal symbols are the basic language of the psyche. Through them the psyche expresses its most profound experiences; it also reads itself in the presence of such symbols. It comes to know its brokenness through the shadow archetype which is collective as well as personal. It meets its possible modes of being in the archetypes of feminine and masculine. Archetypal patterns of journeying, heroic adventure, death and rebirth engage the personality. At the center of the personality is the archetype of the self, the most powerful of the patterns. Jung also calls this archetype the God-archetype because it acts as a God within the psyche.

We have already begun to discuss the archetypal themes of John of the Cross in the symbols of his poetry and the stories from scripture. His imagination found in the archaic images of fire, wound, veil, touch, lamp, cavern, and breath, a language for his soul.

An Example: John's Image of Flame

A key image for John in *The Living Flame of Love* is the flame itself. This symbol has continually evoked typical meanings. Flame and fire are essentially the same symbol. Fire is an image of energy, whether physical or spiritual. It expresses a life force. On the one hand its flames are often linked to a destructive, consuming experience. As a destructive force fire is related to evil and the demonic. But the destruction is often a prelude to renewal, and so fire also represents a purification.

As an elemental force it may symbolize a deity, particularly a creative God. The hearth fire drove away evil spirits, and as center of the home, signaled hospitality. The alchemists thought fire the center of all things.

As we have discussed, the flame symbol in John's poem has this paradoxical nature. It speaks of a wound and its pain. The wounding is an experience of oppression and even a killing. Yet this same flame is delightful, gentle, and life-giving. John identifies the flame with the Holy Spirit.

The flame constellates other symbols as well. It burns in the "center" of the person and swells the "heart." It separates into "lamps" warming and illumining "caverns of feeling." The depths of John's desire, the goal of his quest, is revealed as he asks the flame to "consummate" and "tear through the veil."

Carl Jung would hear in this language of John of the Cross primordial words of the human spirit.

John, Jung, and Human Transformation

In his commentary on *The Living Flame of Love* John describes the effects of his experience on the dynamics of his psyche. The passions no longer war against the will, and the appetites seek only what is proper and healthy. Consequently, the faculties are functioning properly and the entire psychic structure is in harmony, operating in accord with the soul's deepest nature, and with the God who dwells in its center. "What you desire me to ask for, I ask for; and what you do not desire, I do not desire, nor can I, nor does it even enter my mind to desire it."[56]

This language reveals a deep healing within human desire so that now this desire is expressive of the most fundamental current within the human. His psyche has been radically healed and now experiences a gentle, delightful enlivening, an inflaming.

Jung has a view of the goal of human development which resonates with John's description of his transformation. The self which emerges through the dialogue of consciousness and the unconscious is a healed and enlivened individual. The energy of the psyche has an in-built propensity for wholeness, the fullness of life available to the personality. The psyche, formerly at odds with itself, now engages in healing communication.

The ego, center of consciousness, has escaped the danger of isolation. In its religious journey, its "obedience to awareness," it has learned of another law within the personality. It has opened itself to the realm of the collective unconscious, the "objective psyche" and begun to find its orientation around another center, the self.

In this process, the polarities of the psyche are united. The integration is always relative because the self is not an object to be achieved but an objective toward which the personality grows. The unconscious is never finally exhausted, never entirely made conscious. Or, as John of the Cross teaches, the journey is never completed this side of death. Even the "dawn" experience of union which he is describing in *The Living Flame of Love* still partakes of night's darkness; it is always a journey in faith.

Nevertheless, relative wholeness of the psyche means that polarities have reconciled and consciousness has grown. The shadow side of the personality has been acknowledged and accepted, and a positive integration has taken place. (John of the Cross will speak more pointedly about this painful experience of confronting one's "miseries" in *The Dark Night*.)

The masculine and feminine modes of consciousness, one focused and differentiating, the other diffused and uniting, are now available to the individual. This "marriage" allows the person to breathe in rhythm with life. The result of the dialogue between consciousness and the unconscious is a personality which is at the same time uniquely individual, or "individuated," and responsibly communal, nourished from the collective strata of psychic life.

The God-Image

The entire personality is centered on the archetype of the self, or the God-image. Jung observed that he could not differentiate symbols for the self from symbols for God. Both types have the same centering, harmonizing effect on the psyche. When he equates the self with the God-image Jung claims not to be speaking about God as such, but about the inherent readiness of the psyche for someone or something to be its greatest value, and around which the personality will have its orientation.

Jung insists that he is observing effects in the psyche only and not commenting on the objective existence of God. What then is the ultimate source of healing in the psyche? If life is a circumambulation of the center, as Jung believed, who or what resides at the center? Is the self the

final reality at the core of humanity? Are God symbols merely symbols
of the psychological self?

John's Testimony

The testimony of John of the Cross, based on his own experience,
is that he was led by Another into the depths of his personality. His
senses, his spirit, and his very substance were affected. He experienced a
transformation of his personality which was a fulfillment, and not an
annihilation. These realities of a transformed self spoke themselves in
poetic imagery: a living flame, delightful wound, lamps of fire, caverns
of feeling, an awakening heart.

Yet, these self-symbols are also God symbols, expressions of the
Mystery met in the substance of John's soul. His testimony was to a
gracious reality at the core of his existence, but not totally compassed by
his existence. Within the innate structures of his personality he encountered a transcendent source of identity. From within and beyond his
psyche he was drawn into a relationship which totally transformed him.
He did not hesitate to name this presence within him "God." The ancient Christian formula was applied to his experience: ". . . the Father,
the Son, and the Holy Spirit, are they Who effect in it this divine work
of union."[57]

The Mystery at the core of his being, initially mediated by the
psyche's poetic images, now is named as the God of Christians. "The
soul's center is God."[58] The effect of this encounter on the soul is
dramatic and unexpected: "The soul becomes God from God through
participation in Him and in His attributes. . . ."[59] The union is so intense that John, practically, cannot separate the two realities, the soul
and God. The flame images both the life of the soul and the activity of
the Holy Spirit.

Effects of Divinization

John struggles to express this divinization of his humanity. He no
longer is himself, or rather, he is himself but with divine life: "Thus in
this state the soul cannot make acts because the Holy Spirit makes them
all and moves it toward them."[60] And again he attempts to describe this
new relationship: "Thus all the movements of this soul are divine. Although they belong to it, they belong to it because God works them in it
and with it, for it wills and consents to them."[61]

In this experience the person still functions as a human being, making meaning and responsibly choosing, but the person's consciousness is now so totally transformed that John boldly says the intellect, the will, the memory are now God's intellect, will, and memory.

John is attempting to delineate a gradual change in the motivation for human activity. As the senses are purified and united with the spirit, and as the human spirit is transformed by the Holy Spirit, the locus of intentionality shifts.

When we love solely at the sense level, we love because the object of our love pleases us, attracts us, is fulfilling to us. It is a love that tends to extremes, bending all to our good and making a true encounter impossible. A purification by God brings these senses into harmony with the spiritual faculties and we begin to live on the level of spirit in a truly human manner.

When we love at this level of spirit we love with human understanding and deliberate choosing. The motivation for our love is now in consciousness and we love because we should love. We know we are loved by God, and we are to love others because God loves them and invests them with immense dignity and worth. We love now, not because it is satisfying, but because it is the thing to do. We even love those who do not please us, even our enemies. It is our intention to love them, and we freely do so. In this gospel activity we are followers of Christ.

However, when the human spirit is transformed in a deep union of love with the Holy Spirit, motivation for our love shifts. The motivation for our love is no longer in us but now is in God. We now love but essentially do not have the reason for our love. The intention for our love has now moved, so to speak, into God. We love without knowing why; we simply love, and can do nothing but love. In our love, God is loving God and God's world. ". . . The soul here loves God, not through itself but through Him."[62]

John describes the soul as deeply satisfied and happy "to see that it gives to God more than in itself it is worth; and this it does with that very divine light and divine heat and solitude."[63] John says this reality is no more and no less than the life described by Paul: "I live, now not I, but Christ lives in me. (Gal 2:20)"[64]

Human Development and Divinization

John's account of his transformation witnesses to the essence of Christian belief. Human development is not only the emergence of human potential but it is also a growing participation in divine life.

Human divinization means that the intellect and will in some way share in God's knowing and loving. John's language is strong: "The soul becomes God from God through participation in Him and in His attributes. . . ."[65] At the same time John does not collapse the two realities: ". . . the substance of this soul is not the substance of God. . . ."[66]

The paradigm for this experience is the life, death, and resurrection of Jesus Christ. He is the fully divinized human being who demonstrates to humanity the depths of its possibilities. Because of the solidarity of humanity all human development is now open to participation in divinity. More than an openness to divinity, authentic human development is already a process of divinization.[67] Authentic human self-transcendence is at the same time God's self-communication.

Christ and Axial Consciousness

In the long development of human consciousness it could be said that the resurrected Christ signalled an intensification of interiority.[68] Axial consciousness, witnessed in certain writings of the prophets, was the emergence of freedom and autonomy in humanity. The person had a subjectivity, an inward identity; an "I" arose. The human person was more than simply physical or biological, but also had a spiritual dimension. Jesus radicalized this development.

Within human interiority Jesus experienced the immediacy of a divine presence, "Abba." He spoke of a transcendent core in the human personality, the Kingdom which is within. The experience of Christ's resurrection impelled reflection on the part of the disciples which led to a new level of consciousness, a new realization of the spiritual dimension of individuation.

At the center of the human personality is a transcendent source of identity. Jesus' life, death, and resurrection confirmed a divine presence in the depths of the human co-constituting the self. The long history of the development of human consciousness is revealed as the tracing of God's intimate presence within the human, and a continuing invitation to humanity to participate in divinity. In the words of John of the Cross, transformation is the manifestation of "the spirit of God . . . hidden in the veins of the soul. . . ."[69]

Lonergan and "Unrestricted Eros"

Lonergan's articulation of the dynamism of the human spirit as an "unrestricted eros" issuing in the knowing and loving of God provides a further context for understanding the experience of John of the Cross. In John's categories, the transformation of the faculties, particularly the intellect and will, resulted in a knowing and loving which was a participation in God's knowing and loving. John experienced his spirit as a movement beyond knowing and loving any particular thing or person or any representation of God, to an experience of the deep desire hidden within that very knowing and loving. John says that only when the faculties are emptied of particular references is there an awareness of the deep thirst and hunger present in them.

John's experience of God within the "deep caverns of feeling" was an experience of the desire for God which was fundamental to his psychic structure. ". . . It is true that when the soul desires God fully, it then possesses Him Whom it loves. . . ."[70] Lonergan speaks of this mystical experience as occurring when one's categories, formulations, constructs fail to satisfy, and the person simply attends to the yearning itself. The person returns to a "new, mediated immediacy of his subjectivity reaching for God."[71] Or, from Karl Rahner's perspective, the mystical experience is an experience of our basic orientation to God.

For John of the Cross this experience of his transformed desire was itself a participation in God, an experience of divinization: "The more the soul desires God the more it possesses Him, and the possession of God delights and satisfies it."[72]

Lonergan and Conversion

The transformation experienced by John is described as conversion by Lonergan. John speaks of the faculties being transformed. Lonergan identifies intellectual, moral, and religious conversions accompanying the process of authentic self-transcendence. The dynamism of the human spirit involves profound changes in one's understanding, the way one lives and, ultimately involves a surrender to the mystery at the core of our existence.

In particular, John of the Cross gives evidence of what writers have referred to as the psychic conversion which accompanies authentic self-transcendence. Usually they mean the purifying of one's affectivity in the process of transformation. The affective and the cognitive probably can never be totally divorced. John of the Cross struggled in his imagery and prose to communicate both cognitive and affective outcomes: "Yet sometimes in this delicate communication, God wounds and communicates Himself to one faculty more than to the other; sometimes more knowledge is experienced than love, and at other times more love than knowledge and likewise at times all knowledge is felt without any love, or all love without any knowledge."[73]

John did experience a radical healing of the appetites and passions. This healing of affectivity is most powerfully expressed in the love imagery of his poetry and certain lyrical passages of his prose. He explains in his commentary that the "deep caverns of feelings" reveal an affectivity redeemed from false fulfillment; it learns to wait, deeply hungering but hope-filled. And the heart swollen with love speaks of a human desire which is now consonant with God's desire.

The Role of the Spiritual Director

When John of the Cross speaks about the role of the spiritual director in contemplative prayer, as he does at length in this commentary, he appears to be speaking about special periods in the transformation of the individual. He encourages the director to allow the soul to become quiet and idle in prayer and to begin to go to God by an unknowing. Then John leaves the soul in this state.

If the process Lonergan is describing is normative, then times of wordless, imageless prayer will alternate with more focused times of reflection and active prayer as the soul takes responsibility for its living and grows in love with God.

The process of direction could be understood as assistance in moving authentically through the levels of consciousness and the consequent transformations involved. It would include assisting the psyche in finding the symbolic language which captures the affective conversions which result in transformed desire. Along the way the mystical experience of contemplative prayer as absorption in a loving knowledge beyond categories may become the authentic human response for a period of time.

Even John of the Cross returned from these far regions of the human spirit to word his experience in poetry and prose. This communication was probably as much for himself as for us as his spirit continued to seek meaning and value.

John's Commentary Describes the Goal

The Living Flame of Love attempts to describe the outcome of John's spiritual journey. His humanity was healed and transformed so that he lived in accord with God's will. We might say that he functioned in a way which was beautifully human and at the same time in full coopera-tion with the Kingdom of God.

This goal of the mystic journey was presented first so that it may be a guide in reflecting upon John's description of the experiences which occurred on his pilgrimage to union with God. The beginnings of this journey are discussed in *The Ascent of Mount Carmel*, Book One. This work is the focus of the next chapter.

THE DARK NIGHT

One dark night,
Fired with love's urgent longings
—Ah, the sheer grace!—
I went out unseen,
My house being now all stilled;

In darkness, and secure,
By the secret ladder, disguised,
—Ah, the sheer grace!—
In darkness and concealment,
My house being now all stilled;

On that glad night,
In secret, for no one saw me,
Nor did I look at anything,
With no other light or guide
Than the one that burned in my heart;

This guided me
More surely than the light of noon
To where He waited for me
—Him I knew so well—
In a place where no one else appeared.

O guiding night!
O night more lovely than the dawn!
O night that has united
The Lover with His beloved,
Transforming the beloved in her Lover.

Upon my flowering breast
Which I kept wholly for Him alone,
There He lay sleeping,
And I caressing Him
There in a breeze from the fanning cedars.

When the breeze blew from the turret
Parting His hair,
He wounded my neck
With His gentle hand,
Suspending all my senses.

I abandoned and forgot myself,
Laying my face on my Beloved;
All things ceased; I went out from myself,
Leaving my cares
Forgotten among the lilies.

CHAPTER FIVE

Liberation of the Heart

The Ascent of Mount Carmel, Book One
Active Night of the Senses

The first part of this chapter is a brief summary of John's commentary, *The Ascent of Mount Carmel,* Book One. The *Ascent* is the first of a two-part commentary on John's poem *The Dark Night.* The *Ascent* discusses the active night of the senses and the spirit.

The second part of John's commentary is *The Dark Night* and it discusses the passive nights of sense and spirit. This commentary will be treated in chapters six and eight.

Book One of the *Ascent* discusses the active night of sense. It begins by introducing the principal metaphor in these commentaries, the "night." John tells why he chooses "night" to describe the spiritual journey.

This same book contains an insightful discussion of the ways the human heart exhausts itself in trying to find fulfillment. In the process it gives itself to alien gods.

John offers advice on how to liberate oneself from these gods, and once again have a heart free to respond to the love of God deep within our own desire. He insists that this project of liberation is impossible without God's love leading the way and transforming the heart.

The second part of this chapter is a reflection on John's commentary. In it John's description of the debilitating effect of attachment is related to the psyche's refusal to come to consciousness in a situation of projection. Psychological and spiritual perspectives say that the ego will continue to grow in consciousness only when it encounters the self in its mysterious otherness, and when that self is able to remain open to the otherness of transcendent Mystery.

The analysis of the human heart and John's classic ascetical suggestions take on new dimensions when read through the eyes of the poor in our contemporary world. Liberation theologians help us to once again focus on the mystics who offer a spirituality of liberation.

A SUMMARY OF *THE ASCENT OF MOUNT CARMEL*, BOOK ONE

In announcing the theme of this work, John refers to the poem *The Dark Night* and says that it contains all the doctrine he will discuss in his commentary, *The Ascent of Mount Carmel.* The stanzas of the poem speak of movement through a night, but John says they also describe the way to the summit of a mountain, another image for union of the soul with God through love.

In the Prologue John says that his guide in the commentary, especially in important and difficult matters, is not experience or science but sacred scripture, since through it the Holy Spirit speaks to us. Furthermore, in any disputed teachings he defers to the teaching of the Catholic Church.

John writes, not because he has confidence in his abilities, but because people need to hear the teaching. Many are journeying on the road of virtue and are invited to union through the dark night. They do not advance, however, perhaps because they resist entering the night, and perhaps because they do not have a suitable director available.

John declares that he is writing for "beginners and proficients that they may understand or at least know how to practice abandonment to God's guidance when He wants them to advance."[1] The matters are not simple. Often when God is calling an individual along a dark path a director will say it is all the result of mental problems which are an indication of an evil life. Or the director will say the person is falling back. Sometimes these are the actual causes but the person believes he or she is being invited by God into the dark night. Some who claim prayer, are not praying. Others who claim not to be praying, are praying intensely.

John warns that the doctrine he presents may not be pleasant to those who look for satisfaction. "We are presenting a substantial and solid doctrine for all those who desire to reach this nakedness of spirit."[2]

He is mainly addressing certain members of his own reformed branch of
the Carmelite Order.

The Image of the Dark Night

Beginning Book One of the *Ascent* John states that a soul must
enter and pass through two nights in order to attain perfect union with
God. The first night refers to a purgation of the sensory part of the soul.
"This dark night is a privation and purgation of all sensible appetites for
the external things of the world, the delights of the flesh, and the gratifications of the will."[3] This night is the experience of beginners and it
introduces them into the state of contemplation. The second night is the
night of the spiritual part of the soul and it is treated in later books.

In chapter two John attempts to explain why he uses the image of
night as a metaphor for the journey of union with God. It is because the
beginning, the middle, and the end of the journey are dark. In the beginning one leaves the possessions of this world; along the way one lives in
the dark of faith; and at the end, God is still dark to the soul. These
nights pass through the soul—or it may be said that the soul passes
through the nights.[4]

John then alters the image and describes the journey as one night.
And this one night has three phases as does a real night: twilight, or the
night of the senses; midnight, or the night of the spirit and a time of
faith; dawn "just before the break of day," representing God.[5]

The Active Night of the Senses

John then begins to speak about the matter proper to this first book
of the *Ascent*, the active night of the senses. Here night refers to a denial
of the appetites of the senses. John knows that the senses cannot cease
functioning, but a person can mortify the appetites by denying
gratification.

It is easy to misinterpret what John is saying. Being related to this
world through the senses is not the primary problem; the problem is the
way we are related. John clarifies: "For we are not discussing the mere
lack of things; this lack will not divest the soul, if it craves for all these
objects. We are dealing with the denudation of the soul's appetites and
gratifications; this is what leaves it free and empty of all things, even
though it possesses them. Since the things of the world cannot enter the
soul, they are not in themselves an encumbrance or harm to it; rather it is
the will and appetite dwelling within it that causes the damage."[6]

All attachments to this world are dark in comparison with the light of God. Attachment to creatures and a relationship with God are contraries, according to John, and hence one excludes the other. He offers a favorite philosophical principle: ". . . two contraries cannot coexist in the same subject."[7]

Attachments Enslave a Heart

A person who is attached to something or someone becomes like that attachment. Not only does an attachment create an equality between the person and the creature, but the person becomes subject to the creature, "because love not only equates, but even subjects the lover to the loved object."[8] This subjection makes a person unfree for a relationship with God.

John's emphasis on God's sovereignty is seen in these statements: "All creatures in contrast to God are nothing. . . . Now all the goodness of creatures in the world compared with the infinite goodness of God can be called evil, since nothing is good, save God only."[9] And the world's wisdom is ignorance when contrasted with God's wisdom. Consequently union with God is effected through an unknowing rather than a knowing.

John offers one of his rare examples: "A person, then, because he is attached to prelacies, or other such dignities, and to freedom of his appetites, and because he finds unacceptable God's holy teaching, that whoever wants to be the greater will be the least, and that whoever wants to be the least will become the greater (Lk 22, 26) is considered and treated by God a a base slave and prisoner, not as a son."[10]

John emphasizes, again, that the outcome of such attachments is a heart not free to grow in God's love. "For such a one, the royal freedom of spirit attained in divine union is impossible, because freedom has nothing to do with slavery. And freedom cannot abide in a heart dominated by the appetites—in a slave's heart; it dwells in a liberated heart, which is a son's heart."[11] We are made for great things, but little loves make us little. In their possession we are miserable and poor.

John points to scripture for confirmation, and interprets certain stories in the context of his teaching. For example, before building an altar on Mount Bethel, Jacob ordered his people to destroy all idols. Here John hears a call to get rid of attachments which have become alien gods. Then Jacob asks his people to repent and change their garments. John hears a command to enter the night of sense and put on God. (Gn 35, 2)[12]

An Analysis of Human Desire

John then provides an insightful analysis of human desires. Desires, or appetites, bring about a loss of God's Spirit in a person, and "they weary, torment, darken, defile, and weaken him."[13] Here John makes it clear that when he is speaking about an attachment to something or someone he is always assuming it is an *inordinate* relationship. In other words, a person is related to a creature in a manner which is only appropriate for a relationship with God. The creature has become an alien god, usurping God's place.

The appetites weary and tire a person because they are never satisfied and the person is never fulfilled: "Just as a lover is wearied and depressed when on a longed-for day his opportunity is frustrated. . . ."[14]

Desires cause suffering as well. When they rule a person it is like lying on thorns and nails, or like being an enemy held prisoner. We are chained to our appetites.

John portrays the pitiful condition of one who lives with unmortified appetites: "How unhappy he is with himself, how cold toward his neighbors, how sluggish and slothful in the things of God! No illness makes walking as burdensome, or eating as distasteful, as do the appetites for creatures render the practice of virtue burdensome and saddening to a man."[15]

John then further nuances the type of appetites he is talking about. Not only are they *inordinate,* but they are *voluntary* and *habitual* as well. In other words, there is a natural desire for this world which cannot be eliminated. Provided the will does not actively participate in this desire there is no hindrance to a union with God.

John stresses the role of the will because in union with God's will the person's will is transformed and the two wills become one. ". . . This one will is God's will which becomes also the soul's."[16]

John is principally speaking of acts which have become habitual, not scattered and inadvertent. Even the smaller attachments, if habitual, can be a problem. John offers examples: "the common habit of loquacity; a small attachment one never really desires to conquer, for example, to a person, to clothing, to a book or a cell, or to the way food is prepared, and to other trifling conversations and little satisfactions in tasting, knowing, and hearing things, etc."[17] He is quite impressed with the importance of small things. "It makes little difference whether a bird is tied by a thin thread or by a cord."[18]

These voluntary appetites oppose virtue in a person. In the moment of their fulfillment the pleasure is such that the harm done to the person is not recognized. But eventually the appetites take their toll. "An act of virtue produces in a man mildness, peace, comfort, light, purity, and strength, just as an inordinate appetite brings about torment, fatigue, weariness, blindness, and weakness."[19]

Counsels and Maxims

In chapter thirteen, Book One of the *Ascent*, John presents counsels and maxims whereby the soul may attempt to free itself of its enslavements. He refers to them as an "abridged method" for entering the night. They represent an active way of entering the night. John says he will discuss the passive way of entering the night in a "fourth book" (*The Dark Night*).

His first counsel is to "have an habitual desire to imitate Christ in all your deeds by bringing your life into conformity with His."[20]

His second counsel prescribes the manner of imitation: ". . . renounce and remain empty of any sensory satisfaction that is not purely for the honor and glory of God."[21]

These counsels mean, John says, we should not desire to hear, to look at, to speak about anything which is not related to the service and glory of God, or which will not bring us closer to God. This counsel is the same for the other senses as well. John recognizes that there may be unavoidable satisfaction in this sense activity, but "it will be sufficient to have no desire for it."[22] This effort will bring the senses into the night.

These counsels, while sounding painful, actually have the potential to produce a peaceful soul. The natural passions of joy, hope, fear, and sorrow are brought into harmony, and blessings come to the soul as a result.

John offers the following maxims to insure the harmony of the passions:

> Endeavor to be inclined always:
> not to the easiest, but to the most difficult;
> not to the most delightful, but to the harshest;
> not to the most gratifying, but to the less pleasant;
> not to what means rest for you, but to hard work;
> not to the consoling, but to the unconsoling;
> not to the most, but to the least;
> not to the highest and most precious, but to the lowest
>   and most despised;
> not to wanting something but to wanting nothing;

do not go about looking for the best of temporal things,
    but for the worst,
and desire to enter for Christ into complete nudity,
emptiness, and poverty in everything in the world.[23]

John predicts that the soul will find great satisfaction in these maxims if executed with "order and discretion."

Again, John says that what he has recommended will bring a person into the night of the senses. But he recommends a further exercise: "First, try to act with contempt for yourself and desire that all others do likewise. Second, endeavor to speak in contempt of yourself and desire all others to do so. Third, try to think lowly and contemptuously of yourself and desire that all others do the same."[24]

In conclusion, then, to these counsels, maxims, and exercises, John reminds the reader of verses which he wrote to accompany a drawing he made for the nuns and friars of the reform. The drawing was a stylized mountain, the Mount of Carmel, and John drew three paths to the top. Two paths, the way of possessing the goods of the earth and the way of possessing spiritual consolations, are dead ends. Only the middle path of the *nada*, allowing no thing to be God, reaches the top. The accompanying verses are:

To reach satisfaction in all
desire its possession in nothing. (*nada*)
To come to possess all
desire the possession of nothing.
To arrive at being all
desire to be nothing.
To come to the knowledge of all
desire the knowledge of nothing.
To come to the pleasure you have not
you must go by a way in which you enjoy not.
To come to the knowledge you have not
you must go by a way in which you know not.
To come to the possession you have not
you must go by a way in which you possess not.
To come to be what you are not
you must go by a way in which you are not.
When you turn toward something
you cease to cast yourself upon the all.
For to go from all to the all

you must deny yourself of all in all.
And when you come to the possession of the all
you must possess it without wanting anything.
Because if you desire to have something in all
your treasure in God is not purely your all.
In this nakedness the spirit finds
its quietude and rest.
For in coveting nothing,
nothing raises it up
and nothing weighs it down,
because it is in the center of its humility.
When it covets something
in this very desire it is wearied.[25]

Need for a More Intense Love

After apparently specifying an extremely rigid ascetical program for moving into the night of the senses, John then surprisingly says, in effect, "we cannot do it." It is not possible to tear our hearts away from what provides satisfaction and meaning unless a deeper love calls us. "A more intense enkindling of another, better love (love of one's heavenly Bridegroom) is necessary for the vanquishing of the appetites and the denial of this pleasure."[26]

Rather than a laborious, ascetical achievement, detachment becomes the freedom which results when lesser loves fall away in the presence of God's love. Without the experience of this love, attachments remain because the desire of the heart has to go somewhere. John explains: "For the sensory appetites are moved and attracted toward sensory objects with such cravings that if the spiritual part of the soul is not fired with other more urgent longings for spiritual things, the soul will be able neither to overcome the yoke of nature nor enter the night of sense; nor will it have the courage to live in the darkness of all things by denying its appetites for them."[27]

Knowing that this material has become quite challenging and perhaps confusing for the reader, John concedes, "It is better to experience all of this and meditate upon it than to write of it."[28]

John concludes with the metaphor of prison and captivity. Release from the bondage of the passions and appetites is experienced as a "sheer grace." In other words, an active night of the senses is not really possible unless founded upon "the sheer grace" of a passive night of the senses. This passive night is the topic of John's commentary *The Dark Night*.

REFLECTIONS ON *THE ASCENT OF MOUNT CARMEL*, BOOK ONE

On this journey through the night two mysteries are being met: the self and God. Ultimately John experienced the two intertwined in a dance of flames. But the encounter with each is a difficult process. A distorted self reaches for false gods. False gods distort the self. Relationship with the true God requires a discovery of the true self, a self-appropriation. But the true self is not a possibility until the individual is open to the God who is more than the self. Relationship with the true God requires a self-transcendence, a surrendering of the self to the Mystery met darkly.

In this first book of the *Ascent,* John is concerned with those people, possessions, concerns, which begin to take the place of God in the life of an individual. The human being is basically made to be in relationship with God. Our deepest desire is ultimately for God. At the same time that desire is expressed through the faculties of the soul which follow their appetites or desires and reach out to whatever provides fulfillment and meaning. God is met through the mediation of this world.

But John observes that what mediates God slowly becomes God. In effect, the individual begins to relate to something or someone as the person would to God. People and things become idols. Without a conscious attention to one's relationship with God, and without an ability to clearly "see" God, other images slowly allure the psyche.

John does a masterful job of analyzing human desire in the first book of the *Ascent*. He tells about its never-ending quest for fulfillment and its endless frustration as the latest fulfillment, in time, proves unsatisfactory. Speaking of these restless appetites and desires John writes, "they deprive him of God's spirit; and they weary, torment, darken, defile, and weaken him."[29] The pain of attempting to satisfy the desires of the heart is like "lying naked on thorns and nails."[30]

An attachment, for John, is an inordinate relationship. When we relate to a part of creation as we would to God then the relationship is inordinate. John reserves the label "attachment" for a relationship which enslaves the heart and allows someone or something to stand in God's place. John is speaking about the process of creating idols, and the inability of idols to completely fulfill the person. We begin to identify with our idols. Or, as John comments, "an attachment to a creature makes a person equal to that creature. . . . He who loves a creature then, is as low as that creature, and in some way even lower, because love not only equates, but even subjects the lover to the loved object."[31] We cannot grow beyond our God; a lesser god means a lesser person.

The Otherness of Self

The self is as ungraspable by the person as is God. It represents the fullness of life available to the individual. Jung referred to it as an objective toward which the personality develops; it is not an object ever achieved. The self is the central archetype in the collective unconscious. It is the archetype of meaning within the psyche and it centers the entire personality. The recovery of the self is an important concomitant to a deepening relationship with God.

In the individuation process the ego, center of consciousness, learns to relate to the self, the center of the whole personality. Jung commented that there is a great difference between the person whose sun circles her earth, and the one whose earth learns to circle the sun.

Initially, aspects of the self are met in projection on the world around and met as though they were "out there." Ego is finding in the world images of the self, stories of its humanity. The ego does not know that these images, these stories, speak to it of itself, so it is contained within these images as its energy goes out to them, is engaged by them, and finds a degree of satisfaction in them.

In projection there is a strong element of identification. Unaware that it is meeting an aspect of the self in projection, the ego experiences a power and numinosity in the relationship which causes it to unconsciously identify with whomever or whatever is carrying the projected part of self. As long as that projection is in effect, the ego is excused from meeting its wider depths and an encounter with the self is postponed.

The Jungian analyst, Ann Ulanov, writes about the need to experience the "otherness" of the self: "One cannot get in touch with one's deepest subjective self without also feeling confronted with the self as an objective *other;* one cannot meet this other self without, in fact, meeting many *others* other persons or figures in one's dreams."[32]

As long as there is identification with some outer object which is carrying the self, ego does not experience this otherness. The person grows only when the self is met as other. In that dialogue ego establishes a relationship which nourishes the total psychic life of the individual.

Rather than alienation or identification between ego and self, there is a life-giving communication.

The Otherness of God

Just as the otherness of the self is not realized in the process of projection, so the otherness of God is not experienced when the heart is enslaved by people and things in attachment. The promise of the self and the psychic readiness for God find expression in the same outer images. The outer objects become self-images and also God-images.

Jung wrote about the relationship between the God-image and the self: ". . . the God-image does not coincide with the unconscious as such, but with a special content of it, namely the archetype of the self. It is this archetype from which we can no longer distinguish the God-image empirically."[33]

In withdrawing projections and liberating the heart in detachment, both the otherness of the self and the otherness of God are respected. A relationship with these mysteries moves the personality along the complementary paths of self-appropriation and self-transcendence.

God Without and Within

On these journeys there is a complex relationship between the subjective experience of God within the psyche, and the outer expression of that experience. In projections and attachments it may be said that our gods are "all outside." Jung challenged Christian churches to help open the believer to the kingdom within: "So long as religion is only faith and outward form, and the religious function is not experienced in our own souls, nothing of any importance has happened. It has yet to be understood that the *mysterium magnum* is not only an actuality but is first and foremost rooted in the human psyche."[34]

He is aware of the churches' suspicion of psychology: "Yet when I point out that the soul possesses by nature a religious function, and when I stipulate that it is the prime task of all education (of adults) to convey the archetype of the God-image, or its emanations and effects, to the conscious mind, then it is precisely the theologian who seizes me by the arm and accuses me of 'psychologism'."[35]

Using "within" and "without" language, Ann Ulanov speaks about the reciprocity which is necessary between both realms: "We must deal with what traditional systems of value tell us about God in order to gain access to our subjective experience of God; we must deal with our very personal experiences of the Divine, to gain access to the God of which organized religions speak. We must deal with the God-within through the self-archetype in order to meet the God-without. In such a way we recover our religious orientation."[36]

John's Counsels and Maxims

The first book of the *Ascent* offers suggestions for "detaching" from inordinate, habitual, voluntary relationships, i.e., for toppling the idols in our life, for freeing the heart from its slavery. It is clear that John is not counseling avoiding the world. The situation of the individual is that he or she is immersed in the world. This person has necessarily gone out to the world in human development, and desire has found natural outlets. The heart is scattered over the landscape, and the person has fallen to the gods of the land. The question is, how to become free in order to continue the journey that has been begun with so much promise.

John begins by urging the imitation of Christ. Conforming one's life with Christ, Jung suggested, means living the unique life one has been given as faithfully, as authentically as Jesus lived his life. Lonergan would probably echo this encouragement by saying that the one who is imitating Christ is growing in human development through authentic self-transcendence, in obedience to the law of the transcendental precepts to be attentive, intelligent, reasonable, responsible, and in love. The imitation of Christ is an openness to the Spirit in one's own life.

If authentic humanity is the goal, and Jesus is the model, then some of John's sayings regarding self-contempt are overly dramatic.[37] It is difficult to know how he meant these counsels to be taken. He could have been offering a challenge which seemed proper according to his intense, ascetical spirit. And the counsels may have been taken quite seriously.

But our problem today often is not an exalted sense of our conscious self, but an identity that is poorly developed. Much counseling effort goes into building a strengthened ego and a healthy persona. We are much more sensitive to faith's foundation on a positive sense of self. We do know that, however John understood his instructions, he was not counseling a rejection of one's God-given humanity. It is this humanity's destiny to be divinized.

The stories of Jesus' life, the ones he told and the ones he lived, become the fundamental story of the believer's life. John's faith says, and Lonergan's theology presumes, that when the individual Christian tells his or her own authentic story, it finds its archetypal patterns in the Jesus story. And, further, the Jesus story is the supreme telling of the human story begun eons ago. The stories are the stories of the presence of God in creation, "the spirit of God insofar as it is hidden in the veins of the soul. . . .,"[38] loving that creation to life.

John explains that the imitation of Christ is a commitment to "renounce and remain empty of any sensory satisfaction that is not purely for the honor and glory of God."[39] While this counsel sounds absolutely rigorous and conjures up the strictest notions of asceticism, two obvious keys are available for interpreting John's meaning. First, if one is attempting to imitate Jesus, then observing Jesus' life and conjecturing about his relationship to the world around him brings a balanced perspective. Second, the life of John of the Cross provides clues to the actual meaning of his counsel. Think only of his often-proclaimed deep love for his brother, and John's own interpretation of the maxim begins to be clear. John's counsel is an anticipation of a transformed humanity whose every activity is in harmony with God's will and, consequently, all that it does is for the honor and glory of God.

Not Simply a Lack of Things

John was not concerned primarily with being related to life; that relationship is a given. It is the way whereby one is related that was problematical. He writes: "For we are not discussing the mere lack of things; this lack will not divest the soul, if it craves for all these objects. We are dealing with the denudation of the soul's appetites and gratifications; this is what leaves it free and empty of all things, even though it possesses them. Since the things of the world cannot enter the soul, they are not in themselves an encumbrance or harm to it; rather it is the will and appetite dwelling within it that causes damage."[40]

John, therefore, is talking about right relationship, relationship which is not harmful to, and is in accord with, the deepest desires of the human heart, desires which are essentially "for the honor and glory of God." Rather than cravings which distort the human heart and dissipate the energy for the journey, John counsels being single-hearted, having a clear vision. This loving, this vision, provides a context within which other loves are judged. Have one God, he encourages, and then other loves will not be alien gods; they will be fellow-pilgrims and helpful supports.

A Balanced Way

"Endeavor to be inclined always: not to the easiest, but to the most difficult; not to the most delightful, but to the harshest, etc."[41] Here

John prescribes a tough program. Ever suspicious of the heart's inclination to rest in the first point of comfort and satisfaction, John introduces a wedge with which the inclination may be countered: "Endeavor to be inclined . . ." the other way. Was it his hope that a person would then find a balanced way?

Teresa of Avila, too, preferred the difficult to the easy. Even when she was experiencing the depths of union which she identified as the "spiritual marriage" in the Seventh Dwelling Place of her *Interior Castle,* she wrote that one of the effects was a desire to suffer. But even in this suffering it is the will of God that must be served: "If He desires the soul to suffer, well and good; if not it doesn't kill itself as it used to."[42]

Again, John appears to be trying to bring a balance to an already imbalanced situation. He trusts the life that costs, more than the life that is comfortable and without challenge. His natural suspicion is that the comfortable life has stopped seeking God and has settled for far less, for other gods. It appears to be a life of satisfaction but it is a life of slavery.

A further understanding of John's point of view is seen in his reference to the verses he wrote to accompany his drawing of a soul's journey to the summit of Mount Carmel. The verses are a type of koan: "To reach satisfaction in all, desire its possession in nothing. To come to possess all, desire the possession of nothing, etc."[43]

The bipolar structure of these sayings is striking. Similarity with the parables of Jesus comes to mind: the good Samaritan story, the banquet for strangers, the search for lost sheep, and the feast for the lost son. Images of faith are presented as a juxtaposing of opposites. The scriptures have a wealth of such faith images: the last who shall be first, the grain of wheat that must die to grow, the virgin mother, and the cross of Jesus.

The point is not to deny a person of what is desirable. John believes that our desires should be fulfilled. The first part of each instruction describes the goal: "To reach satisfaction in all. . . . To come to possess all. . . ." John agrees with the goal. But he says the way to the goal is far different from what we would assume. It is so different that it makes no sense. Jesus, too, through the parables, taught that our normal judgment will be deficient in matters of the kingdom of God.

John's Sketch of the Crucifixion

The sketch of Jesus on the cross made by John when he was confessor at the Incarnation in Avila gives insight to his point of view. The drawing is unusual because the normal view of the crucifixion is from the perspective of the spectator looking up at the man hanging on the cross. John's perspective is from a point above the scene looking down at an angle upon the man leaning out from the cross with blood dripping from his wounds. It is God's perspective upon this scene. From this point of view all things, in comparison with God, are of little consequence. John writes "Now all the goodness of creatures in the world compared with the infinite goodness of God can be called evil, since nothing is good, save God only." (Lk 18, 19)[44] John is unremitting in his testimony to God's claim upon this world.

Carl Jung understood the crucifixion to represent the passion of the ego. "This great symbol tells us that the progressive development and differentiation of consciousness leads to an ever more menacing awareness of the conflict and involves nothing less than a crucifixion of the ego, its agonizing suspension between irreconcilable opposites."[45] John would claim that the crucifixion is more than the ego's passion; it is the entire self which has passed over to the realm of the holy in surrender to the Mystery in its deepest center. But involved in that total surrender would be the reconciling process among the polarities of the psyche, and the ego would die its deaths. John wrote: "To undertake the journey to God the heart must be burned and purified of all creatures with the fire of divine love. Such a purgation puts the devil to flight, for he has power over a man attached to temporal and bodily things."[46]

The Perverted Self

John suspects that the human heart can pervert anything. His counsels and maxims are an effort to keep the heart from hardening, from being closed to the ground of reality. And Jung understood that the disordered psyche does not stay open to its true reality, the self; hence his description of sin as a refusal to come to consciousness. The counsels and maxims of John of the Cross would have the effect of undermining the psyche's projections.

William Thompson has described John of the Cross as a perceptive "pneumopathologist"—one who has studied the sinfully dark side of humanity. John has attempted to distinguish between symptoms and root cause when he says it is not the possession of something which is wrong but the disordered heart, the craving, which is vitiating the relationship. Thompson understands John to trace the source of evil and our sinfulness to a self closed to God. "Reason, passions, Church, society, indeed the entire world, all can be perverted by the perverted self."[47]

Still, the symptoms and the cause affect one another. Thompson writes:

John shares, I think correctly, the "bias" of the great tradition of tracing the source of evil to the perverted self, rather than to one or another individual or social symptom of evil. A perverted self can corrupt the best of realities if it remains perverted. Still, this does not lead John to slight or ignore symptomatology. . . . The disoriented passions and beclouded thoughts of one's life, as well as the varied social pressures of one's society, are the realities which can contribute toward the self's perversion, habituating and blinding it. Of course, it works the other way too: the perverted self can further pollute all the passions, reasoning processes, and realities of Church and society.[48]

Enslaved Hearts and Societies

Liberation theologians such as Gustavo Guttierez and Segundo Galilea find in John's discussion of the disordered desires of the heart a powerful critique of our human situation, both personal and social. Galilea hears in John's counsels a contemporary call to return to a renunciation and asceticism which will counteract a selfish consumerism and a life oblivious to the struggling poor. The *nadas* can be a path to solidarity with others in this world. The issues are both in society and deep in the human soul. "Justice and asceticism go hand in hand," writes Galilea.[49]

The experience of John of the Cross and the experience of those involved in social liberation have resulted in a sense of the radical nature of sin. It is rooted in the rejection of God and God's kingdom, which leads to enslaved hearts and societies. If read through the eyes of the poor, John's writings become a source for a spirituality of liberation. He is convinced that only the love of God, inviting and leading the soul, is powerful enough to effect the necessary transformation.

A More Intense Enkindling

After all the talk of spiritual counsels and maxims by John of the Cross, in which he appears to be urging the reader to strive through rigorous asceticism to free the heart for God, John then says simply, it cannot be done. In chapter 14 of the first book of the *Ascent* John makes an extremely important observation: because the appetites and passions are so powerful, an individual will not be able to be free of inordinate attachments through sheer willpower. It is only with God's help that this effort can be made. And the help of God which John experienced was a call to a deeper love which helped free him from what was not God. "A more intense enkindling of another, better love (love of one's heavenly Bridegroom) is necessary for the vanquishing of the appetites and the denial of this pleasure."[50]

John does not counsel an affective vacuum. He does not ask the person to rip her heart away from what is fulfilling and wait without support or direction. God takes the lead and enkindles the heart with "longings of love." "For the sensory appetites are moved and attracted toward sensory objects with such cravings that if the spiritual part of the soul is not fired with other more urgent longings for spiritual things the soul will be able neither to overcome the yoke of nature nor enter the night of sense; nor will it have the courage to live in the darkness of all things by denying its appetites for them."[51]

The asceticism that follows this experience of a deeper love comes much more easily to a soul. The perverted self is transformed in God's love. Mysticism is the prelude to asceticism. John refers to this enkindling as the passive night of sense. Only in the light of this passive night is the active night possible.

Initially, however, this enkindling is not a happy experience. The soul feels as if it is being negated by something over-against it. John discusses this passive night and its effects in Book One of *The Dark Night*.

The "Day" of Human Development

It is evident from John of the Cross' description of human desire and its fickleness that he is presuming a "day" of development before the coming of the night. He portrays a person whose heart is given to this world, who has been committed to it, passionate about it. This attachment is just the problem. It has led so far in the journey to God, but now no farther until the coming of night. John is not saying the human personality has traveled the wrong road; he is saying that these complications are the inevitable result of the right road taken.

If this day of development is not presumed, then John's talk of the night and his counsels appear to express a preference for disengagement from life. He would appear to be saying that one would be better off, and would journey straight to God, if one did not get mixed up with this world.

On the contrary, John's writings speak to the one who has gone out to the world in engagement, and who now asks how to continue the journey. Segundo Galilea's comment is apt: "One arrives at the mystics; one doesn't begin with them."[52]

In order to set the stage for the discussion of the passive night of senses in the next chapter, the following section is a brief review of Jung's understanding of the day of development, or outer journey, which precedes the inner journey.

Journey into Consciousness

Jung observed that the personality begins in an unconscious state; this state has been called by Erich Neumann the "uroboric state."[53] The uroborus was a primal Egyptian deity symbol; it is an image of a circular snake swallowing its tail. This circular image represents the state of the psyche of the newly-born; all is unconscious and the polarities of the personality exist together in an undifferentiated state. It is an image of the primordial night, that vast realm of darkness out of which consciousness grows and an individual personality begins to emerge.

In the adult years the person will have to reenter this dark in order to touch the wellsprings of deeper life. It is truly a "night" experience. Jungians even refer to this archetypal descent into the unconscious as paralleled in the "night-sea journey" of the sun in mythology.

The infant's consciousness slowly develops. This realm of development was not a major focus for Jung's studies, but he hypothesized that the ego is not truly present until about the age of three.[54] Prior to that time Jung believed that ego-consciousness was sporadic, much like stars twinkling on and off in the vast sky. This coming of consciousness in an individual human echoes the emergence of consciousness in the human race and the slow awareness of the African skies and landscapes. But eventually there is a perduring "I," and consciousness is on firm ground.

In Jung's view the personality is not fully born until puberty, because at that time there appears to be an emergence from the psychic womb of the parents. The individual is no longer "contained" in an unconscious manner, and now begins to experience the inner contradictions of the psyche's polarities. For the first time the human being may have personal problems.

This day of development is called by Jung a "necessarily one-sided journey." In other words, one cannot develop both sides of the psychic polarities simultaneously; consequently one side is developed in consciousness while its opposite in the unconscious awaits its opportunity.

The movement is out to the world as consciousness emerges from the dark of the unconscious.[55]

The miraculous nature of this coming of consciousness makes one pause. From the Christian perspective it is a graced-development which situates the human in eons of divine activity within creation. The evolutionary view, rather than reducing the human to what is far less, exalts the graciousness of God at work in a vast panorama. This realization also makes strikingly evident the importance of human consciousness in this process, and leads to an awareness that for the first time in the history of the world creation itself, in human consciousness, is aware of the project taking place and can responsibly cooperate with grace. Our prayer is an openness to ever greater awareness, to a listening to what is afoot in the universe.

The Persona

For Jung, a major task in the first half of life is the development of a "persona." A persona is a mask, or perhaps many masks, which a person begins to wear in her relationship with the environment. We do not relate to life around us as raw psyches, but we learn to live roles, to tell our stories in certain ways.

These masks, these stories, are partially the result of the masks we are given, the stories we are told about ourselves. Society joins the individual in creating this persona. It is a healthy development, in Jung's view, but should always keep in touch with the very real dimensions of the individual personality.

I am not only the person others want me to be, nor am I even only the person I want to be. There are other "persons" within me, other stories, which are part of who I am and which need to be contacted. The one who lives solely in the persona, solely in the roles given by society, is living a fragile existence because such a life does not have solid foundations in reality.

The initial chapters of Book One of *The Dark Night* may be understood as an analysis of a religious persona, and its neglected shadow side. The night invites a healing and a deepening of life. John's elaboration of the symbol of "night" and his description of the experience are a major contribution to Christian spirituality. These are the topics of the following chapter.

CHAPTER SIX

The Dark Night and Contemplative Prayer

The Dark Night, Book One
Passive Night of the Senses

In this work John describes the spiritual condition which he calls "the dark night." Specifically he treats the dark night of the senses, a time when God's love is difficult and painful, but ultimately liberating. It brings other loves into harmony.

John addresses the situation of "beginners," those who are experiencing satisfaction in their devotions and prayers. He insightfully analyzes their "imperfections," the ways the spiritual life is twisted by egoism. No effort can free this soul; only the passive purgation of the night brings transformation.

The dark night is contemplation. John presents the classic signs for the beginning of the dark night. He recommends how to proceed in the night; and he tells of the healing benefits of this prayer.

The first part of this chapter summarizes John's work. The second part, a reflection on John's commentary, makes use of Jung's categories of ego, persona, and shadow. Jung's description of the inner journey, the second half of the individuation process, resonates with John's description of the beginning of contemplative prayer. Both John and Jung discuss the "right" ways and the "wrong" ways of proceeding through these passages.

The relationship between contemplative prayer as described by John of the Cross, and psychological transformation as described by Jung is far from clear. The night is a psychological experience, as is all human experience, but its roots are not found solely in a psychological condition, such as depression. The relationship between contemplation and individuation is briefly examined in this chapter.

A SUMMARY OF *THE DARK NIGHT*,
BOOK ONE

John draws the reader's attention to the fact that the poem was written when the soul had already reached a loving union with God. It is now on the other side of its severe trials. The narrow road leading to this union with God is called a dark night. The dark night, or purgative contemplation, is a passive experience in which the soul dies to itself and begins to live a life of love with God.

This night happens to those people whom John calls "beginners." Beginners are those who are converted to God and practice meditation; through the night they will be led into contemplation which is the prayer of proficients. The goal is the state of the perfect who are in union with God.

God nurtures the beginner "like a loving mother who warms her child with the heat of her bosom, nurses it with good milk and tender food, and carries and caresses it in her arms."[1] God gives the beginner enthusiasm and satisfaction.

The beginner, then, experiences a false sense of security: "The soul finds its joy, therefore, in spending lengthy periods at prayer, perhaps even entire nights; its penances are pleasures; its fasts, happiness; and the sacraments and spiritual conversations are its consolations."[2]

The problem, as John analyzes it, is that the beginner relies upon, and actually is motivated by, this satisfaction and consolation. Although feeling strong, the beginner is actually in a feeble condition. It is this condition which is changed in the experience of the night. "But as the child grows older, the mother withholds her caresses and hides her tender love; she rubs bitter aloes on her sweet breast and sets the child down from her arms, letting it walk on its own feet so that it may put aside the habits of childhood and grow accustomed to greater and more important things."[3]

The Imperfections of Beginners

Before discussing this night experience, John describes the fragile situation of beginners by analyzing their imperfections. In this extended profile he uses the seven capital vices as a framework: pride, avarice, lust, anger, gluttony, envy, sloth. Because of their initial conversion, beginners do not manifest these vices as they formerly would; the vices are now hidden within an evidently spiritual life.

Pride

Pride grows in beginners who can become complacent and even vain in their spiritual life. They can be critical of others and quite competitive, desiring to be thought holy in comparison with others. If superiors, confessors, or spiritual directors do not agree with their high opinion of themselves, they look elsewhere for someone who will congratulate them.

These beginners downplay their faults and explain away their sins, using the sacrament of penance as an opportunity to excuse themselves. They do not mind, however, telling about the good they do. And when they are aware of their faults, they often become discouraged at not being saints. John observes that "their motive is personal peace rather than God."[4]

John contrasts these people with other beginners who are truly growing in God's love. Their spirit is quite different. No matter how much good they do, they are always more impressed with the inadequacy of their efforts. In their love they view their efforts as nothing, and certainly nothing to talk about; they prefer to talk about their faults and sins.

In their humility they are open to the teaching of others. They are "ready to take a road different from the one they are following, if told to do so."[5] They rejoice when others are praised. They want to cooperate with all who serve God. Their own faults are suffered by them with humility, docility of spirit, loving fear, and hope. John then returns to the faults of beginners.

Avarice

Avarice manifests itself in beginners as a restless spirit striving to obtain more consolation through religious reading, spiritual discussions, and devotional objects. "Many never have enough of hearing counsels, or of learning spiritual maxims, or of keeping them and reading books about them."[6] John is also critical about a preoccupation with workmanship or the decoration of religious objects. His concern is for an interior poverty which frees the heart from its possessiveness.

Sometimes objects are valued for their beauty, but at other times one finds security just in their possession, beautiful or not. John tells a story: "I knew a person who for more than ten years profited by a cross roughly made out of a blessed palm and held together by a pin twisted around it. He carried it about and never would part with it until I took it from him. . . ."[7]

The spiritual person does not want to know or have more than is necessary to do good works. They are generous with their possessions. "Their pleasure," writes John, "is to know how to live for love of God or neighbor without these spiritual or temporal things."[8]

But John admits that no amount of effort will eliminate all the imperfections of a beginner. Only the passive night can finish the work. John walks a fine line by saying that we must do our part, and in so doing we merit God's cure. At the same time he resolutely maintains: "No matter how much an individual does through his own efforts, he cannot actively purify himself enough to be disposed in the least degree for the divine union of the perfection of love. God must take over and purge him in that fire that is dark for him. . . ."[9]

Spiritual Lust

In discussing spiritual lust, John observes that the lust itself is not spiritual, but it accompanies spiritual activities. He speaks of impure feelings which may be present during prayer, or while receiving sacraments of penance and eucharist.

The first source of these impure feelings John identifies as human nature, which experiences a sensory pleasure as the spiritual part of the soul is experiencing satisfaction in God. "It will happen that while a soul is with God in deep spiritual prayer, it will on the other hand passively experience sensual rebellions, movements, and acts in the senses, not without its own great displeasure."[10] In particular, these experiences may take place at communion time. John teaches that the sensory and spiritual parts of the soul form a whole and consequently they resonate with one another.

John also names the devil as another source of impure feelings and thoughts. These thoughts may even involve people who have been helpful to a soul. There is a danger that a person may abandon prayer because of the fear of the accompanying movements and thoughts. It is an especially difficult situation for people suffering from "melancholia." The fear of impurity adds to the weight of their depression. Even here, however, John says that the night can overcome this oppressive fear.

The fear itself is another distinct source of continuing feelings of lust. The very fear of impure thoughts and feelings stirs up impure feelings, through no fault of the individual.

Again, John is very aware of the unity of our human nature: "Some people are so delicate that when gratification is received from the spirit or from prayer, they immediately experience a lust which so inebriates them and caresses their senses that they become as it were engulfed in the delight and satisfaction of that vice; and this experience will endure passively with the other. Sometimes these individuals become aware that certain impure and rebellious acts have taken place."[11]

Observations on Friendship

In this context, John offers observations about friendship. Begun for spiritual reasons, a friendship may actually have its origin in lust and not the spirit. John's rule of thumb is that when the love of God increases as a result of affection for another person, this friendship is good and spiritual. "For this is a trait of God's spirit: the good increases with the good, since there is likeness and conformity between them."[12]

A person loving another with an inordinate love will experience a coldness in the love for God, and vice versa. The dark night brings order to these loves, John counsels. The night extinguishes the inordinate love, and it strengthens the love of God. But initially the night darkens both loves.

Anger

John discusses the capital vice of anger in a brief but pointed section. He has observed that some people become peevish and angry when they cannot sustain a sense of satisfaction in their religious practices. When listless times follow delightful times in prayer these people are often dejected.

At times, beginners may express anger toward those whose behavior is sinful. They may reprove them righteously, and angrily, "setting themselves up as lords of virtue."[13]

And at other times, they may turn their anger upon themselves, because of their imperfections. John is critical of this impatience to become "saints in a day." But, the other extreme is unattractive as well.

"Some, however, are so patient about their desire for advancement that God would prefer to see them a little less so."[14]

Spiritual Gluttony

Spiritual gluttony is a common vice of beginners who engage in spiritual practices because they are satisfying. They go beyond the mean to an extreme. The delight they experience is so attractive that they impose extreme penances upon themselves, even against others' advice or commands under obedience. "But corporal penance without obedience," John writes, "is no more than a penance of beasts."[15] John judges these people to be spiritually gluttonous and proud. They do only what they are inclined to do, convinced that it is the only way to serve God.

John is even critical of those who boldly insist upon frequent reception of Communion. Counseling against frequent reception is an anachronism today. However, John's underlying concern is not the practice but the motivation. "Not only in receiving Communion, but in other spiritual exercises as well, beginners desire to feel God and taste of Him as if He were comprehensible and accessible. This desire is a serious imperfection. . . ."[16]

As always, John's focus is not on the possession or the practice, but on the relationship one has to it. Possessions we will have, and practices we will do; the challenge is to possess and practice with a heart free to be submissive to God.

If pleasure is the motivation, John warns, then people will avoid the way of the cross and the accompanying self-denial. He offers spiritual sobriety and temperance as virtues to counter self-seeking. "An individual thereby becomes aware that the perfection and value of his works does not depend upon their number, or the satisfaction found in them, but upon knowing how to practice self-denial in them."[17] John encourages beginners to practice this self-denial until God places them in the dark night.

Because he is eager to discuss the dark night, John hurriedly ends his listing of the seven capital vices of beginners with a brief discussion of envy and sloth. He leaves the beginner nowhere to hide.

Envy and Sloth

Envy may occur when others are praised for their goodness. The beginner experiences a sadness, and an annoyance, because others are farther down the road of holiness. The beginner may even try to undermine compliments paid to others.

Their envy could be a proper "holy envy" if they rejoiced in the goodness of another, as St. Paul urges, and sorrowed over their own lack of virtue. In this case the service of God is the preeminent concern, and not the reputation of the beginner.

At times, bored with spiritual practices and receiving little satisfaction in them, beginners may begrudge prayer or give it up entirely. In their sloth, John criticizes, they have substituted their own will for God's will. His analysis is challenging: "Many of these beginners want God to desire what they want, and become sad if they have to desire God's will. They feel an aversion toward adapting their will to God's. Hence they frequently believe that what is not their will, or that which brings them no satisfaction, is not God's will, and, on the other hand, that if they are satisfied, God is too. They measure God by themselves and not themselves by God. . . ."[18]

Necessity of the Night

John concludes his analysis of the imperfections of beginners by saying that earnest efforts at mortification will not be enough to remedy the situation. God must wean the person from imperfections through the passive purgation of the dark night. John then makes a brief prayer asking God to help him explain this difficult matter of the dark night, which he begins to discuss in the next section.

The Dark Night of the Senses

The dark night *is* contemplation. John observes that this night causes two kinds of darkness. One darkness affects the senses and brings them into harmony with the spirit. The other darkness affects the spirit and prepares it for union with God.

The night of the senses happens to many people and is a difficult experience. The night of the spirit happens to a few people and is much more difficult.

The night of the senses occurs not long after the initial stages of the spiritual life. For a time the beginner prays faithfully and with satisfaction, and perseveres in virtuous living. God then desires to liberate them from the bondage of the senses. "Consequently, it is at the time they are going about their spiritual exercises with delight and satisfaction, when in their opinion the sun of divine favor is shining most brightly on them, that God darkens all this light and closes the door and spring of the sweet spiritual water they were tasting as often and as long as they desired."[19]

This experience is evident in the scriptures, especially in the Psalms and Prophets, but John does not think it is necessary to cite passages since the experience is quite common.

Three Signs of the Dark Night

John then presents three signs for identifying a true dark night. Discernment is necessary since aridity may come from sin and imperfection rather than from the sensory night.

"The first is that as these souls do not get satisfaction or consolation from the things of God, they do not get any out of creatures either."[20]

If the night were the result of sin then there would still be indications of satisfaction somewhere. But in a true dark night dryness invades prayer and all other human activity. Still, the same sign could be the result of solely psychological problems, and consequently a second sign is needed.

"The second sign for the discernment of this purgation is that the memory ordinarily turns to God solicitously and with painful care, and the soul thinks it is not serving God but turning back, because it is aware of this distaste for the things of God."[21]

If the darkness were the result of a lukewarm spiritual life, the painful care would not be present. In the true night there is a desire for things to be different, but there is also an inability to change them. The dryness remains, and the soul suspects the darkness is the result of its own betrayal of God. The experience may be accompanied by, but is not wholly rooted in, a psychological state such as "melancholia or some other humor."[22]

John says the dryness is the result of God weakening the senses and strengthening the spirit. Initially, only weakness is felt. But, in time, if the soul follows its inclination to be alone and quiet, it will realize God's nourishing and strengthening activity. As difficult as the night may be, through it emerges a peace which is "quiet, delicate, solitary, satisfying. . . ."[23]

"The third sign for the discernment of this purgation of the senses is the powerlessness, in spite of one's efforts, to meditate and make use of the imagination, the interior sense, as was one's previous custom. At this time God does not communicate Himself through the senses as He did before, by means of the discursive analysis and synthesis of ideas, but begins to communicate Himself through pure spirit by an act of simple contemplation, in which there is no discursive succession of thought."[24] Some people in the beginning of the night may still be able to meditate and experience satisfaction in their prayer. But John says advancement comes when the work of the senses is left behind.

Those whom God does not call to contemplation may experience darkness mixed with their active prayer, but the darkness is not a continual state. It is a humbling experience meant to assist the spiritual life, but it is not contemplative prayer strictly speaking. "For God does not bring to contemplation all those who purposely exercise themselves in the way of the spirit, nor even half. Why? He best knows."[25]

John's Recommendations for Proceeding in the Night

Souls suffer in the night because they fear, simultaneously, that they have gone astray, and that God has abandoned them. Because they are unable to pray as before, they think they are doing nothing. Their anxious search undermines God's work. John writes, "They are like someone who turns from what has already been done in order to do it again, or one who leaves a city only to reenter it, or they are like the hunter who abandons his prey to go hunting again."[26] They become tired and overwork themselves. Without someone to understand them they may not continue their journey, or at least they will impede their own progress.

John recommends that souls in the night persevere patiently with trust in God. They should "allow the soul to remain in rest and quietude. . . ."[27] With patience and perseverance in this prayer they will have a freedom of soul, which is all the activity God asks of them. "They must be content simply with a loving and peaceful attentiveness to God, and live without the concern, without the effort, and without the desire to taste or feel Him."[28]

Any movement born out of a desire just to do something will disturb God's work, just as the movement of a model disturbs the painter. "For contemplation is nothing else than a secret and peaceful and loving inflow of God, which, if not hampered fires the soul in the spirit of love. . . ."[29]

What is perceived at the beginning of the night is dryness and void.

Within the experience is a care for God and a fear about not serving God. In time the aridity experienced by the senses gives way to an enkindling of love in the spirit. The soul may begin to feel a longing for God which greatly increases through the night. This desire for God may be so intense that it is like the thirst of dry bones.

Enduring the night is similar to entering the small gate. "This small gate is the dark night of sense, in which the soul is despoiled and denuded—in order to pass through it—and grounded in faith, which is foreign to all sense, that it may be capable of walking along the narrow road which is the night of spirit. The soul enters this second night that it may journey to God in pure faith, for pure faith is the means whereby it is united with God."[30]

The Benefits of the Night

The first benefit of the night is the "knowledge of self and of one's own misery."[31] When prayer was satisfying and consoling, the soul believed it was strong and was serving God well. In the experience of the night, however, the soul learns of its lowliness, its inability to do anything on its own. The easy assumption of virtue has been undermined in the dryness and desolation of the night.

This self-knowledge leads to a new knowledge of God. John notes that "a person communes with God more respectfully and courteously, the way one should always converse with the Most High."[32] Reverence replaces presumption. John says Moses, too, had to learn to be more respectful of God. When he dared to approach God he was ordered to stop and take off his shoes.

Life's journey is over sacred ground. The dark night renews the sense of Mystery and reminds the soul to walk reverently. The knowledge of one's lowliness opens the soul to the awareness of God's grandeur. John quotes Augustine: "Let me know myself Lord, and I will know you."[33]

A further benefit of the night is a spiritual humility which allows the soul to see his sisters and brothers in a new light. "From this humility stems love of neighbor, for he will esteem them and not judge them as he did before, when he was aware that he enjoyed an intense fervor while others did not."[34] One's own frailties are so evident that there is "no opportunity to watch anyone else's conduct."[35] Competition and self-righteousness fall away in the night.

The overall effect of the night on a person is a softening. The soul is open to being led on the spiritual journey. Humility and docility characterize its life. John observes, "The affective presumption they sometimes had in their prosperity leaves them."[36]

The Night Undermines the Seven Capital Vices

The night liberates the soul and brings it peace and consolation. Virtue replaces imperfections, the imperfections John analyzed through the framework of the seven capital vices.

Pride gives way to spiritual humility, and avarice for spiritual objects and excess is replaced with moderation. The soul has been freed from the impurities of lust, and gluttony has been replaced by spiritual sobriety.

Anger and impatience have been transformed into meekness in the individual who has been "softened and humbled" in the difficulties of the night. In John's description of the changes one can perceive the presence of gentleness and compassion in the soul purified in the night.

Envy is now a humble determination to imitate the goodness of others rather than be distressed by their virtue and its praise. And slothfulness, which was due to frustration at not always having consolation in prayer, has been replaced by an acceptance of powerlessness in the aridity of the night.

John claims innumerable benefits flowing from this dark night, including the twelve fruits of the Holy Spirit. The soul is "liberated from the hands of his enemies, the world, the flesh and the devil."[37] Because of these outcomes, the soul can say in the poem, *The Dark Night*, "My house being now all stilled."

In his final chapter of this first book of *The Dark Night* John warns that souls who are being prepared for the even more intense night of the spirit may be tried by the spirit of fornication, or a blasphemous spirit, or even the *spiritus vertiginis* which floods the soul with "a thousand scruples and perplexities."[38]

Length of the Night

Only God knows why some nights are longer than others. John believes that the length and intensity have to do with the amount of imperfection. For persons with a capacity for suffering the night may be intense but brief. For weaker souls the night is gentler and longer, and God intersperses it with consolations. "They arrive at the purity of perfection late in life. And some of them never reach it entirely, for they are never wholly in the night nor wholly out of it."[39]

In the end, John appeals to experience: "Yet, as is evident through experience, souls who will pass on to so happy and lofty a state as is the union of love must usually remain in these aridities and temptations for a long while no matter how quickly God leads them."[40]

REFLECTIONS ON *THE DARK NIGHT*, BOOK ONE

In discussing the situation of beginners about to enter the dark night, John is assuming a "day" of development. The beginner is one who has had an initial conversion to God and a religious way of living. It may be said that John is describing a person who has taken on a religious persona; and John's analysis of the beginner's imperfections using the schema of the "seven capital vices" could be understood as a discussion of the shadow side of this religious persona.

It is evident that the night of sense is not necessarily connected to any specific time in human development. John is talking about a maturation of spirit which may not parallel chronological growth. Nevertheless, it stands to reason that the issues involved in the dark night are usually not issues for a very young person. The young person may be in touch with such issues, but these issues are not available to the young person in the way they are available to the adult.

The developmental psychologist Daniel Levinson identifies the years between seventeen and forty-five as Early Adulthood, and the years beginning with age forty until sixty-five as the era of Middle Adulthood. Numerous indications lead to the possibility that the experiences John terms the night of sense are related, psychologically, to the beginning of the transition from one era or season to the other, or from Early to Middle Adulthood. It is in this transition that the events John describes would be most probable and powerful. His own mystical poetry was written between the ages of thirty-six, the time of his imprisonment, and forty-nine, the age of his death.

The imperfections of beginners which John describes in chapters two through seven remind one of the situation of young adults. Some early developmental issues appear to have been tentatively and temporarily settled. For example, the person has assumed a basic identity in life and is not taking on a spiritual project solely for the sake of establishing an identity. Nevertheless, the person's identity is thoroughly interwoven with a religious persona.

John assumes, also, that the person is able to enter into a loving relationship. Consequently some initial resolution of the problem of intimacy can be inferred. In his analysis of human desire in *Ascent*, Book One, John was discussing people who were in relationship with this world and were deeply aware of the frustration involved in attempting to fulfill one's desires. This frustrated lover of the *Ascent* is the imperfect beginner in *The Dark Night*.

When John talks about an inability to meditate he describes meditation in terms of discursive thought and analysis of ideas. He obviously assumes a fairly well-developed cognitive ability which has been functioning adequately but is now no longer sufficient for continuing on the religious journey.

A Religious Persona

From a Jungian point of view, John's beginner sounds like someone who has a well-developed ego-consciousness and whose persona is in place. The persona is one of a religious person whose self-understanding and identity in society involves being associated with religious activities: "The soul finds its joy, therefore, in spending lengthy periods at prayer, perhaps even entire nights; its penances are pleasures; its fasts, happiness; and the sacraments and spiritual conversations are its consolations."[41]

Teresa of Avila describes a similar person when she discusses the condition of one who has entered the third dwelling place of the *Interior Castle*. She depicts a model adult Christian: "They long not to offend His Majesty, even guarding themselves against venial sins; they are fond of doing penance and setting aside periods for recollection; they spend their time well, practicing works of charity toward their neighbors, and are very balanced in their use of speech and dress and in the governing of their households—those who have them."[42]

It is an attractive picture and one would conclude that the heights of Christianity have been reached. But the reader is suspicious because it is only the third dwelling place and there are many more rooms in the Castle to enter. Teresa's Christian in the third dwelling place is more positively described than is John's beginner, but the underlying problems are the same.

Both John and Teresa understand the conditions they describe to be the result of a person traveling the right road. Teresa's Christian has come a long way, but eventually such a well-ordered and structured life becomes an end in itself. In order to continue, Teresa concludes that the individual needs much more freedom of spirit.

And John's beginners are involved in activities which are good in themselves, but start to be taken to an extreme and are undermined by egoism. Living at this sense level all things are turned back to the consolation of the individual.

Further conversions are required of Teresa's model adult Christian and John's beginner. Teresa notices that God begins to undermine the stability of her prayerful Christian with trials of dryness. John identifies similar trials in the life of the beginner, which indicate the beginning of the night of sense.

It was Jung's view that, in time, a persona built up in the first half of life will no longer be adequate to express all the psychic life emerging in the individual. The ego finds itself out of touch with the unconscious. Meaning begins to erode and life's map blurs. At this time Jung observed that the individual is experiencing a religious problem, a loss of contact with the nourishing life of the depths.

Often it is only when the persona begins to dissolve or disintegrate that the ego is open to listening to the dark, unconscious life of the psyche. The language needed for this dialogue is the language of imagination. The experience of the night is an experience both of God subverting the Christian's stable condition, and of the self breaking through the confines of a too-limiting persona.

John's Three Signs for the Beginning of Contemplation

The signs John offers to judge an authentic experience of the dark night (dryness in prayer and life, powerlessness to restore the former satisfaction, and an inability to meditate) indicate a radical transition in an individual's life. John views the occasion as the time in a life of prayer when, after initial conversion and enthusiasm and satisfying religious practices, the spiritual journey wanes in excitement and the certainty of the soul weakens.

The initial stage of the journey is dominated by the words, choices, and vision of the individual. Prayer then is still a response to God, but the person feels strength and satisfaction. The night, unexpected and unwanted, slowly undermines the soul's noble project. The enthusiasm dies, the vision blurs, and the tongue goes quiet.

John indicates that this dark situation affects more than a person's time in formal prayer. One's whole life is being wrung out through cognitive and affective aridity. Unable to word life as before, and with no burning desire beckoning the soul, the world grows dark and cold.

Shift to an Inner Orientation

This time in life is quite similar to the time Jung described as the shift from an outer orientation in life to an inner orientation; in his view it marked the major turning point between the first and second halves of life.

For Jung, the first half of life is necessarily a one-sided journey. As ego emerges it struggles against the primordial chaos of the unconscious and through consciousness establishes order and control in the personality. In terms of the polarities of the psyche, one side of a polarity becomes established in the conscious personality; the other side of the polarity remains dormant in the unconscious.

In Jung's theory, when one pole of the personality has reached its maximum development in consciousness, its opposite pole in the unconscious begins to be activated through a reversal of energy which now runs into the neglected pole. When this process happens, and the unconscious life forces itself upon the personality, ego-consciousness experiences a loss of control. The wider life of the psyche, the self, is seeking expression. And this self is so "other" to ego that it is a dark experience.

Ego would not willingly give up its hard-earned position as center of consciousness, the only life it knows. To make an inner journey and connect up with parts of the self which have not been integrated in consciousness is an extremely difficult task for the ego.

Jung wrote that the fear of going into the unconscious is the fear expressed in the mythological journey to Hades. The ego fights returning to the dark, losing structure and control. But the movement of the undeveloped parts of the self slowly, and with more or less intensity, begins to darken the light of consciousness.

John of the Cross' signs describe well this psychological condition: loss of meaning, an inability to restore it, and a powerlessness to word one's existence as before. The ineffectual prayer John describes is a prayer of wording, thinking, analyzing, resolving; all are activities of the mode of consciousness which Jung terms "masculine."

The Night Not Solely a Psychological Experience

If there is congruence between the process Jung is describing and the condition John is identifying, then what Jung is attributing to a spontaneous psychological transformation of the psyche, John is attributing to the activity of God in the personality.

It makes sense to say that the spiritual crisis John is describing has psychological reverberations as well, and that hypotheses, such as the individuation process of Jung, capture some of the psychological ramifications of such a crisis. John's own description of the dark night experience is in psychological categories of his day. He attempts to present the impact of Mystery on his personality, and to describe the ensuing transformation of the innate structures of his psyche.

John of the Cross is careful to say, however, that the dark night condition is fundamentally an activity of God and not solely a psychological state. He writes: "Even though the dryness may be furthered by melancholia or some other humor—as it often is—it does not thereby fail to produce its purgative effect in the appetite, for the soul will be deprived of every satisfaction and concerned only about God. If this humor is the entire cause, everything ends in disgust and does harm to one's nature, and there are none of these desires to serve God which accompany the purgative dryness."[43]

Given all that is happening to the individual, one would seem to have a right to some depression. But John says the depression cannot be the whole story. If it is the whole story, it is a destructive state and not the true dark night.

Psychiatrist Gerald May has noted some of the differences he has perceived between those people who are experiencing the dark night and those who are experiencing a state of primary psychological depression. One whose condition is basically depression does not function well, loses a sense of humor, is self-absorbed, experiences the condition as destructive, and is struggling for help to be relieved of the depression.

One who is in a true dark night may continue to function well, often retains a sense of humor about the situation, has a growing compassion for others, experiences the condition as confusing but basically "right" for the soul, and is not urgently trying to eliminate the condition.

A final difference May notes is the effect on those who attempt to be with people in these experiences. To be with someone in a primary psychological depression can be a draining, frustrating, angry experience. Time spent with a person who is in a dark night condition is usually not draining, and often may be a consoling, graced experience.[44]

Self-Transcendence and the Dark Night

Once again, Lonergan's interiority analysis provides a framework for linking the spiritual and psychological transformations. The authentic self-transcendence of one who is attentive, intelligent, reasonable, and responsible is understood as the result of God's love within the human spirit calling the individual to an ever deeper union. The process continually undermines one's current understanding and meaning, and requires a letting-go which temporarily produces a dark condition.

Or it could be said this way: When the desire that we are exhausts itself in the ultimately unsatisfying places where it seeks fulfillment, then the personality experiences an eclipse. John of the Cross appears to be describing a time in this interior process when the eclipse is total and the conversions are quite radical.

Ineffectual Remedies: John and Jung

The recommendations by John of the Cross for entering the dark night, and by Carl Jung for making the inner journey are remarkably similar. First, they warn what not to do.

John warns the soul not to redouble its efforts at meditation. The temptation will be to attempt to restore the former satisfaction and sense of direction with renewed activity, activity which brought the person to the present state. John says such a solution would be missing the invitation from God to let God work quietly in the soul. John writes: "They are like someone who turns from what has already been done in order to do it again, or one who leaves a city only to reenter it, or they are like the hunter who abandons his prey to go hunting again. It is useless then for the soul to try to meditate, because it will no longer profit by this exercise."[45] The challenge will be to not word one's life as was done previously. It is time to listen.

Jung's warnings are similar. The invitation to enter into the darkness of the unconscious can be refused or resisted. Jung talks about two ways of responding poorly to the opportunity, through inflation or through regressive restoration of the persona.

Inflation

One poor solution is to give way to the unconscious totally and to identify with the collective psyche in a state of inflation. In this inflated state, rather than dialogue with these parts of the self and maintain a conscious point of view in order to integrate the material, the ego collapses into the archetypal realm and the person begins to live a mythological life, an unreal and eventually tragic imitation of the gods. The fate of Icarus whose wax wings melt when he flies too near the sun captures the hubris involved in identifying with the archetypal realm.

All people, observes Jung, are drawn by a "longing for the mother," a return to the source. In this longing is the beginning of the story of the hero. Jung writes: "It is precisely the strongest and best among men, the heroes, who give way to their regressive longing and purposely expose themselves to the danger of being devoured by the monster of the maternal abyss. But if a man is a hero, he is a hero because, in the final reckoning, he did not let the monster devour him, but subdued it, not once but many times. Victory over the collective psyche alone yields the true value—the capture of the hoard, the invincible weapon, the magic talisman, or whatever it be that the myth deems most desirable."[46]

But Jung goes on to warn: "Anyone who identifies with the collective psyche—or, in mythological terms, lets himself be devoured by the monster—and vanishes in it, attains the treasure that the dragon guards, but he does so in spite of himself and to his own greatest harm."[47] Jung especially warns about the person who identifies with the collective psyche and suddenly appears as a "prophet." "I would not deny in general the existence of genuine prophets," he writes, "but in the name of caution I would begin by doubting each individual case; for it is far too serious a matter for us lightly to accept a man as a genuine prophet. Every respectable prophet strives manfully against the unconscious pretensions of his role. When therefore a prophet appears at a moment's notice, we would be better advised to contemplate a possible psychic disequilibrium."[48]

Because the inflated "prophet's" role is too demanding, many people choose the equally inflated role of "disciple of the prophet." The disciple can feign unworthiness while growing in stature and dignity. The disciple can make the same demands on others as does the prophet, without the prophet's dangerous responsibility. "And these people," Jung observes, "who creep about behind an apparently modest persona, are the very ones who, when inflated by identification with the collective psyche, suddenly burst upon the world scene. For, just as the prophet is a primordial image from the collective psyche, so also is the disciple of the prophet."[49]

Jung's observations begin to describe some of the terrain John's beginner will have to traverse in the night.

Regressive Restoration of the Persona

A second poor way of responding to the psyche's invitation to make an inner journey is to attempt to regain control of life through a type of intentional restructuring which Jung referred to as a "regressive restoration of the persona."[50] In other words, if the persona one has is being undermined by the demands of life outside and within the individual, there is a temptation to scale back the persona and wrap it around oneself more tightly. Life's demands are then filtered out, and only that which affirms a person's present condition is allowed in. No journey has to be taken because all is well. Where no one asks, no one need answer, wrote Jung.

However, "circling the wagons" may protect the ego from extremely difficult times and unwanted sufferings, but it is not done without a penalty. This refusal to come to consciousness was Jung's psychological definition of sin. The person stops growing because the unlived life within the personality is stillborn. Wrapped in a defensive persona, the personality dries up because it is unable to be open to psychic nourishment. And this person is unable to be generative of new life in others.

Others pay dearly when a person refuses to continue on life's journey. The unlived life in a person is projected out on the environment in its unadapted form. The person hates it, lusts after it, feels threatened by it, fights it, all without realizing it is her life, her potential. It is all "out there" in the other. The other person becomes competition to be feared or kept at bay, or is seen as evil incarnate, or the other becomes an object of desire to be appropriated. It is then that the refusal to come to consciousness leads to sinful activity.

The heart of this condition of projection, as was previously discussed, is an unconscious identification with the other person who is carrying part of one's unlived life. It is only when the other person is known as truly "other," when projections are withdrawn, that the self within a person is met as truly other and a trustworthy partner for a dialogue with ego.

Both Jung's person with the regressive persona, and John of the Cross' beginner have their gods all outside, giving their life away to the world around because of the fear of meeting it within in its mysterious "otherness."

Recommended Behavior

In the experience of the night, John of the Cross recommends entering into the dark condition with patience and trust. It is an experience of God's love which is affecting us, initially in a disturbing manner. At this time the soul has a natural inclination to be in solitude and quiet, and John encourages this movement. Amidst all the fears and doubts,

John counsels a waiting in perseverance. It is his belief that deep work is being done by God who is bringing order and harmony into a scattered existence. "For contemplation is nothing else than a secret and peaceful and loving inflow of God, which, if not hampered, fires the soul in the spirit of love. . . ."[51]

It may not be possible for a person to actually have physical conditions of solitude and quiet. Family demands, work responsibilities, living situations may all make such a setting impossible. But John is not essentially urging a physical retreat as much as an interior stance in life. Even while going about normal activities and responsibilities, and apparently unchanged in the view of others, a person may take up another attitude, another stance toward life, which is far different from their previous stance.

John is urging people to admit the experience of the night, accept the condition, and within it listen attentively, persevering in prayer without knowing the outcome. Resist naming it failure, or the wrong road taken in life, or blaming oneself. In effect, become a "watch in the night" interiorly. It is a time of "sheer grace."

A Careful Descent

Carl Jung, too, urges cooperation with the condition one is experiencing. The psyche is asking ego to let go of conscious control and let itself be engaged by unknown parts of the self. In Jung's view we may as well make the descent into the unconscious with a rope and torch and carefully examine what is there, or we will probably walk off backward anyway. One way or another the journey will be made.

He, too, encourages letting the light of consciousness be dimmed in the experience, and entering into the dark carefully listening, trusting that there is a process underway which ultimately is for the health of the psyche. We are not the source of the river, he once said, we only take from it a hatful of water. It is a religious process because for Jung religion is "obedience to awareness."

Symbolic Living

Different from John, who simply leaves one in the dark waiting for the light, Jung recommends a step after listening. He assumes that the psyche will eventually begin to record the experience in its own language, the language of imagination. Consciousness may not be able to formulate concepts about the experience, but images will arise from the unconscious which symbolize, give word to the deep events. The inner journey for Jung is a process of learning to live "the symbolic life."

When the ego has listened in the dark experience, and imagination has begun to speak its language, Jung encourages the ego to relate to the images from the imagination. Pay attention to them and search for the meanings which are being born through them. They are the result of the psyche's natural process of imaging its depth experiences in projections on the environment, in dreams, and in images hidden within its feelings. But they are not symbolic in themselves until ego begins a dialogue with the self through them. Both the conscious and the unconscious viewpoint are linked through the image, which then becomes symbol.

For Jung the symbol is the best possible expression of something which is basically unknown. It is a bridge thrown out to an unseen shore. In the presence of symbol one finds the heart and mind continually challenged.

John's Example

In his commentaries, John of the Cross does not explicitly address the next step after listening. He leaves one in the dark, generally, and continually reminds the reader that *nada* is God. But he does predict light and warmth coming into the situation as God illumines the mind and warms the heart in a kindling of love.

Meaning does return and the journey is resumed with further intentionality. Lonergan's view that the human spirit is eventually driven to word its experience, and so be responsible for what it has heard, would allow us to predict that John's contemplative person does not remain in a wordless, imageless state. An imageless state may be impossible in any event if, as Jung maintains, psyche "is" image.

While he did not write about a further process, John exemplified a process beginning with his poetry. He obviously did not remain unknowing, beyond word and image, in a perduring cloud. He produced image-filled poems and wrote thousands of words of commentary about imageless, wordless prayer. (Somewhat like the monk who traveled the world preaching stability.)

A Rhythm in Prayer

Teresa of Avila, through her own experience and natural symbolic attitude, mistrusted a permanent, silent, dark prayer. In *The Interior*

Castle she said that "life is long" and there is no sense in just sitting there in the dark if nothing is happening. Get back to the humanity of Christ, she urged, and the celebrations of the church. "I believe I've explained," she wrote, "that it is fitting for souls however spiritual, to take care not to flee from corporeal things, to the extent of thinking that even the most sacred humanity causes harm."[52]

In other words, there is a rhythm to the dark and light times in prayer. The dark cannot be forced but should be accepted when it is present. But it should not artificially be sustained when it is time for the soul to word and reflect upon its experience.

Jung would maintain that the soul needs to tell and hear its own story in order to appropriate that story. Let it attend to its symbols, make narrative of them, and reflect on the story in a responsible way. This process coincides with Lonergan's understanding of the development of human consciousness. We are driven, through attentiveness, to meaning and responsible choices. But the process begins not in conscious decision but in the experience of being grasped by God's love, the very experience John is describing as a "dark night."

Benefits of the Night

John describes the effects of this night experience as self-knowledge, knowledge of God, and greater respect for others. The self-knowledge he describes is quite painful in part, because it includes an awareness of one's "misery." In a condition of complacency a person is unaware of a need for healing. The night breaks through this complacency and reveals the brokenness of the human condition, our alienation from our true selves. The outcome is a chief reason for an increase in respect for God and others.

The Shadow

Jung wrote that one of the first parts of the self which will be encountered on the inner journey is the alienated, rejected, shameful part which he termed the "shadow." This shadow consists of material which is the result of human development in the first half of life. It generally is identified with the personal unconscious, that layer closer to consciousness which contains the residue of past relationships, our unadapted power and sexual drives, and other matter that may have been conscious at one time but for one reason or another now resides in the unconscious.

In describing the shadow, Jung is concerned about the freedom of the ego. He generally interpreted images arising from contact with shadow material in a reductive manner, that is, looking back into the development of the individual. This personal unconscious material points to a lack of psychic integration which may still be influencing the ego and holding it bound to unconscious forces. For example, unhealed past relationships may be skewing present relationships.

Jungian analyst Murray Stein has discussed the necessity for integrating shadow material in the therapeutic process. In the initial movement in analysis it is important to determine if there is any material in the personal unconscious, matter from an individual's past, which may be affecting the ego in its ability to function properly. Bringing this matter to light assists the ego in becoming free of past baggage. Images at this point are interpreted reductively.

The ego needs to have a relative autonomy and be freed from the past so that it can then freely give itself to the true center of the personality, the self. The self material is rooted in a deeper layer of psyche, the collective unconscious, and images which are expressive of this wider self are interpreted prospectively, that is, with a view to future development.[53]

The Night and Shadow

Much of John of the Cross' description of the difficulty of the night of the senses sounds quite similar to the challenge of integrating shadow material. Jung attributes the process to a spontaneous healing dynamic in the psyche. John attributes the experience to a passive prayer in which God is leading the person to an awareness of the reality of the self, others, and God.

Jung was quite positive about the shadow dimension of the personality, saying that it represented energy available for the development of the full life of the individual. Because it was unadapted and did not see the light of consciousness, it acted in a negative way in the personality. Consequently, the initial confrontation with one's shadow side is an experience of otherness and generally not pleasant.

It would make sense that prayer, such as described by John of the Cross which leads one into the reality of one's existence, would bring a person face to face with the shadow, one's "misery." This encounter would add to the negative quality of the night.

Jung observes that the shadow material is psychic matter which one would be ashamed to admit to others, and to oneself. Therefore, a generalization might be that the shadow is the underside of the persona, the mask one presents to the outer world. If this is so, and if John's beginner may be understood to have taken on a religious persona, then John's analysis of the imperfections of beginners is also a preview of the shadow material the beginner will encounter in prayer. John's use of the seven capital vices as a framework for understanding the beginner's lack of freedom, even while enjoying a relatively satisfying prayer life, is a look at the neglected side of the personality.

John's Contributions

Theologian William Thompson has identified three contributions of John of the Cross: a shattering of the illusion whereby we pretend all is day and ignore the night; a warning to avoid utopianism in which selfishness is overlooked, and pessimism which sees no possibility of liberation; and a call for a continual critique of everything, including society, church and one's own preferences, because we are capable of perverting anything.[54]

In general, the vices of the beginner represent something good which has been taken to an extreme; the shadow represents material which is mainly positive but is unacknowledged and is therefore acting negatively. The situation is one of living in illusion (John), refusing to come to consciousness (Jung), engaging in inauthentic self-transcendence (Lonergan).

The night painfully reveals the true situation, and begins a healing process. More than shadow is revealed as a person confronts his sinfulness and realizes his inability to forgive himself. At the same time the "otherness" of God impresses itself upon the person in the dark night. The soul is softened, loses arrogance, and grows in reverence. Life's journey is on sacred ground and we learn to show respect and remove our sandals. And with this new-found sense of self and God, other people are seen in their true light. One begins to honor them rather than judge and condemn them.

When Gods Die

John of the Cross is describing a difficult situation, one which people generally would want to avoid. Nevertheless he says that it is part of the prayer process, part of life's journey, and it is a suffering which surprisingly brings life. His insight is that nothing (*nada*) is God, and therefore nothing finally fulfills us as God. The death of false gods is another way of describing the experience of the night.

When a person's desire attempts to find total fulfillment in someone or something, that person or thing begins to take the place of God. Slowly life revolves around whatever is loved in this way, and the personality attempts to derive full meaning and satisfaction from what is ultimately incapable of providing such a return.

Two deaths begin to occur. First, whomever or whatever is being asked to be a god cannot bear it. No community, ministry, future plan, relationship, or reputation can sustain that kind of role. The expectation is too much for any part of creation and it begins to die under the pressure.

Second, a lesser god means a lesser human. We cannot grow past our god. The self-transcending process which Lonergan identifies as necessary for human development is truncated as ultimate truth and goodness are attributed to something which is not truly ultimate. The personality stops growing and becomes distorted.

If the relationship, family, project, or whatever, is to live and grow healthily, then we need to release our hold on it. We need to be open once again to the deeper love which drew us to these loves in the first place. In the context of this love we can then love others and live in this world in a way which is life-giving, and not killing.

The night is an experience of our desire's inability to find its depth and intensity matched by anything in this world. The night reveals that we are "deep caverns of feeling" with hungers for which only God is the proper food. As tough as John of the Cross sounds in his discussion of the dark night, he is doing no more than describing life as it is experienced at depth by people, and recommending a prayerful passage through it with a trust that in these depths lives a graciousness.

The pain and sorrow of the night are the grief that accompanies the death of gods. When gods die, Jung explained, the personality begins to disintegrate. In Jung's understanding, what is needed is the birth of a new and more appropriate image for the god-archetype within the psyche. Projections are withdrawn in the night and the other is allowed to be "other," and not a screen for the unconscious. Ego is opened to an encounter with the self, and listens attentively for its symbolic expression.

In the understanding of John of the Cross, alien gods lose their hold on a soul in the night experience. What was transfixing in the light of day becomes blurred and indistinct at twilight. It is now possible to see past the idols of one's life. The night is God whose light pierces to the heart of things and in whose presence all is as though dark.

Contemplation and Individuation

Jung himself is rather ambiguous regarding the relationship between the dark night of John of the Cross and the individuation process. In one of his letters, when asked if the integration of the collective unconscious is the same process John of the Cross was describing, Jung wrote: "John of the Cross' 'Dark Night of the Soul' has nothing to do with this."[55]

However, the question put to Jung was about the *integration* of the collective unconscious, and perhaps because he viewed this particular aspect of the individuation process as a conscious dialectical process involving a relatively small amount of constellated material, it was therefore not the passive experience of John of the Cross. Or perhaps Jung was making a distinction between an ego-transcendence, which he discusses as the individuation process, and a self-transcendence, which John described in the dark night experience. The latter process involves relationship to a realm beyond psyche which Jung would maintain is unknowable. And perhaps he was the victim of a theology which was uncomfortable relating psychological and spiritual processes.

Jung did not necessarily deny that the dark night was equivalent to some aspect of the individuation process. In a paper on *The Psychology of the Transference*, in which he studied plates from a 1550 alchemical text, *The Rosarium Philosophorum*, Jung referred to one plate as reminiscent of John's dark night of the soul.

The plate is a picture of a King and a Queen who have died in one another's embrace and now lie in a watery sarcophagus in an hermaphroditic form. The soul, in the form of a cherub-like figure, is leaving this scene of decay and is ascending to heaven.

In Jung's interpretation, the plate depicts the state of the psyche when two poles have confronted one another as thesis and antithesis and the personality has gone into a regression with the energy moving deeply into the unconscious where these poles were originally undifferentiated. Psychologically the plate reveals a state of disorientation; it shows a flooding of consciousness by the unconscious as the Nile floods in order to make fertile.[56]

It is Jung's opinion that the fundamental polarity being wed here is the polarity of matter and spirit. The relationship signifies, in Jung's words, "man's longing for transcendent wholeness."[57] And he says that the psychologist is in no position to explain fully the meaning of such psychological facts.

But he did observe that John of the Cross attempted to explain similar realities. Jung wrote: "It is not immediately apparent why this dark state deserves special praise, since the *nigredo* is universally held to be of a sombre and melancholy humour reminiscent of death and the grave. But the fact that medieval alchemy had connections with the mysticism of the age, or rather was itself a form of mysticism, allows us to adduce as a parallel to the *nigredo* the writings of St. John of the Cross concerning the 'dark night.' This author conceives the 'spiritual night' of the soul as a supremely positive state, in which the invisible—and therefore dark—radiance of God comes to pierce and purify the soul."[58]

In another letter, Jung describes the disorientation which precedes growth in consciousness as a psychological equivalent of the dark night. He wrote: "Considering that the light of Christ is accompanied by the 'dark night of the soul' that St. John of the Cross spoke about, and by what the Gnostics of Irenaeus called the *umbra Christi* . . . the life of Christ is identical in us, from the psychological point of view, with the unconscious tendency toward individuation. That is what forces us to live life completely, an adventure which is often as heroic as it is tragic."[59]

Spiritual and Psychological Journeys

The discussion continues in the fields of spirituality and psychology regarding the relationship of one to the other. Do the two deal with the same realm of interiority, but each having a different focus?

The religious journey involves slowly surrendering one's being to the God who created it. Gerald May believes that this process is deep and hidden and continues throughout a lifetime. Times such as the dark night are "noticings" of what is happening at depth.[60] Lonergan's assumption is that it is the experience of God's love which impels this journey. John of the Cross appears to be noting just such an experience, hidden within a dark time for the soul. It is essentially a passive experience and John identifies it with true contemplative prayer. The process is one of self-transcendence.

The psychological journey deals with intrapsychic and interpsychic realities, but it is always affected by the transpsychic. To a great extent this journey is assisted by focused attention, reflection, analysis. The accent is on what theologian Robert Doran called self-appropriation.

Authors seem to agree that one does not grow in religious development without also maturing psychologically, within one's limitations. Teresa of Avila observed that we cannot know God if we do not know ourselves. The situation of the human psyche today, and our understanding of the human stance in experience, necessitates that the human journey is one of self-appropriation. Without it, in Jung's framework, we give ourselves away in projection. The individual does not grow, but begins to die, and others are forced to carry our unlived life, which is a crushing burden to them.

On the other hand, Teresa of Avila said we cannot truly know ourselves unless we also know God. It is only in this relationship that our humanity is revealed. John of the Cross, too, assumed that the human psyche functions healthily only when the soul is in relationship with God. The journey through the night is a healing process which is the result of an openness to and a deeper union with God.

But there may be psychological processes and frameworks which foreclose the process of self-transcendence. They may leave no "door" open at the center of the self for nourishing contact with Mystery. In that case there would be a truncated religious journey and distorted human development.

Authentic Individuation Implies Contemplation

It might be said that authentic experiences of individuation contain at least moments of contemplation, understood as attentiveness to Mystery passively experienced. In accord with Bernard Lonergan's interiority analysis, authentic self-transcendence of the human spirit is religious development, named or not. Human development is a graced reality which, when lived in accord with the dynamism of the human spirit to know and to love, leads a person into processes of conversion.

These processes of conversion entail shifts of horizon for the individual consciousness, and those shifts include a darkening of former horizons. These moments, or even quite long periods, naturally invite the person to a listening in the dark. It is a psychological experience because it inevitably registers on the psyche. It is passive because the ego does not structure or control the experience, and as a matter of fact, usually feels negated in the process.

This experience is at least implicitly a contemplative experience because ultimately it is the Spirit relating to the individual in such a way that an unknowing is occurring. If there is no conscious attention to a relationship with God, or no explicit faith dimension in the experience, then the experience does not appear to have the quality or openness of a contemplative experience as identified by John of the Cross. But it will be a relationship to some aspect of the true self and therefore, implicitly, it is an experience of God.

In sum, the individuation process, understood as a process of authentic self-transcendence in accord with the dynamism of the human spirit, has rhythms of contemplation as described by John. The quality and depth of that contemplation will, to an extent, depend upon the maturity and faith stance of the individual. Ideally, it is one journey, psyche and spirit reverberating one with the other, with occasional palpable moments revealing the graciousness at the heart of this reality.

Faith Development

In the next chapter this spiritual and human development will be examined in the context of a faith journey. John encourages a way of unknowing in *The Ascent of Mount Carmel,* Books Two and Three. Examining these writings will also provide an opportunity to look at certain contemporary studies regarding faith development.

CHAPTER SEVEN

Toward a Mature Faith

The Ascent of Mount Carmel, Books Two and Three
Active Night of the Spirit

In these books John discusses the active night of the spirit. Book Two discusses the night of the intellect, and Book Three the nights of the memory and will. He tells what a soul must do to live a life of faith, hope, and charity. Along the way he offers practical advice regarding, among many other topics, visions, statues, oratories, ceremonies, spiritual direction and preaching.

Because nothing (*nada*) is a proximate means to union with God, John encourages a way of unknowing, a dark, silent prayer. He seems to set an impossible goal. However, when he speaks about the process of growing in contemplative prayer John demonstrates a more nuanced teaching, which nonetheless remains challenging.

Part one of this chapter summarizes John's work. The second part of this chapter, a reflection on John's commentary, concentrates on his presentation of faith. More recent studies of faith development, namely the studies of James Fowler and Gabriel Moran, are briefly described and related to John's thought. These developmentalists provide a contemporary expression of the journey mapped by John. In particular, the role of image as a symbolic expression of religious experience is discussed.

A SUMMARY OF *THE ASCENT OF MOUNT CARMEL,* BOOKS TWO AND THREE

Book Two

John reports that this night of the spirit is not begun through the experience of urgent longings as was the case in the night of the senses.

The spiritual night is a negation of one's understanding through faith. The night of the spirit is more interior than the first night, and darker. This faith is comparable to midnight.

"Faith, the theologians say, is a certain and obscure habit of soul," writes John.[1] It comes through hearing, and so we believe what faith teaches. John describes this faith as a dark night illumining our soul. It is a union with God which does not depend upon understanding, or experiences, or feelings or imagination. While these modes and methods are no longer necessary, John claims that a person in this state actually possesses all methods.

Of course, there is always a union between God and creatures; otherwise creatures would cease to exist. But the union he is writing about is a union and transformation which consists in a likeness of love. "Indeed, it is God by participation."[2] The soul, however, is still naturally distinct from God.

Even in this intense union there are degrees. The degrees are similar to people's abilities to discern the qualities of a fine painting. Everyone appreciates the painting, but some appreciate it more.

The three virtues of faith, hope, and charity affect the spiritual faculties of intellect, memory, and will. "Faith causes darkness and a void of understanding in the intellect, hope begets an emptiness of possessions in the memory, and charity produces the nakedness and emptiness of affection and joy in all that is not God."[3]

Seek God in Self

John observes that self-love usually hinders this spiritual journey. He returns to a basic image of the journey when he says this high mount of perfection is narrow and steep. One cannot be burdened by the soul's lower part, the senses, nor can one be burdened by the higher part, for example the understanding. He encourages the soul not to seek self in God, which is a subtle distortion of spirituality, but he urges a seeking of God in self.

He repeats that ". . . the road leading to God does not entail a multiplicity of considerations, methods, manners, and experiences."[4] He admits these may be necessary for beginners. But eventually only one thing is necessary: "true self-denial, exterior and interior, through surrender of self both to suffering for Christ and to annihilation in all things."[5]

Here is the strong language of John of the Cross. Often when he is establishing principles of the spiritual life his writing is stark. But when he discusses the process whereby one honors the principle, the language changes considerably. He allows for a gradual, gentle transformation, which in the long run is no more, and no less, than the following of Christ.

Christ is our model and light, John writes. "He proclaimed during His life that He had no place whereon to lay His head (Mt 8:20). And at His death He had less."[6] He experienced extreme abandonment by his Father, and so reconciled humanity with God through grace. In imitation of Christ, "the journey, then, does not consist in recreations, experiences, and spiritual feelings, but in the living, sensory and spiritual, exterior and interior death of the cross."[7]

This death to everything is predicated on the principle that nothing is a proximate means to union with God. One advances by an unknowing. Contemplation is mystical theology, a secret wisdom of God. John recalls Pseudo-Dionysius calling contemplation a "ray of darkness."[8] Faith alone is the proximate and proportionate means to union with God.

Knowledge of the Intellect

In chapter ten John begins to write about the natural and supernatural knowledge of the intellect. Natural knowledge refers to knowledge received through the senses or by reflection. Supernatural knowledge refers to what is known by the intellect in a manner which is beyond its natural ability. This supernatural knowledge is both corporal and spiritual, relating to the two parts of the soul.

Corporal supernatural knowledge may come from the exterior or interior senses. Spiritual supernatural knowledge may be distinct (visions, revelations, locutions, spiritual feelings) or vague, dark, and general (contemplation).

The goal is to lead the soul to this last knowledge, contemplation, leaving behind all the other ways of knowing.

John then makes recommendations regarding supernatural experiences received by the exterior senses (visions, angels, lights, words, smells, tastes, touches). His rule is never to rely on them or accept them; and he warns against even trying to discern whether they are good or bad. Consider them diabolical, he recommends.

A a rule of thumb, the more exterior something is, the more it is suspect. If such experiences are truly from God they have already produced their effect. If they are diabolical they will cause unrest, but John says such unrest will usually not last long. He counsels that "diabolical communications are not as efficacious in doing harm as God's communications are in doing good."[9]

John names six kinds of harm which result from accepting exterior communications, even if they are from God: first, faith diminishes as the senses feast; second, they keep the spirit from soaring; third, the person becomes possessive; fourth, they gradually lose their effect because the soul attends only to the sensible aspect; fifth, God's favor is lost as the soul assumes the communications to be its own; sixth, they open the door to the devil.

Natural, Imaginative Knowledge

In chapter twelve John begins to discuss natural, imaginative knowledge. This knowledge is derived from the interior bodily senses of imagination and fantasy. John says there is no need to distinguish between them. Here he is talking about our usual way of working with images. He is discussing what the soul can actively construct through "forms, figures, and images." When we meditate we are using these faculties, for example in imagining Christ crucified.

As usual, John prescribes emptying the senses of these images, leaving the senses in the dark, since these images are not an adequate means of reaching union with God. He warns that images are always less than the real thing. The images of pearls and mountains are certainly less than real pearls and mountains. But, such images are necessary for beginners, says John. Only when faculties come to the end of their usefulness do they cease to function. Even then we may put faculties to work imaging, at times, with gentleness and love, and without excessive effort or studied reasoning.

Here John appears to be allowing for a natural process of imaging which seems to contradict his strongly stated teaching regarding the inadequacy of images. Nothing before its time, he seems to be saying. And as long as images aid one's spirituality they are to be acknowledged, even when one's prayer is more contemplative.

Three Signs for the Beginning of Contemplation

As in *The Dark Night*, Book One, John again gives three signs which indicate the beginning of contemplative prayer. One should not abandon imaginative meditation until all of these signs are present. "These signs will indicate that the time and season has come when one can freely make use of that loving attentiveness, and discontinue his journey along the way of reasoning and imagination."[10]

"The first is the realization that one cannot make discursive meditation nor receive satisfaction from it as before."[11]

"The second sign is an awareness of a disinclination to fix the imagination or sense faculties upon other particular objects, exterior or interior."[12] However, the imagination does wander.

"The third and surest sign is that a person likes to remain alone in loving awareness of God, without particular considerations, in interior peace and quiet and repose, and without the acts and exercises (at least discursive, those in which one progresses from point to point) of the intellect, memory and will; and that he prefers to remain only in the general, loving awareness and knowledge we mentioned, without any particular knowledge or understanding."[13] This third sign differs from the three given in *The Dark Night*, although in that work John does discuss this growing inclination to remain in solitude with a loving attentiveness to God. In both works, John warns that initially the loving knowledge is almost imperceptible.

This third sign is quite important. Without it, the person who stops meditating will simply be doing nothing. The soul cannot force contemplative prayer.

When Meditation Is Appropriate

In chapter fifteen John again acknowledges that the process is not either/or. He says he did not mean to say that those entering the general, loving knowledge of contemplation should never try to meditate. One can meditate on scenes as before, and find something new in them. When the three signs are not present, and all three must be present, meditation is appropriate. As a matter of fact, he says that until reaching the stage of proficients, both meditation and contemplation are appropriate. When a person attempts to meditate, but has no desire to do so, and notices a quiet, loving knowledge, then it is time for contemplative prayer.

In *The Dark Night* John said there are many ways of being in and out of the night. People's experience differs. Presumably, then, a mixture of meditation and contemplation may last most of a lifetime, or all of a lifetime, or it may be mainly meditation with occasional contemplative moments.

Nevertheless, John points to the most desirable outcome: "The manifest conclusion is that, when a person has finished purifying and voiding himself of all forms and apprehensible images he will abide in this pure and simple light, and be perfectly transformed into it."[14] The light is always offered. When things move out, God moves in, because ". . . there can be no void in nature."[15]

Fantasy and Imagination

In chapter sixteen John discusses "imaginative visions," which include everything represented to the interior senses of fantasy and imagination supernaturally; that is, without the aid of the exterior senses. Everything that can be received by these internal senses naturally through the external senses can also be received supernaturally.

Here John examines the role of the fantasy and imagination:

> This interior sense, the fantasy coupled with the memory, is for the intellect the archives or receptacle in which all the intelligible forms and images are received. Like a mirror, this faculty contains them within itself, whether they come to it from the five bodily senses or supernaturally. It in turn presents them to the intellect, and the intellect considers and makes a judgment about them. Not only is the fantasy capable of this, but it can even compose and imagine other objects resembling those known.[16]

Both God and the devil can provide images to the interior senses without the aid of the exterior senses. God's work is evidenced in scripture in the visions of Isaiah, Jeremiah, Daniel, and the dream of Pilate's wife.

> The devil ordinarily comes with his wiles, natural or supernatural, to this sense, the imagination and fantasy, for it is the gate and entry to the soul. Here the intellect comes as though to a seaport or market to buy and sell provisions. As a result, God—and the devil too—comes here with the jewels of images and supernatural forms to proffer them to the intellect.[17]

Discerning Visions

John is not interested in providing signs for discerning good visions from bad ones. As with external visions, one should pay no attention to them, no matter what the source. The reason is that these visions are always limited in mode and manner and therefore cannot adequately represent God's wisdom.

The best approach is to deny and reject these visions. If they truly are from God no resistance is possible and they produce their good effect in the soul regardless. "I affirm, consequently, that the unintelligible or unimaginable element in these visions is communicated to it passively, exclusive of any effort of the soul to understand."[18]

God Respects the Human Process of Knowing

In chapter seventeen John asks why, if such revelations get in the way of true faith, does God grant them? Because, answers John, God respects the soul and brings it to union in an orderly and gentle way, following the soul's natural process. "Since the order followed in the process of knowing involves the forms and images of created things, and since knowledge is acquired through the senses, God, to achieve His work gently and to lift the soul to supreme knowledge, must begin by touching the low state and extreme of the senses."[19]

John then demonstrates how God leads a soul according to human nature. First God uses natural exterior objects such as sermons, masses, holy objects, and penances. Then God may present a supernatural favor such as a vision of a saint. At the same time the interior senses of imagination and fantasy are using meditation and reasoning which instruct the spirit. At the proper time God may assist these interior senses with supernatural imaginative visions. Gradually the spirit is reformed and refined.

John concludes: "This is God's method of bringing a soul step by step to the innermost good, although it may not always be necessary for Him to keep so mathematically to this order, for sometimes God bestows one kind of communication without the other, or a less interior one by means of a more interior one, or both together. The process depends on what God judges expedient for the soul, or upon the favors He wants to confer. But His ordinary procedure conforms with our explanation."[20]

John concludes this important chapter by reiterating his stance toward supernatural visions, whether of the exterior or interior senses: they must all be renounced. When they are from God they inevitably benefit the soul's spirituality. By distancing itself from visions, the soul safeguards the true purpose of the visions which is to engender a spirit of devotion.

Spiritual Directors

John begins chapter eighteen by apologizing for the length of his discussion of visions. He then has advice for spiritual directors regarding these supernatural visions. He has noticed that both penitent and director can become bewildered in this matter, with the blind leading the blind.

John's advice is simple: Just as an individual should pay no attention to these visions, so too should the spiritual director ignore them. The director should not make the visions a topic of conversation, nor should the director show esteem for them. Any curiosity on the part of the director may cause the individual to overestimate the visions. Imperfections result: "He thinks his visions are significant, that he possesses something profitable, and that he is prominent in God's eyes."[21]

Consequently, John again discourages the director from providing signs for the discernment of good and bad visions. They all can easily mislead. Even visions and locutions from God can mislead, for two reasons: one, the true meaning is not always found in the literal meaning; two, people and times change and so the communications become flexible (for example, something predicted does not happen because people have repented). John provides numerous examples from scripture.

Christ and the Church

In chapter twenty-two, John's focus on Christ is evident. He writes that people should not desire supernatural visions or revelations because it is offensive to God. John provides a lengthy response from God which reads, in part:

> If I have already told you all things in My Word, My Son, and if I have no other word, what answer or revelation can I now make that would surpass this? Fasten your eyes on Him alone, because in Him I have spoken and revealed all, and in Him you shall discover even more than you ask for and desire. You are making an appeal for locutions and revelations that are incomplete, but if you turn your eyes to Him you will find them complete. For He is My entire locution and response, vision and revelation, which I have already spoken, answered, manifested, and revealed to you, by giving Him to you as a brother, companion, master, ransom, and reward.[22]

One should believe only the teachings of Christ, and Christ's ministers. Even when visions are from God, the church must be consulted. The vision or revelation itself contains an inclination to consult appropriate persons about it. God is present where two or three are gathered, not one. "For God will not bring clarification and confirmation of the truth to the heart of one who is alone."[23]

John's conclusion is that supernatural visions should be told to the spiritual director in full. This consultation appears to be essential to the revelation. Some people maintain that the revelation or vision truly took root in them only after they conferred with others.

John is not contradicting his principle of ignoring these visions. When they are told to the director, the director then has the opportunity to guide the individual in the way of faith. John's basic attitude is apparent in his instructions to directors: ". . . they should explain how one act done in charity is more precious in God's sight than all the visions and communications possible . . . and how many who have not received these experiences are incomparably more advanced than others who have had many."[24]

"Visions of the Soul"

In chapter twenty-three John begins to write about even more interior events which he calls supernatural, spiritual, "visions of the soul." He is still speaking about the various ways the intellect can apprehend something. He has just finished writing about the types of knowledge gained from the outer or inner senses, naturally or supernaturally. Now he is writing about knowledge which comes without any mediation of the senses, outer or inner. This knowledge is immediately present to the intellect.

John speaks of four categories of "visions of the soul": visions, revelations, locutions, feelings. John subdivides the categories and so presents a complex schema.

As a general conclusion, John gives the same advice regarding these "visions of the soul" as he did for the other visions; namely, disregard them and do not desire them.

Visions are either corporal, dealing with material things of heaven and earth, or incorporeal which can only be seen by the light of glory (angels and souls). Visions from God produce in the soul "quietude, illumination, gladness resembling that of glory, delight, purity, love, humility, and an elevation and inclination toward God."[25] If a vision is from the devil it produces dryness, self-esteem, and causes the person to value the vision.

Revelations are disclosures of a hidden truth, secret, or mystery. Two types are intellectual knowledge, and God's secrets.

Intellectual knowledge may be about God, or creatures. Intellectual knowledge about God is pure contemplation, union with God, a touch of divinity. John is *not* negative about this type of vision. "He should simply remain humble and resigned about it. . . ."[26] If the knowledge is about creatures, it should be rejected and the person should continue journeying to God by unknowing.

God's secrets involve both knowledge about the Trinity, and knowledge about God's activity in creation, such as revelatory prophecies, promises, and threats. John advises us to close our eyes and ears to these revelations of mysteries, and "rest simply on the doctrine of the Church and its faith. . . ."[27]

Locutions include successive, formal, and substantial locutions. Successive locutions are the words and reasonings of a recollected spirit. John warns the soul to mistrust such reasonings. It is difficult to discern if the source is God, the natural light of the intellect, or the devil. Words from God leave the person more deeply united with God in a love marked by humility and reverence.

Formal locutions are words spoken to the soul by another, e.g., by an angel. It is clear the words are from another because the soul may not even be recollected. Again, John says to pay no attention to formal words.

Substantial locutions bring about what they express in the substance of the soul. If God were to say, "Be good!" the soul would be substantially good. As with revelations about God which are pure contemplation, John is positive about substantial locutions. Nothing need be done here. It is not important to desire or reject them. "The soul should rather be resigned and humble about them."[28] They greatly assist union with God; the more interior and substantial, the better.

Feelings, the last of the "visions of the soul," may relate to the will, or they may occur in the substance of the soul. Matters of the will are discussed in Book Three of *The Ascent*, so John is reluctant to include the will in this discussion concerning the knowledge of the intellect. But, because the intellect does gain knowledge from feelings in the will, and feelings in the substance of the soul, he briefly mentions them here. The intellect registers a particularly sublime perception of God as a result of these feelings. John counsels that ". . . the intellect should do nothing about them other than behave passively and refrain from meddling through the use of its natural capacity."[29] A humble and unpossessive attitude is best.

Finally, John judges that he has provided a schema which will account for all forms of intellectual knowledge or apprehension. He is confident that any form of knowing is reducible to one of these categories, "even if it may seem different or unincluded."[30]

Book Three

Book Three discusses the active night of the memory and will. John declares his exposition will be brief because his lengthy instructions concerning the intellect are applicable to memory and will as well.

Active Night of Memory

John divides the objects of memory into three parts: natural, imaginative, and spiritual.

Natural objects of memory include anything which can be formed from the senses. His prescription is clear: "The annihilation of the memory in regard to all forms is an absolute requirement for union with God."[31] Distinct knowledge in the memory cannot unite a person with God who is beyond any form or figure.

In speaking about annihilating the memory, John recognizes that he gives the appearance of tearing down rather than building up a person's spirituality. This objection would be true, he responds, if he were speaking about beginners; but he is writing for those whom he would call proficients, those advancing in contemplation.

John describes rather unusual effects which may occur in experiences of union. A touch of union may jolt the brain and cause a loss of consciousness. The memory, now united with God, may not be aware of what has taken place. Such strong effects happen at the beginning of union, John reports, but are not present in one who lives in a more constant state of union.

When the memory is absorbed in such contemplation John says that the person may be quite forgetful about everyday activities, such as eating and drinking. Yet, once this union with God is habitual, such forgetfulness does not occur. The memory functions appropriately, but now in a supernatural manner. "As a result all the operations of the memory and other faculties in this state are divine. . . . As a result the operations are not different from those of God; but those the soul performs are of God and are divine operations."[32]

John's descriptions reveal a transformed humanity now functioning in harmony with God's will. "For God's Spirit makes them know what must be known and ignore what must be ignored, remember what ought to be remembered—with or without forms—and forget what ought to be forgotten, and makes them love what they ought to love, and keeps them from loving what is not in God."[33]

John reminds the reader that only the passive night can actually bring about such a union. For now, he is discussing what the soul can do to lessen attachment to objects of memory.

Although John describes how the memory should ideally function, he realizes he is speaking about a rare situation. He writes: "Although it is true that a person will hardly be found whose union with God is so continuous that his faculties, without any form, are always divinely moved, nevertheless there are those who are very habitually moved by God and not by themselves in their operations. . . ."[34]

John speaks of the harm caused by memory. Memories disturb the soul and bring much that is evil. The devil, too, makes use of memory to influence the person. And when memory is not darkened the person cannot remain free for the "Incomprehensible Who is God. . . ."[35]

Supernatural *imaginative* objects of the memory such as visions, revelations, and locutions leave vivid impressions. Once again, the person should attempt to empty the memory of such objects. "Every possession is against hope. . . ."[36]

Such memories harm the soul in numerous ways, such as encouraging vain presumption and confining God to the forms of these memories. As with forms of knowledge of the intellect, these supernatural objects of memory are recalled only to deepen love for God.

John's third category of objects of memory is *spiritual*. Reflections and reminiscences of the spirit which are held in the memory are either about creatures or the Creator. Knowledge of creatures will not further union, but knowledge of the Creator may be recalled because it will have a beneficial effect.

John summarizes his teaching regarding memory:

> Our aim is union with God in the memory; the object of hope is something unpossessed; the less other objects are possessed, the more capacity and ability there is to hope for this one object, and consequently the more hope; the greater the possessions, the less capacity and ability for hope, and consequently so much less of hope; accordingly, in the measure that a person dispossesses his memory of forms and objects, which are not God, he will fix it upon God and preserve it empty, in the hope that God will fill it.[37]

What should a person do with memories? "As often as distinct ideas, forms, and images occur to him, he should immediately, without resting in them, turn to God with loving affection, in emptiness of everything rememberable."[38] As he finishes this discussion of the active night of memory, with its strong language of forgetfulness, John makes rather remarkable statements which greatly help clarify his teachings about the dark night:

There is no delusion or danger in the remembrance, venera-
tion, and esteem of images that the Catholic Church proposes
to us in a natural manner, since in these images nothing else is
esteemed than the person represented. The memory of these
images will not fail to be profitable to a person, because this
remembrance is accompanied with love for whoever is represented. Images will always help a person toward union with
God, provided that he does not pay more attention to them
than is necessary, and that he allows himself to soar—when
God bestows the favor—from the painted image to the living
God, in forgetfulness of all creatures and things pertaining to
creatures.[39]

One might not have expected such a reasonable process to be com-
patible with John's call to actively enter the night.

Active Night of the Will

John then begins a discussion of the active night of the will. He says
he can find no more appropriate passage for educating the will than
chapter six in Deuteronomy: "You shall love the Lord, your God, with
all your heart, and with all your soul, and with all your strength. (Dt
6:5)" John continues: "This passage contains all that a spiritual man
must do and all that I must teach him here if he is to reach God by union
of the will through charity."[40]
    The will rules the soul directing the faculties, passions, and appe-
tites toward God. But feelings or passions affect the will. These passions are four: joy, hope, sorrow, and fear. When they are focused on
God the soul is in harmony. When they are directed to something else in
place of God the feelings are inordinate. Union with God requires
purging these feelings and appetites so that the will is made identical
with God's will. Then the soul "rejoices only in what is purely for
God's honor and glory, hopes for nothing else, feels sorrow only about
matters pertaining to this, and fears only God."[41]
    John provides an extensive discussion of the passion of joy. He
never does discuss the other three passions—his assumption is that
when one passion is recollected, the others are as well.
    Joy is satisfaction of the will with a fitting object, and there are six
kinds of objects or goods: temporal, natural, sensory, moral, supernatu-

ral, and spiritual. John discusses these objects of joy at great length listing the harm done by these goods when not directed to God, and the benefits derived when joy is withdrawn from them and focused on God. His discussion follows the pattern of previous discussions regarding the objects of intellect and memory.

Joy in *temporal* goods includes rejoicing over "riches, titles, status, positions, and other similar goods. . . ."[42] John teaches: "Man should not be joyous over riches, neither when he possesses them or when his brother possesses them, unless God is served through them. If it is in some way tolerable to rejoice in riches, it is so when they are spent and employed in the service of God."[43]

John's critique is timely: "Out there in the world, their reason darkened through covetousness in spiritual matters, they serve money and not God, and they are motivated by money rather than by God, and they give first consideration to the temporal price and not to the divine value and reward. In countless ways they make money their principal god and goal and give it precedence to God, their ultimate end."[44] John says that when someone is unpossessive of things, that person enjoys them as though they were possessed. The principle continues to be: freedom of the heart for God.

Joy in *natural* goods means rejoicing in "beauty, grace, elegance, bodily constitution and all other corporal endowments; also in the soul, good intelligence, discretion, and other talents pertinent to the rational part of man."[45]

Natural grace and beauty can be particularly harmful. He writes: ". . . we hear everyday of many murders, lost reputations, insults, squandered fortunes, rivalries, quarrels, and of so many adulteries, rapes, and fornications, and of fallen giants. . . ."[46]

In being unattached to anyone even though these natural graces are apparent, a person is able to love neighbors with a great freedom. There may be attachment involved, but the attachment to God is greater. And one increases with the other.

Joy in *sensory* goods includes rejoicing in anything the senses are able to receive, both exteriorly and interiorly. Gratification of the senses, such as hearing music and smelling fragrances, is beneficial only when the thoughts and affections are immediately directed to God. Here the senses are being used properly, to increase knowledge and love of God.

And John speaks about joy in food. Such joy "directly engenders gluttony and drunkenness, anger, discord, and lack of charity toward one's neighbor and the poor. . . ."[47]

Joy in *moral* goods includes rejoicing in "virtues and their habits insofar as they are moral; the exercise of any of the virtues; the practice of the works of mercy; the observance of God's law; urbanity and good manners."[48] In all God should be served.

Even doing good works is often perverted. John complains: ". . . I believe most of the works publicly achieved are either faulty, worthless, or imperfect in God's sight, because people are not detached from these human respects and interests."[49] Try to hide your good deeds, John counsels, so that only God sees them.

Joy in *supernatural* goods includes rejoicing in "all the gifts and graces of God that exceed our natural faculties and powers. . . ."[50] Included among these gifts are the gifts of faith, healing, miracles, prophecy, knowledge, discernment of spirits, interpretation of words, and the gift of tongues. These supernatural gifts are given for the sake of others. In exercising them the individual is serving God. But the person should be detached about using them because God will guide the person in the manner and time of their use. In John's view, God only works these marvels out of necessity. Faith should not depend on these testimonies and signs.

Joy in *spiritual* goods includes rejoicing in "all those that are an aid and motivating force in turning the soul to divine things and to converse with God, as well as a help in God's communications to the soul."[51]

Statues, Paintings, Oratories, Ceremonies, Preachers

John establishes many divisions once more, including spiritual goods which are motivating, provocative, directive, and perfective. He comments only on motivating and provocative spiritual goods by the end of the book.

Motivating spiritual goods are statues, paintings of saints, oratories, and ceremonies. John's strict teachings regarding images find a more nuanced context here. Statues are helpful when they assist a person in giving reverence and having devotion to a saint. He criticizes those who pay more attention to the decorations than to the saint. When that happens, he says, the statues become idols, and devotion is reduced to "little more than doll-dressing."[52]

John encourages choosing an image which fosters devotion. But if one is sad if the image is taken away, then one was too attached. "One rosary is no more influential with God than is another."[53]

But if God gives favors through one statue it is not because of the statue itself, but because the statue awakens greater devotion in individuals. An image of Our Lady may be no more than a painting, but it may awaken great faith and devotion.

Frequently God grants favors through images which are in remote places. God wants the journey to become a pilgrimage during which individuals withdraw from noise and other people. On such a pilgrimage devotion grows and prayer deepens. It is better to make a pilgrimage alone. John says, "I would never advise going along with a large crowd, because one ordinarily returns more distracted than before. Many who go on pilgrimages do so more for the sake of recreations than devotion."[54]

Where there is faith, any image suffices; where there is no faith, no image suffices. John offers one maxim for all cases: "Since images serve as a motivating means toward invisible things, we should strive that the motivation, affection, and joy of will derived from them be directed toward the living object they represent."[55]

Places of Prayer

John then begins to talk about oratories and the excessive care some take in decorating these places of prayer. While John is critical of those who pay more attention to the quality of the painting or statue than to prayer, he is not indifferent to the workmanship. "Some artisans so unskilled and unpolished in the art of carving should be forbidden to continue their craft."[56] Even John of the Cross has limits to his indifference.

He is critical of festivals when people are actually celebrating themselves, in their socializing and eating, rather than celebrating God.

John then returns to the topic of oratories. Beginners need to take some satisfaction in the setting for their prayer, but more spiritual people should choose places which least occupy the senses, and least hinder raising the senses and spirit in prayer. Churches should be such places, and should be used only for prayer. But other places may be chosen, especially solitary and austere places which assist an ascent of the spirit to God.

John identifies a type of person who continually searches for the right place: ". . . now you see them in one spot, and now in another; now choosing one hermitage, now another. . . ."[57] This restlessness involves more than places for prayer: "Some also pass their time here below changing states and modes of life."[58] He believes they lack spiritual recollection and seek only sensible satisfaction.

John identifies three types of places which assist devotion. "The first includes those sites which have pleasant variations in the arrangement of the land and the trees, and provide solitary quietude, all of which naturally awakens devotion."[59]

Even in beautiful sites the person should forget the place and be interiorly with God. "The anchorites and other holy hermits, while in the loveliest and vastest wildernesses, chose for themselves as small an area as possible, built narrow cells and caves, and enclosed themselves within."[60]

The second type of place "includes those localities, whether wildernesses or not, in which God usually grants some very delightful spiritual favors to particular individuals."[61] Returning to these places does not guarantee that God will grant favors. But John recommends returning there for prayer sometimes, since it will at least awaken devotion.

"The third kind of place comprises those in which God chooses to be invoked and worshiped."[62] John offers examples such as Mount Sinai, and a place where Mary, through a miracle of snow, designated that a church be built. John admits that only God knows why God chooses one place rather than another.

Ceremonies and Devotions

Ceremonies are another means of motivating devotion. They may be perverted when people pay more attention to the methods of prayer in the ceremony than to the prayer involved.

> For example, they demand that the Mass be said with a certain number of candles, no more nor less; or that it be celebrated at a particular hour, no sooner nor later; or that it be said after a certain day, not before; or that the prayers and stations be a particular number and kind and that they be recited at certain times and with certain ceremonies, and neither before nor after, nor in any other way; and that the person performing the ceremonies have certain endowments and characteristics. And they are of the opinion that nothing will be accomplished if one of these points is lacking.[63]

And, even worse, some expect to be granted a favor, such as an answer to a petition, as a result of these superstitious ceremonies.

Christ taught only the seven petitions of the Our Father. He taught perseverance, not many words. And he taught only two ceremonies:

one, by his teaching, when he said go in your room, close the door, and pray; the other by his example, when he prayed in a solitary wilderness at a quiet time of night.

Prayer is not a matter of this time, or this day, or these prayers, other than the ones the church uses, which even then are reducible to the Our Father. But John does not want to be misunderstood: "By this I do not condemn—but rather approve—the custom of setting aside certain days for devotions, such as novenas, fastings, and other similar practices. I condemn the fixed methods and ceremonies. . . ."[64]

Preachers

John's final words in *The Ascent of Mount Carmel* concern preachers. They are included among the provocative spiritual goods, the next ones to be discussed after the motivating spiritual goods of paintings, statues, oratories, and ceremonies.

John urges preachers to consider preaching a spiritual practice. The efficacy of preaching comes from the interior spirit of the preacher. Certainly a good style, good theology, and a good vocabulary produce an effect when accompanied by a good spirit. But without the good spirit, the preaching may please but it will not move the listeners' will.

John writes, ". . . the better the life of the preacher the more abundant the fruit, no matter how lowly his style, poor his rhetoric, and plain the doctrine. For the living spirit enkindles fire."[65] St. Paul told the Corinthians that he did not preach with the rhetoric of human wisdom, but he preached in the power of the Spirit.

But John does not want to dismiss skilled preaching: "Indeed, neither is it the Apostle's intention nor mine to condemn good style, and rhetoric, and effective delivery; these rather are most important to the preacher, as they are in all matters."[66]

John then inexplicably ends *The Ascent of Mount Carmel* in the middle of a sentence: "Elegant style and delivery lifts up and restores even those things that have fallen into ruin, just as poor presentation spoils what is good and destroys . . ."[67]

REFLECTIONS ON *THE ASCENT OF MOUNT CARMEL*, BOOKS TWO AND THREE

In these books of the *Ascent* John discusses the role of faith, hope, and charity in transforming the spiritual faculties of intellect, memory, and will. John relates faith to the faculty of the intellect, which is in accord with Scholastic teaching. Faith is involved in specific expressions of belief, but it also moves the person into a dark contemplation beyond concrete expressions.

It becomes clear in John's overall treatment of faith, hope, and charity that faith is the total, trusting response of an individual to God's love. Intellect, memory, and will are transformed in this love which obliterates all categories.

John's mapping of faith's journey through successive nights contributes to contemporary studies in faith development. His description of the nights may find support and amplification in these studies, and his writings may help elucidate the actual dynamics involved in such faith development. In particular the works of James Fowler and Gabriel Moran provide a helpful framework within which the writings of John of the Cross may be examined.

Faith Development Studies of James Fowler

Fowler does not appear to be studying faith itself, but perhaps the underlying structures whereby this faith is expressed. He is sensitive to the uncertainty and risk involved in human living. "We have," he writes, "imaginations, intuitions, and moments of awakening that disturb us into awareness of dimensions of circumambient reality that we can only name, on our own, as 'mystery'."[68]

And how do we attempt to express this mystery? "We are language-related, symbol-borne and story-sustained creatures. . . . We live by forming and being formed in images and dispositions toward the ultimate conditions of our existence. And for at least 300 millennia these images and dispositions have been the province of religion. Faith has been religious faith from the first red ocher and flower-decked cave burials to Chartres Cathedral."[69]

In his research Fowler is asking these questions: "How do persons awaken to and begin to form (and be formed) in the life stances of trust and loyalty, of belief and commitment that carry them into the force fields of their lives? Are there predictable stages of revolutions in the life of meaning-making? Must we, in order to become fully adult and to be fully human, have a deep-going and abiding trust in and loyalty to some cause or causes, greater in value and importance than ourselves?"[70]

Fowler is not studying particular beliefs, but the underlying cognitive and affective structures that are operating in faith. "Our stages describe in formal terms the structural features of faith as a way of construing, interpreting, and responding to the factors of contingency, finitude, and ultimacy in our lives."[71]

The writings of John of the Cross describe the faith response of the Christian as the Mystery who is God undermines certainties and evaporates meaning. He reports the effects on his humanity of an intimate encounter with this dark love. Cognitive and affective structures are transformed in the night as the soul gradually participates in the knowing and loving of God. Contemporary studies, such as Fowler's, are continuing to explore this process as it is manifested in people's lives.

Stages of Faith Development

The experiences John of the Cross writes about are related more closely to the later stages of faith development in James Fowler's schema. But it is informative to know the stages which precede the experiences of the dark night. Fowler identifies the following stages of faith:

Primal Faith, is the faith of the infant. It is sometimes discussed as the initial situation prior to the actual faith stages. The basic struggle is to develop some sense of trust, and not mistrust, in the worth of the self and the reliability of one's environment. The baby "begins to wrap the coils of centration around primal images of the felt goodness and badness of *self-world.*"[72]

Among the primal images conveying trust or mistrust are probably those of the mother and the father. These primary care givers provide experiences for the child which later inform the early images of God, images which begin forming by the fourth or fifth year.

Freud and Jung present striking contrasts in their understanding of the dynamics regarding images of God within the early human. For Freud, the experience of the parents was primary. Then, when the individual outgrew parental care, there was still a need for someone to play that role. God becomes an illusory projection allowing the individual to remain dependent and secure. God is mother and father writ large.

Jung, on the other hand, believed that the human being was born with a readiness for God, someone or something to be the supreme value for the psyche. The first images which filled in this readiness were the parental images. The mother and father, therefore, are "little gods." During the course of life, as the individual outgrows the parental images for God, there is a need to find more and more appropriate images for the God-archetype.

The spirituality of John of the Cross appears to identify the ongoing process in the personality to find more adequate images for God. Not only in the early years of development is the God-image changing, but later through the nights of sense and spirit our humanity is still attempting to find the words and images which satisfy and express our yearning. The path of the *nadas* is the spiritual heir to, and continuation of, the earlier psychological process of establishing a primal faith through parental images, which then give way to more and more appropriate images in the course of human development.

Intuitive-Projective Faith, Fowler's first stage, begins about the age of two and is marked by the emergence of language and greater physical mobility. The child has a lively imagination and an intuition which can penetrate beneath the surface of life. Fowler writes, "For now, stimulated by experience and by stories, symbols, and examples, children form deep and long-lasting images that hold together their worlds of meaning and wonder."[73]

The child is aware of limitations, including the limitation of death. Still unable to distinguish between the symbolic and the literal, the child anthropomorphizes God. Fairy tales, stories of religious traditions, and religious celebrations help a child make meaning of the world.

Religious educator Gabriel Moran refers to this time in the life of a young person as a time of being *simply religious*. This stage lasts from birth until about seven years of age. The child is naturally open to wonder and mystery. Moran quotes G. K. Chesterton, who captures movements within this stage: "A child of seven is excited by being told that Tommy opened a door and saw a dragon. But a child of three is excited by being told that Tommy opened a door."[74]

The time of dragons, especially, is a time of image and story in the young person's life. Gods and goddesses are alive in the world, and ordinary experience is, at the same time, quite religious. These religious experiences may be awesome or frightening. Children are aware of a cosmic battle going on; fairy tales and religious stories help assure and comfort them that good prevails.

This ability to "see" the transcendent through the windows of everyday life does not remain long in the life of the child. A developing cognitive ability apparently shuts down this openness to mystery. Later, in the adult years, the ability to attend to the world more imaginatively becomes an important process for further psychological and spiritual development.

Mythic-Literal Faith, Fowler's second stage, is the faith of a school-age child, beginning about six or seven years of age. According to

Piaget, the child has developed "concrete operational thinking." Fantasy and imagination are less important now as the child begins to think in an orderly, linear manner, with little ability for abstract thought.

The individual is in an affiliative stage of faith. "Faith becomes a matter of reliance on the stories, rules, and implicit values of the family's community of meanings."[75] The child wants to know the "lore, the language, and the legends" of the communities to which she belongs. These stories are taken literally, but the child does not yet have a "story of her stories."

Synthetic-Conventional Faith, the third stage, begins to emerge in adolescence, and may perdure throughout one's adulthood. Abstract thought is now possible as the person reaches the stage of cognitive development which Piaget terms "formal operational thinking." A certain self-consciousness emerges and there is a new depth of awareness and interest in the interiority of persons, their personalities, emotions, thoughts. The young person is able to pull together the various mirrorings of self seen in the faces and reactions of others. An identity is forming.

The young person struggles to formulate a "story of her stories." The adolescent is a member of various groups—family, school, church, and peers, among others. There is a synthesis of these stories, sometimes subordinating all to one story, or sometimes compartmentalizing stories so that the individual takes on the values of the particular group she is with at the moment.

It is a "conventional" story in that, although it may be a unique configuration, the story is drawn from the beliefs and values of significant others in one's life. "The synthesis is supportive and sustaining; it is deeply felt and strongly held; but it has not yet become an object of (self) critical reflection and inquiry. In this stage, one is *embedded* in her/his faith outlook and one's identity is derived from membership in a circle of face-to-face relations."[76]

Individuative-Reflective Faith, a fourth stage, may begin to arise in late adolescence at the earliest, but for many people it does not begin until their mid-thirties or forties, and for other adults it just never begins. A new quality of self-authorization enters into life. The self, or ego, emerges from behind the personae or masks and roles one has been wearing and playing. The individual is able to step away from the story in which he was embedded, and now begins to critically reflect upon it. Faith is becoming more interiorized and owned. The individual begins to take personal responsibility for values, beliefs, and lifestyle.

When people in their thirties and forties begin to experience this individuating process their life-structure may be quite disturbed. There is a beginning awareness of the paradoxes and polarities of life, such as self-fulfillment versus service to others, feeling versus thinking, etc. The tendency is to collapse the tension in favor of one side or the other.

At this time in life a person may join a group which has a strong ideology and which eliminates the tensions of ambiguities in life. It is a chosen commitment, and yet in some ways it may be a retreat back into a conventional stage, thereby absolving the individual from further personal reflection and decision.

Gabriel Moran describes the school years as a time of *acquiring a religion*. It is the great middle of religious development when the ego emerges and directs the religious quest. Beginning about five or six and lasting until late adolescence, this stage receives the most attention in religious education. It is a time to learn about and practice being Catholic, Jewish, Muslim.

Moran identifies two phases within this stage of religious development. Initially the individual wants to learn the story of "our people." What are the specific beliefs and practices of this religion? What is its history, and who are its heroines and heroes? And later the individual may enter a phase of "disbelief." Intruding adult issues and a developed critical ability challenge the teachings of a religion. This critical reasoning is the beginning of a process of owning the faith.

Moran sees the possibilities of at least three major times of conversion in religious development. One conversion occurs when the person moves from the stage of being simply religious to the time of acquiring a religion. Then within that second stage is a conversion to disbelief and the willingness to wrestle with personal questions of belief and meaning. And a third conversion occurs when the individual moves into an adult faith.

Fowler's last two stages, which he terms Conjunctive and Universalizing, respectively, involve this adult faith.

Conjunctive Faith is a fifth stage of faith development in Fowler's schema, and it may begin in the 30s and 40s. "The stage of faith that emerges with mid-life or beyond involves the integration of elements in ourselves, in society, and in our experience of ultimate reality that have the character of being apparent contradictions, polarities, or at the least, paradoxical elements."[77] Conjunctive faith is related to the idea of God being a "coincidence of opposites."

The adult at this age is aware of being part of the "bridge generation," linking elders with the young. Perhaps the parents have already died. Some peers have died as well. An adult is aware of having lived more than half a lifetime, and aging is beginning to be felt.

Fowler's description of the psychic dynamics of this stage owes much to Jung. The conscious self believes that its awareness exhausts the person's total selfhood. But the firm ego boundaries become porous at this time. Fowler writes: "The confident conscious ego must develop a humbling awareness of the power and influence of aspects of the unconscious on our reactions and behavior—the individual, the social, and the archetypal unconscious."[78]

The transition to conjunctive faith is marked by certain character-istics. The individual becomes aware of polar tensions in life and is challenged to hold them together without collapsing the tension. Fowler names such polarities as old and young, masculine and feminine, con-structive and destructive, conscious and unconscious. "Conjunctive faith comes to cherish paradox and the apparent contradictions of per-spectives on truth as intrinsic to that truth."[79] This statement is reminis-cent of Jung who said that when something is true psychologically, its opposite is true as well.

The adult in this stage of faith development is ready to approach the tradition with a "second naivete," to reappropriate the tradition at a deeper level. This faith is marked by an openness to other traditions and a willingness to be corrected and challenged by them. The common story of humankind is now entered into through the particular faith tradition of the adult.

Fowler's description of the movement into the next, and last, stage of faith has echoes of John's dark night: "Being in but not of the world, they feel a cosmic homelessness and loneliness. For some, this longing and discomfort becomes the means by which they are called and lured into a transformed and transforming relation to the ultimate conditions of life—and to themselves and everyday existence with the neighbor. This transforming and transformed relation we call Universaliz-ing faith."[80]

Universalizing Faith, a sixth stage, is the situation of a person whose community has slowly expanded from the family, in the stage of primal faith, to an ever wider circle of communities, to eventually the community of humankind. Fowler speaks of the process as a decentra-tion from self. One's perspective is balanced by the perspective of others in an expanding radius. At the same time the adult is growing in a participation in the valuing of the Creator and is able to value the world from the standpoint of God's love for that world.

Fowler further describes the emptying process involved in Universalizing faith: "Often described as 'detachment' or 'disinterestedness,' the *kenosis*—literally, the 'pouring out' or emptying of self described here—is actually the fruit of having one's affections powerfully drawn beyond the finite centers of value and power in our lives that promise meaning and security."[81]

Here is a blend of contemporary and traditional language for the process of divinization described by John of the Cross. Mystics such as John no doubt have provided a language which assists developmentalists in describing these later stages of faith development.

Gabriel Moran equates his third and final stage of religious development with the last two stages described by Fowler, the Conjunctive and Universalizing faith stages. Moran describes his third stage as a time for becoming *Religiously Christian* (Jewish, Muslim, etc.).

In this stage of faith the individual retains the rationality of the second stage (Acquiring a Religion) and weds it with the natural contemplative ability of the first stage (Simply Religious). The individual has an ability to return to the tradition learned in a one-dimensional manner in the school years, and let the tradition speak symbolically of the realities it attempts to express. The adult approaches the tradition with a "second naivete."

In the early part of this stage the adult develops a "parabolic" attitude. Parables are stories which eventually subvert the assumptions of the hearers. Religiously Christian adults realize that life will not be reduced to certainties and rational systems. Faith involves tolerance for ambiguity and outright paradox. Life does not get simpler but more complex, and an authentic response finds one standing within the tensions. Moran doubts that a person will attain a parabolic attitude before one's thirties or forties.

Jung's understanding of the psyche as arranged in polarities complements this discussion of paradox. The inner journey in the second half of life could be understood as a journey to encounter the neglected poles of personality. The conscious and the unconscious poles are united by the psyche through the language of the imagination. Symbols hold in relationship that which consciousness would separate. Attentiveness to God in faithful prayer would lead one into such fundamental realities.

Moran discusses an attitude of "detachment" which flows from the parabolic attitude. The parabolic simply deepens as a contemplative center emerges in the person. The person still acts, but it is action expressing a transformed humanity.

Moran attempts to capture the meaning of such detachment: "Detachment means the willingness to wait, the determination and the patience to stay at what one feels called to. Whether one's work is to design a cathedral, mop floors, govern a nation, or lie flat on one's back in pain, the human vocation is to stay at one's post and do the best one can. And after doing the best possible, the detached person takes no credit but returns glory to the source of all gifts."[82]

While this description, and the language of detachment, evoke the highest stages of the mystical life, Moran believes it is common in later life, and not the preserve of a few. And he observes that the very old and the very young share a sense of the underlying unity in life. "If the world has a future at all, that future largely depends upon the child a few years from birth and the old person a few years from death speaking, in their own secretive way, of mysteries that the rest of the race is too old or too young to comprehend."[83]

John of the Cross and Faith Development

John's account of both the active and passive nights of sense and spirit have elements recognizable in these faith development studies. The very sequential structure of the nights is a type of stage construction, confirming the insight that faith results in transformations of one's humanity over a period of years. Neither John nor the developmentalists are talking about specific doctrine or beliefs, but the underlying transformation of one's knowing and loving which slowly seems to participate in the knowing and loving of God.

Faith development, or perhaps more accurately, religious development, is imaged as a movement inward to a center, and as a movement outward to the communities of God's world. It is an intensely interior process which draws one into paradoxical depths of humanity in response to a graciousness at the core of that humanity. Moran writes: "The least inadequate image of the religious journey is that of a journey toward the exact center of a sphere. One can speak of moments, periods, phases, stages, etc., along this journey. The most explicit religious language might refer to stations on a pilgrimage."[84] John says simply, "The soul's center is God."[85]

Moran describes the journey as moving past false selves and false gods. "A lesser self sets its heart upon a lesser God; as false selves are stripped-away, idols are revealed for what they are: substitutes for the Nameless One beyond all gods."[86]

Continually suspicious of the process of setting up idols, John of the Cross calls for an active night of spirit, which entails efforts to enter the night and be open to its purification. The work is only completed in the passive night in which faith darkens the intellect, hope empties the memory of possessions, and charity removes affections for all that is not God. And, again, the language of "emptying" and "detachment" used by both John and the developmentalists speaks of the soul's gradual surrender to God's love.

For John of the Cross the world is known as it truly is only when one is related to God. Without this relationship as central, the heart goes askew and human development is distorted. Fowler's description of a Universalizing stage wherein the individual has a new perspective on the world, and values it now from God's standpoint resonates with John's descriptions of the unitive stage of the mystical life.

However, Moran doubts that one ever moves beyond a conjunctive stage with its polarities. Such tensions seem to be an inevitable part of life. He writes: "The mature person has to live with paradox which can be done only if one's language and imagery are capable of supporting apparent contradictions."[87]

The language of John of the Cross is striking in its expressions of paradox. He writes of a wounding flame which also heals, and a night in which darkness becomes a guide. Still, his language of paradox is used to express an experience of oneness, a union with God in which the flame of the Spirit and one's own flame join in one movement. As intense as this union is, John cautions that the veil of mortal life still remains and the soul has not reached the "perfect state of glory." The human still struggles to express its situation of paradox.

Religious Experience and Symbol

This discussion of religious development, along with John's description of his experience of the dark night and union, raises the question of religious experience today. What is religious experience? And where may we look to find God in our own lives?

I have found the work of theologian Dermot Lane helpful in understanding the mystic's experience of God, and how we today experience God in our lives. Lane has provided a helpful synthesis drawn from contemporary theology as it wrestles with the question of the experience of God. The following brief discussion is drawn, for the most part, from his synthesis.

Human experience today is regarded as interactive. Lane writes, "Experience . . . is the product that arises out of the interaction that takes place between the subject and reality."[88] Neither reality nor the self is solely responsible for creating experience.

Theologians speak of different levels of human experience. The primary level of human experience may be called the sense level, or outer experience. Think, for example, of the sensory effects when a person watches a sunset.

A secondary level of human experience is the depth level, or inner experience, where the world is mediated by meaning. Watching a sunset can be much more than a sensory experience. It may contain worlds of meaning. It may lead to reflection and insight. It may put one in touch with regions of the unconscious which Jung maintained were as vast and unknown as the cosmos without.

And then there can be the religious level or dimension of human experience. At this level one becomes aware of the transcendent present within experience, and the relationship one has to this Mystery. "Religious experience," therefore, is a shorthand way of speaking about the religious dimension of ordinary human experience.

In this understanding of religious experience, or the religious dimension of human experience, the experience of God is always mediated, never face-to-face. It is referred to as a "mediated immediacy." John of the Cross certainly concurs with that understanding. Even dawn at the end of the night still partakes of the dark because we must live in faith.

The experience of God occurs within ordinary human experience. God is so intimate to the experience that God is not a third thing, so we do not have the self, a sunset, and then God. In the interactive experience of the self and the sunset God is co-experienced, co-present, co-known.

Not Every Depth Experience Is a Religious Experience

In this understanding of the levels of experience, every religious experience is a depth experience, but not every depth experience is a religious experience. And herein lies a challenge for the catechist, and for the church generally as it attempts to assist people in being open to the graciousness at the core of their lives.

One avenue of explanation for the fact that the transcendent remains hidden within depth experiences has to do with the "interactive" aspect of experience. It is not just a matter of God's presence within experience, but the experience itself is co-created by the individual. A religious tradition, through its stories, images, beliefs, may provide a context within which the individual is open to the transcendent dimension of experience.

Without some such language inviting the person to listen more carefully, experience remains too opaque. For example, a person whose tradition includes parables may perhaps be more open to being subverted by experience and drawn into conversion processes. This person may more readily follow John's advice to stay in the dark night with trust and patience.

Gabriel Moran writes about this subversive role of the religious tradition. "Religious traditions in a variety of ways turn the mind against itself, not in a destructive way but in a discipline of receptivity to reality. Through the use of pun, paradox, parable, and other literary devices, religious literature strains at the limits of language and prepares the mind for the One that cannot be named."[89]

In accord with religious experience as we have been discussing it, the pure mystical experience occurs when whatever mediated the experience of God, e.g., watching a sunset, temporarily fades and there remains simply an awareness of this divine presence. Even this awareness is still mediated even though in a very indistinct, dark way. John of the Cross would understand that we are experiencing our desire for God, which, in his estimation, is the possession of God.

The Role of Symbol

John has stated that the experience of God is basically inexpressible. Once we begin to reflect on the experience or communicate it, we are in the realm of metaphor and symbol, the land of the imagination which John traversed so well. "Religious development," writes Moran, "thus occurs by means of metaphors that are based on imagination, nourished in community, and rooted in tradition."[90] John's reflection upon, and communication of, his deepest experiences are rooted in his imagination and its symbols, and in the community's tradition expressed in scripture.

It may be said that symbol precedes and prepares for an experience of God, and is the vehicle for communication of the experience. John's discussion of the active night of the spirit acknowledges that God leads the soul through external sensory means (sermons!), to internal images and reflection, and he warns that one should not turn away "from the breast of the senses" until God brings one to contemplation.

John seems to be trying to come to terms, through Scholastic categories, with what today is understood as psyche, and especially with that dimension of psyche known as the unconscious. He accepts, although with some reluctance, the presence of products of the imagination, whether from exterior or interior sources. Some of these products, such as the dream of Pilate's wife, must be supernatural, in John's view, since such knowledge is inexplicable otherwise.

If we hold that image is fundamental to the operation of the psyche and that the experience of God will always be within human experience, then John seems to be talking about symbolic expressions of these transcendent levels as he discusses the various forms of knowledge, these images, which lead us to a deeper union with God.

Johns seems to indicate that the image may be totally divorced from the reality as he urges moving past the image to the Mystery expressed through it. A contemporary theologian might hold that the image, as symbol, is related to the experience in a more integral way. As symbol, however, the image does not exhaust Mystery.

John says, renounce them all. Jung would say, attend to them symbolically. These two processes may not be totally opposed since John counsels against abandoning images until the right season.

Psyche and Image

Contemporary psychology, too, warns us not to dismiss the image too quickly in going to God who is no image. We have no other route. There is no standpoint outside the psyche. Jungian analyst James Hillman urges respect for the psyche's processes: ". . . following Jung I use the word fantasy-image in the poetic sense, considering images to be the basic givens of psychic life, self-originating, inventive, spontaneous, complete, and organized in archetypal patterns. Fantasy-images are both the raw materials and finished products of psyche and they are the privileged mode of access to knowledge of soul. Nothing is more primary. Every notion in our minds, each perception of the world and sensation in ourselves must go through a psychic organization in order to 'happen' at all. Every single feeling or observation occurs as a psychic event by first forming a fantasy-image."[91]

Hillman and others believe a distinction should be made between spirit and soul in order to maintain the integrity of psychic processes. For them soul is the middle ground between body and spirit. The theologian may understand spirit as referring to the human subject involved in a process of self-becoming which is radically open to God. The psychologist understands soul as that which deepens events into experiences, is communicated through love, has a religious concern, is related to death, and refers to the imaginative possibilities in our natures. Soul is expressed in fantasy-image.

Hillman would understand John of the Cross to be concerned primarily with "spirit," a *via negativa* which says "not this, not that." But by acknowledging God's process of working through the outer to the inner, and in his poetry and commentaries, John is in the land of "soul" which says "this too."

Hillman writes in defense of soul: "For soul, says spirit, cannot know, neither truth, nor law, nor cause. The soul is fantasy, all fantasy. The thousand pathologizings that soul is heir to by its natural attachments to the ten thousand things of life in the world shall be cured by making soul into an imitation of spirit. . . . There may well be more psycho-pathologizing actually going on while transcending than while being immersed in pathologizing. For any attempt at self-realization without full recognition of the psychopathology that resides, as Hegel said, inherently in the soul is in itself pathological, an exercise in self-deception."[92]

John of the Cross understood well the pathologizings of both the senses and the human spirit. The night, active and passive, is a process of revealing and healing. Or as Gabriel Moran writes, "The de-absolutizing of idols remains the constant religious vocation until death."[93]

Night of Faith

The next chapter focuses on John's intense experience of a passive night of the spirit. It is a time when all human and spiritual support is taken away and the soul learns to go on with a dark faith. False selves and false gods are radically uprooted and the soul journeys deeply into its center, who is God.

CHAPTER EIGHT

The Fear of Losing God

The Dark Night, Book Two
Passive Night of the Spirit

Part one of this chapter summarizes John's commentary *The Dark Night,* Book Two. In it he describes a period of illumination after the passive night of the senses, which then leads to the more radical purgation of the passive night of the spirit. With various descriptions John attempts to convey the suffering of this extremely trying time. Still, his intent is to show that this powerful experience within our weak souls is the result of the fire of God's love. Nothing in this love is dark or painful in itself, John maintains, but "the brighter the light, the more the owl is blinded." This night is prelude to the dawn of union.

The second part of this chapter is a reflection on John's commentary, describing the night as an experience of sinfulness, human finiteness, and God's transcendence. In particular, it discusses the dissolution of God-images in the night.

Both John of the Cross and Carl Jung used the biblical story of Job as an archetypal expression of human suffering. They drew different conclusions. Was Job's painful night experience the result of a dark side of God, or was it the result of a love which is dark to us?

This chapter also talks about the possibility of a collective dark night, especially among people who struggle for justice in their lives, or who walk in a world without meaning. The church itself is purified in the struggles of its mystics.

A SUMMARY OF *THE DARK NIGHT,*
BOOK TWO

John begins Book Two of *The Dark Night* by speaking about the period of time following the night of the senses. The person is now in the state of proficients (the illuminative state), and may spend many years here. The experience is one of greater freedom and satisfaction, and the soul enjoys a serene contemplation.

Still, because the spirit has not been purified and the sensory purgation is incomplete, the person is subject to occasional darknesses, as if in anticipation of the coming night. For some souls the dark and dawn alternate throughout life and they never fully enter the night of the spirit.

God's communications to these proficients may sometimes be quite disruptive, since the senses are still weak. John speaks of the possibility of raptures, transports, and the dislocation of bones. These dramatic occurrences are not meant to last. "For in the perfect, these raptures and bodily torments cease, and they enjoy freedom of spirit without a detriment to or transport of their senses."[1]

In the state of the proficients there are imperfections which John labels habitual and actual. The habitual refer to the remaining imperfect affections and habits which are quite deep in the soul. The difference between removing them and removing imperfections in the night of the senses is the difference between pulling up roots and merely cutting branches; or it is the difference between trying to remove an old stain, and removing a new stain.

Actual imperfections refer to the pride and arrogance which undermine the proficient's spiritual journey. Such vanity gives evidence of a need for further purification.

John refers to the night of the senses as a reformation of the appetites, not a real purgation. The real purgation of the senses occurs in the night of the spirit. The first night prepares the senses to be strong for the purgation of the second night.

The Night of the Spirit

In the second night, the night of the spirit, "God divests the faculties, affections, and senses, both spiritual and sensory, interior and exterior. He leaves the intellect in darkness, the will in aridity, the memory in emptiness, and the affections in supreme affliction, bitterness, and anguish, by depriving the soul of the feeling and satisfaction it previously obtained from spiritual blessings. . . . The Lord works all of this in the soul by means of a pure and dark contemplation. . . ."[2] John refers to this night of the spirit as contemplative purgation, poverty of spirit, an inflow of God, infused contemplation, and mystical theology. He calls infused contemplation the loving wisdom of God which prepares the soul for union with God.

For the soul, this contemplation is a "ray of darkness," again using a term from Pseudo-Dionysius. With a more captivating image, John says "The brighter the light, the more the owl is blinded."[3]

The soul becomes a battlefield, and John gives several reasons for this condition:

First, the soul feels that God has rejected it. The bright light of contemplation is received by the weak soul in a painful manner and it is aware of its unworthiness, miseries, and evils.

Second, whatever had upheld the person seems to have ended; there is no one who will take pity on the soul. The senses and spirit suffer greatly, but John reassures that it is the condition of the soul which is causing the suffering, not God. John writes: "For the hand of God does not press down or weigh upon the soul, but only touches it; and this mercifully, for God's aim is to grant it favors and not chastise it."[4]

Third, the soul feels that it is dying a cruel spiritual death. John writes of the experience as similar to being swallowed by a beast and finding oneself in a dark belly, as was Jonah in the whale; or it is like being in a sepulcher of dark death, awaiting resurrection. The soul feels vividly "the shadow of death, the sighs of death, and the sorrows of hell," reflecting the feeling of God's absence, rejection, and anger.[5] It seems this condition will last forever. As was the case with Jonah, the situation is like being immersed in the heart of the sea, or caught in the "locks" of the earth. And the person feels abandoned by everyone, especially friends.

Fourth, the soul experiences its emptiness and poverty. The senses are in aridity; the spirit in thick darkness. It is "like hanging in midair, unable to breathe."[6] At times it is like peering into hell with perdition opening before it. It is purgatory on earth, and John reports that the full intensity of this situation is felt only at intervals, otherwise a person might literally die.

No Relief, Perhaps for a Long Time

John continues to try to convey the situation. It is like Job's wound upon wound, or the terrible tribulations of Jeremiah. Doctrines and

spiritual directors are of no help, no matter what the director says about
the blessings of such a condition.

The person in this night is like one who is bound hand and foot in a
dark dungeon. This situation may last some years if it is to be truly
effective, although with intervals of illumination and love. The feeling
then is one of having an enemy within oneself which may awaken at any
time; and this purgation erupts again when the person feels safest and
least expects it.

Even though the soul knows that it loves God, in this night experience such knowledge provides no relief, but actually adds to the suffering. The soul cannot believe that God returns the love. The soul is
convinced that there is "every reason for being abhorred not only by
God but by every creature forever."[7]

Prayer is very difficult at this time. The soul cannot raise mind and
heart to God. "Indeed this is not the time to speak with God, but the
time to put one's mouth in the dust," suffering patiently, waiting for
hope.[8] Not only is it impossible to pray, but the person cannot concen-
trate on temporal matters and business.

John goes into an extended discussion of the similarity of this condition to the situation of light entering and passing through a room.
Unless the light strikes something to reflect its light, it passes through
the room darkly. God's love is dark to the soul unable to receive it.

Goal: "The Enjoyment of All
Earthly and Heavenly Things. . . ."

Chapter nine begins with a statement about the goal of this journey
through the nights:

> It remains to be said, then, that even though this happy night
> darkens the spirit, it does so only to impart light concerning all
> things; and even though it humbles a person and reveals his
> miseries, it does so only to exalt him; and even though it im-
> poverishes and empties him of all possessions and natural af-
> fection, it does so only that he may reach out divinely to the
> enjoyment of all earthly and heavenly things, with a general
> freedom of spirit in them all.[9]

Because the soul is called to live such a divinized life it must undergo an annihilation of its natural operations. The soul is called to be

poor in spirit in order to live a new life of union with God. John emphasizes again that nothing in the contemplation or the divine inflow causes pain; it is the soul's weakness which does so.

In chapter ten John compares the effect of contemplation on the soul to that of fire on a log. Initially the fire causes the wood to be ugly and emit a bad odor. Once the wood is dried out it then begins to be transformed into fire itself.

Similarly, contemplation initially purges and darkens the soul, because of the soul's weakness. "The suffering of the soul becomes more intimate, subtle, and spiritual in proportion to the inwardness, subtlety, spirituality, and deep-rootedness of the imperfections which are removed."[10] But in time the soul participates in the light of the contemplation.

In this spiritual night the soul is wounded by a strong love and the soul begins to share in the properties of God. John testifies to the strength of this enkindling of love: "God gathers together all the strength, faculties, and appetites of the soul, spiritual and sensory alike, that the energy and power of this whole harmonious composite may be employed in this love."[11] The soul can finally fulfill the first commandment to love God with its whole heart and soul.

A Heightened Desire

John comments on the poetic line, "Fired with love's urgent longings." This love is experienced as a burning wound which finds rest in nothing. The soul finds everything small and narrow, both within itself and outside itself in heaven or on earth.

So the soul suffers in two ways: first in a darkness which fills the soul with fear; second, through God's love which heightens the soul's desire.

Yet, says John, in the midst of this dark and loving suffering the soul can feel a presence and an interior strength, such that when the darkness passes the soul feels "alone, empty, and weak."[12]

At first the soul is aware of only darkness and affliction. But eventually it begins to feel the burning and warmth of love, which sometimes affects the will and sometimes only the intellect. "All of this is similar to feeling the warmth of fire without seeing its light or seeing the light without feeling the fire's heat."[13]

The result is that there can be a mystical knowledge, but no union of love. Sometimes the contemplation acts upon the intellect and will together in an enkindling of love. When they are purged together the union is much deeper. But until then, the more usual experience is a "touch of burning in the will, rather than a touch of understanding in the intellect."[14]

John calls the enkindling the "passion of love" whereby the will loses its freedom. The will is more susceptible to this movement since it need not be so purged, as must the intellect to receive knowledge. The will is assisted in receiving this love by the passions.

A Growing Boldness

John returns to the suffering of the night. The burning love is not felt in the beginning because there is anguish about losing God. John calls this anguish the greatest suffering of the dark night, and it produces a deep fear that God is angry with the individual.

The experience of love changes the individual, who begins to act boldly in seeking God. John describes Mary Magdalen's boldness in approaching Jesus at dinner, and in seeking him in the garden after his death. The longings of love cause the soul to search. "The wounded soul rises up at night. . . . ; as the lioness or she-bear that goes in search of her cubs when they are taken away and cannot be found, it anxiously and forcibly goes out in search of its God."[15] John observes, ". . . it is the nature of love to seek to be united, joined, equaled and assimilated to the loved object. . . ."[16]

We could never do this work ourselves. It has to be God's work:

Accordingly, God makes the soul die to all that He is not, so that when it is stripped and flayed of its old skin, He may clothe it anew. Its youth is renewed like the eagle's (Ps 102:5), clothed in the new man which is created, as the Apostle says, according to God. (Eph 4:24) This renovation is: an illumination of the human intellect with supernatural light so that it becomes divine, united with the divine; an informing of the will with love of God so that it is no longer less than divine and loves in no other way than divinely, united and made one with the divine will and love; and also a divine conversion and change of the memory, the affections, and the appetites according to God. And thus this soul will be a soul of heaven, heavenly and more divine than human.[17]

John further reflects on this condition of the night. Why not enjoy the good things God gives us for our spiritual health? At this time, John counsels, there should not be any activity or satisfaction relative to spiritual objects. Some people can direct their appetites to any object, including spiritual, and so their satisfaction is simply natural. The dark way is surer.

A Dark Way, a Mystical Theology

The dark way is such a new way that the soul thinks it is getting lost, rather than marching on profitably. The soul is traveling to a new and unknown land. And suffering is a more advantageous road than joy and action; the soul is undergoing a cure to regain its health.

John begins to explain the poetic line, "By the secret ladder, disguised." John refers to this dark contemplation as a "secret" process since "contemplation is the mystical theology which theologians call secret wisdom and which St. Thomas says is communicated and infused into the soul through love."[18]

This contemplation "hides a soul within itself." John describes these realms saying the person will have the "keen awareness of being brought into a place far removed from every creature. He will accordingly feel that he has been led into a remarkably deep and vast wilderness, unattainable by any human creature, into an immense, unbounded desert, the more delightful, savorous, and loving, the deeper, vaster, and more solitary it is."[19]

A Ladder of Love

John also describes contemplation as a ladder. It is a process of descending and ascending, being humbled and being exalted. Just naturally the soul will recognize that it experiences many ups and downs. Perfection cannot come without knowledge of self and knowledge of God, and the soul alternates between the two. Jacob's vision in his sleep of angels ascending and descending a ladder between earth and heaven prefigured this contemplative ladder of love.

John notes that tradition identifies ten steps on this ladder of love:

The first step of love makes the soul sick in order to be healthy. "As a sick person changes color and loses his appetite for all foods, so on this step of love the soul changes the color of its past life and loses its appetite for all things."[20]

The second step of love inspires the soul to continually search for God. "In all its thoughts it turns immediately to the Beloved; in all converse and business it at once speaks about the Beloved; when eating, sleeping, keeping vigil, or doing anything else, it centers all its care on the Beloved, as we pointed out in speaking of the yearnings of love."[21]

The third step of love encourages the soul to be fervent in acting, thinking all that it does is little.

The fourth step of love causes the soul to serve God alone, and not find consolation elsewhere. "Spiritually speaking, the desert is an interior detachment from every creature in which the soul neither pauses nor rests in anything."[22]

The fifth step of love produces impatient longing and desire for God. "On this step the desire of the lover to apprehend and be united with the Beloved is so ardent that any delay, no matter how slight, is long, annoying, and tiresome."[23]

The sixth step of love results in a purified love and the soul runs swiftly to God, and "experiences many touches in Him."[24]

The seventh step of love makes the soul bold and daring. Moses was on this step when he asked God to forgive the people or take his name out of the book of life. John warns: "It is illicit for the soul to become daring on this step if it does not perceive the divine favor of the king's scepter held out toward it (Est 5:2; 8:4), for it might then fall down the steps it has already climbed."[25]

The eighth step of love brings a possession of the Beloved, but it is not a continual state. "If one were to remain on this step, a certain glory would be possessed in this life; and so the soul rests on it for only short periods of time."[26]

The ninth step of love is "the step of the perfect who burn gently in God."[27] All the goods and riches a person enjoys here could never be told. It is the highest union of love in this life. After this step the soul leaves the body.

The tenth and last step of love unites the soul completely to God. These souls do not enter purgatory. All that the soul is becomes like God. "Thus it will be called, and shall be, God through participation."[28]

The soul which leaves the house by the secret ladder is also disguised. It wears the white tunic of faith, a green coat of mail of hope, and a red toga of charity. "Because these virtues have the function of withdrawing the soul from all that is less than God, they consequently have the mission of joining it with God."[29]

Hidden from the Devil

Because contemplation is infused passively and secretly the soul's journey is hidden from the devil. From the quiet of the senses the devil may detect something is happening, and may try to agitate the senses, without effect. But when communications from God affect the senses as well as the spirit, as do the communications from the good angel, then the bad angel is able to stimulate the senses as well.

However, when God communicates with the soul directly there is such complete darkness that the enemy cannot penetrate it. "The reason for this concealment is that since His Majesty dwells substantially in that part of the soul to which neither the angel nor the devil can gain access and thereby see what is happening, the enemy cannot learn of the intimate and secret communications there between the soul and God. Since the Lord grants these communications directly, they are wholly divine and sovereign."[30]

John's commentary on *The Dark Night* poem ends as he begins to comment on the line, "On that glad night. . . ."

REFLECTIONS ON *THE DARK NIGHT*, BOOK TWO

The distinction between the night of the senses and the night of the spirit can be overdrawn. By separating these experiences into two discrete "nights," although he said there is really only one night, John himself leads the reader into possibly artificial divisions. But his commentary relates the nights. He says that the night of the spirit is a more intense experience of what occurred in the night of the senses. And, actually, the work of the first night is only completed in the second night.

The dark night, in general, reveals the pathology of our psyche, both personal and collective. It manifests the finite limitations of our humanity, and it heightens awareness of the transcendence of God.

Perhaps the first night may be understood as undermining a situation where some part of creation has become of infinite value, has taken the place of God, and therefore has become central to a person's existence. The night of the senses severs the dependent relationship and allows the person or thing to die as a god-substitute. The dark experience submerses a person deeper into one's humanity and into an experience of God, or at least into the infinite desires for a truer God.

The night of the spirit may be understood as involving a situation where, instead of something finite having been made God, God has now been made finite. Our faith has domesticated God and, effectively, denied God's transcendence. This transcendence reasserts itself in the night of the spirit and challenges our understandings, attitudes, relationship, and actions, relative to God.

The night of the spirit discloses our finiteness, contingency, mortality; it awakens us to the tragic in life. It questions the meaning of one's life, hints at the nothingness which we suspect is at our core. But within it all, the night comes to be accepted and known as the activity of God's love.

A Transformation of Images

Although the night experience far surpasses psychology's ability to analyse and explain, nonetheless any effort at communication of the experience inevitably entails a psychic process, as seen in John's use of the very symbol of the "dark night." Psychological categories remain helpful, even if less and less adequate.

To use psychological categories already introduced in this book, the night of the senses may be understood as involving transformations of self-images. The night of the spirit may be understood as involving transformations of our God-images. This distinction is somewhat artificial since both types of transformation occur in both nights and, psychologically, self-images and God-images similarly affect the personality. But this core reality of the self, which Jung described as the "God-within," could be considered from the two perspectives of self-images and God-images, and the two nights might be understood as giving weight to one or the other dimension.

Self-Images and the Night of the Senses

The night of the senses attacks the religious persona and its rigid hold on the ego. It helps free the ego from the collective consciousness on which it relies for identity and meaning. Projections of the self are withdrawn as people and objects lose their numinosity. The power of these symbols to hold the personality diminishes as psychic energy seeks a fuller outlet. These symbols are inadequate as ultimate symbols—every symbol is inadequate—and the psyche's need to move beyond them undermines their power. They no longer fascinate. The energy of the psyche, having for now no other expression, regresses into the unconscious, and darkness settles in. The self-images die.

Much of what is dying in the night are projections of material from the personal unconscious, shadow content which make the night intensely personal. As projections are withdrawn the person enters the personal unconscious and meets the shadow side of the persona. The night exposes the "imperfections" of the complacent beginner. The beginner also becomes aware of her sinfulness in refusing to come to consciousness. The night of the senses invites the ego to make an inner journey to encounter the otherness of the self.

God-Images and the Night of the Spirit

The night of the spirit leads the soul into collective depths of the psyche, and beyond. The human being which developed out of primal chaos now returns to this enveloping darkness. John images this condition as similar to being in the belly of the whale, or in a sepulcher of dark death, facing the "sorrows of hell." The soul becomes acutely aware of a need for help, for salvation, and it is aware of its powerlessness to save itself. All supports are failing.

In particular, the psyche's God-symbols are exposed as deficient. The self as a "God-within" is seen in the explicitly religious images the psyche uses, and in the images it uses for whatever has become ultimate. In loosening the hold of God-images the night forces questions upon the psyche: Is there anyone home at the center of the personality? Is there any hope of fulfillment for the deep desires of the heart? Is the ultimate gracious?

Whatever impinges on the psyche from within and yet beyond it, and Jung as a psychologist claimed professional ignorance of the imprinter, is received and expressed by the psyche according to its own laws. Jung argued that we could know nothing else. Here Victor White, a Dominican theologian, parted company from him claiming Jung had left his own competency and entered the realms of philosophy and theology. Jung retorted that White, and many theologians, could not follow a psychological argument.

Yet, to discuss this second night, the night of the spirit, as a purification of inadequate symbols of the God-archetype does provide some explanatory power. These symbols can be beliefs, understandings about who God is, and assumptions about our relationship with God. The night safeguards the transcendence of God which has been diluted in the necessary psychic activity of imaging, reflecting, and wording.

The Dark Night of Thérèse of Lisieux

Thérèse of Lisieux attempted to express the pain of this purification:

And now, all of a sudden, the mists around me have become denser than ever; they sink deep into my soul and wrap it round so that I can't recover the dear image of my native country any more—everything has disappeared.

I get tired of the darkness all around me, and try to refresh my jaded spirits with the thoughts of that bright country where my hopes lie; and what happens? It is worse torment than ever; the darkness itself seems to borrow, from the sinners who live in it, the gift of speech. I hear its mocking accents: "It's all a dream, this talk of a heavenly country, bathed in light, scented with delicious perfumes, and of a God who made it all, who is to be your possession in eternity! You really believe, do you, that the mist which hangs about you will clear away later on? All right, all right go on longing for death! But death will make nonsense of your hopes; it will only mean a night darker than ever, the night of mere non-existence."[31]

Ego, Self, and God

It might be possible to describe the night of the senses as a process of ego-transcendence, as ego is challenged to meet the wider psychic life of the self. The night of the spirit may be understood as a process of self-transcendence in which the person is challenged to surrender to the Mystery of God and to allow the entire psychic structure to be transformed by God's love.

Some theorists have argued that Jungian psychology primarily describes ego-transcendence in its description of the individuation process, but it does not describe self-transcendence, the process of giving way to God who emerges as the core of the personality.

However, the movement from ego to self to God cannot be a step process. The processes are happening simultaneously. Ego-transcendence, if it truly relates ego to its depths is, at the same time, self-transcendence. Ego is part of the self; it is the self that is known in consciousness, the only part of the self which can responsibly give of itself to the mystery of God. One never finally gathers the total self and then offers it to God. What is gathered is the self which is related to ego-consciousness.

When this ego-consciousness trustingly goes into the dark it is also the self which enters the darkness. Dark is dark, and since the Mystery of God is met within the psyche, and is expressed in psyche's images, in this dark ego meets both a fuller self and God.

Teresa of Avila said we cannot know God unless we know our self, but, she cautioned, we cannot truly know our self without knowing God. And John's anthropology assumes that the authentic self emerges only when that personality is related to God in its center.

When ego undergoes conversions as the deeper psychic life emerges, it is involved in a graced process of self-transcendence. At a theoretical level one can agree that beyond the transcendence of the ego into the self, there is a further transcendence in which the ego and the self move into an encounter with God. But experientially, psychologically, these are relative conditions. When is one ever dealing only with the psychic self? And when is one encountering only the Divine? Jung said he could not distinguish self-symbols from God symbols. Gabriel Moran argues that we never leave the paradoxical condition of faith where we live within the tensions, learning to accept both this *and* that.

Often, however, the religious dimension of psychological experiences is only implicit. But the dark night of John of the Cross is a depth experience in which ego encounters the mystery of the self, and it is also a religious experience in which the transcendent dimension of human development is experienced in an explicit manner. The graciousness of the human journey is manifest. The personality, conscious and unconscious, finds itself more and more deeply healed, and the graciousness of this healing is more and more apparent. It is gift from an Otherness whose love darkens to enliven.

Psychologist Gerald May understands the dark night to be a movement which involves all of these processes at one time or another. He writes:

> To be fully accurate one should not call the dark night an "experience" at all. It is more a deep and ongoing process of unknowing that involves the loss of habitual experience. This includes, at different times and in different ways, loss of attachment to sensate gratification and to usual aspirations and motivations, loss of previously construed faith-understandings, and loss of God-images. Accompanying this, of course, are loss of self-image/importance and of preconceptions about one's own identity.[32]

This movement is deep and gradual with occasional "sightings" such as the experiences John of the Cross is relating. Rather than being an experience or phase of development, May understands the dark night to be "the essence of one's ongoing spiritual journey."[33]

The Dark Love of God

In The Book of Job, John of the Cross found words for his suffering in the night. He knows what Job is experiencing when Job says to the Lord: "Why have You set me against You, and I am heavy and burdensome to myself? (Jb 7:20)"[34] Job's cries are from human depths: "I who was wont to be wealthy and rich am suddenly undone and broken; He has taken me by the neck, He has broken me and set me up as His mark so as to wound me. (Jb 16:12)"[35]

Carl Jung, too, was drawn to Job as an expression of human grief in the face of suffering, especially the suffering of the innocent. The psychologist was deeply sensitive to the wounded condition of humanity. In his therapy he entered into a relationship with a patient in such a way that the doctor's wounds were revealed as well. Jung talked about swallowing the sickness of the patient, and then as the doctor's own psyche worked toward a resolution, passing the possibility of healing back to the patient, often in an indirect, empathic way.

Job's story presents a God who appeared to Jung to be short-sighted, needlessly cruel, often indifferent to Job's condition. Jung writes: "One must bear in mind here the dark deeds that follow one another in quick succession: robbery, murder, bodily injury with premeditation, and denial of a fair trial. This is further exacerbated by the fact that Yahweh displays no compunction, remorse, or compassion, but only ruthlessness and brutality."[36]

In *Answer to Job* Jung writes with much emotion, as one who has swallowed Job's sickness, and it has stirred up within him his own woundedness. His charged writing mirrors back the irrational behavior of God toward Job.[37] Jung, the therapist, admires in Job his eventual acceptance of this dark side of God, and Jung is critical of the Christian God-image for not being able to similarly incorporate a God who is somehow a source of human misery.

The suffering of Job, Jung wrote in *Answer to Job*, was due to a darkness in God. God seemed to need more consciousness, and Job was the occasion of God's growth. At times Jung appeared to predicate evil in God—a fourth in an expanded Trinity. He also said that evil represented a value judgment by humans; we do not know what it may be in itself, and God was beyond our categories of good and evil.

Jung was quick to remind the reader that he was not talking about God as a metaphysical reality apart from humanity, but about the God-archetype and its expression in consciousness. It was this human consciousness which was archaic, undifferentiated. Humanity needed more consciousness, and then, presumably, its God-image would change and incorporate the apparent contradictions within the human experience of God. Jung was writing of the earth-bounded travails of humanity which the Christian God-image could not address in its rejection of the feminine and its disassociation from evil.

The Answer to Job: Jung and John

The first answer to Job, in Jung's analysis, was the Incarnation, an expression of God's loving side. But evil was split off from God. A second answer to Job will have to account for the sufferings of the human condition. As one analyst summarized Jung's thought: "The religious task now is to prepare for the next development, which is the incarnation and integration of God's dark side."[38]

Beyond the technical discussion of whether Jung was speaking of God or human consciousness, or both, and beyond complaints about Jung's theology, one can hear in Jung's writings an aggrieved cry on behalf of humanity. How and why does humanity live with such immense suffering?

John of the Cross has his own answer to Job, or perhaps to Jung, which also comes from powerfully moving human experience. His answer was found in a trusting entry into the dark of the human condition, and there facing humanity's responsibility for its selfish, sinful living in this world. In the dark, too, John challenges humanity to come to terms with its reality. In the dark humanity reaches its limits, the boundaries of its condition, and learns there that it has no resource within itself to change the condition, heal its estrangements, forgive its sins, renew its hopes, or comprehend its suffering. In the night humanity knows its poverty.

But John of the Cross experienced more than his misery and humanity's limits. In the core of his suffering, at the heart of his pain, he experienced a graciousness which sustained him and walked with him. This love which awaited him in the night was beyond the sinful and tragic in life, and beyond the exhaustion of men and women to save themselves. In this "dark love" he found a knowledge of himself and this world which did embrace the tragic, and he found a will for this world which gathered up the desires of humankind into its own desire. This God was beyond light and beyond dark, and past unknowing.

John's answer to Job lies not in the ultimate reconciliation of opposites in a heightened consciousness which would then somehow be able to locate the source of suffering and evil in God. John's answer to our suffering is Jesus' answer: to bear the suffering trusting in the dark, incomprehensible love of God.

Robert Doran articulates the Christian response: "In this voluntary acceptance of innocent suffering—what in Christ we call the law of the cross—evil loses its power, and we are elevated into a relationship beyond the perfect symmetry of nature's finest achievements."[39]

The ambiguity of being human, the contradictory experiences within God's creation, are burned to a single vision and heart. John's submission to Mystery brought him through paradox to a oneness with God whom John affirmed was wise, merciful, loving, just.

Humanity is not subject to a cruel God. It is subject, at times, to incomprehensible suffering and, at times, to a cruel humanity. It is this humanity's destiny to be transformed into a participation with God and a life fired with a Spirit who simultaneously fuels humanity's journey, and waits ahead.

In the experience of John of the Cross, this dark love of God found expression in human image and word which sought to express the dark, earthy, sensual, affective and, yes, feminine reality, both of humanity and of God.

A Societal Dark Night

We are aware of the communal nature of our lives. Our psyches open to collective levels where we share life with our brothers and sisters. And we live in societal networks where each affects the other.

One person's dark night experience may be conditioned by society's influence, and its lack of health. At times a whole people may be undergoing together invitations to live their conditions with a faith that is open to the transforming love of God. It is not just the difficult time which announces the dark night; it is the attentiveness to God in such conditions which allows the darkness to be a night of faith.

Liberation theologians, from the heart of the experience of their people, write about the communal night of suffering and injustice. For example, Gustavo Gutierrez writes:

> The passage through what has been called "the dark night" of injustice is part of the spiritual journey in Latin America. On this journey of an entire people toward its liberation through the desert of structural and organized injustice that surrounds us . . . it is very important to persevere in prayer, even if we hardly do more than stammer groans and cries, while in this

struggle the image of God in us is purified in an extraordinary "dark night."[40]

The struggles in Central and South America situate the experience of the dark night in the context of mission. The very effort of liberation may lead to impasses which drive the church to a deeper spirituality. Such nights purify and challenge the church to continue efforts to alleviate conditions, even when sociopolitical realities appear impervious to change.

It is this transformed humanity whose living is in cooperation with the coming Kingdom of God. Doran writes: "The requirement for peace and justice in our world is still the same as it always has been; accepting the divinely originated solution to the problem of evil that comes to us in Christ Jesus; allowing God to transform us into agents of love and justice and reconciliation; and *bearing the suffering* that the powers of evil will unleash on us because of our option."[41]

The dark night of Thérèse of Lisieux, in the opinion of William Thompson, gave her an understanding of the mystery of love in Jesus' life, suffering, and death. Her own night taught her "something of the *broken* and even martyrdom-producing love of Jesus which stretched him out beyond himself and his intimates to all, unknown, unintimate, unwanted, and even sinners."[42]

The Purification of the Church

The nights of its mystics, and the nights of its struggles for justice, also purify the church. Thompson and Harvey Egan note how John of the Cross, guided by no light other than "the one that burned in my heart," balanced a profound interior attention to the Divine, with counsels to follow Christ in his church and ministers. The night did not separate the mystic from ecclesial life, but allowed a participation which assisted in transforming the church. In the case of Teresa of Avila and John of the Cross, the reform began with their own religious community.

For people in the churches of North America and Europe there has been an experience of a night of faith. For many people the churches are no longer adequate containers for the desires of their hearts. The teachings of Christianity often do not seem relevant to adults. Meaning has evaporated. "What has this to do with me?" they ask. Their lives are not addressed by the churches. And so they find themselves "outside" the church, even if still "within" as a member, in the darkness of meaninglessness.

The "night of the spirit" image is not too strong to apply to those who formerly found identity and vision in the church and now stumble in darkness. Their plight was apparent to Carl Jung. He wrote: "I am not . . . addressing myself to the happy possessors of faith, but to those many people for whom the light has gone out, the mystery has faded, and God is dead."[43]

Karl Rahner observed that one of the most common "mystical" experiences today is found in the lives of those who get up in the morning and who go on through the day, but who can give themselves no good reason. Explicitly or implicitly they accept a Presence offered within their unknowing.

Telling the Story

I do not think the night of the spirit of many contemporary people is due to the fact that the church has nothing to say. But just as a God-image dies so that a new image may be reborn, so too the way the Christian Story has been told in the recent past perhaps has to die and the Story has to be retold in a way which will engage people's lives. We need to hear the Story and recognize ourselves in it. It is *our* story as well. The night of faith purifies Christians and their church.

Retelling the Story of Christianity in a way which correlates with human experience is not the whole solution. The night also reveals human limitations and sinfulness. These conditions affect the individual's relationship to God and the Christian symbols. Personal and communal conversions are also required so that a people may be open to hearing the Story. New symbols, and new ways of relating to traditional symbols can be the outcome of our contemporary nights. People need to be purified of old gods, and symbols need to be purified of distorted meanings.

The Dark Night Results in a Loving Humanity

Bernard Lonergan's understanding of the human spirit suggests that we never find a final place of complete meaning and heart's fulfillment. But along the way certain plateaus are reached, and the tendency is to rest with meanings, values, identity, now in place. The constant quest of the human spirit, or, God's love driving us into consciousness, will eventually bring about a dissatisfaction, a dis-ease with the status quo. The light of certainty will begin to dim.

The intensity of the night varies. Hence, perhaps, John's delineation of two "nights" or two phases of the night. The second night is much more radical, and appears deeper than even dying God-images. It is no longer a question of a lack of consciousness, or more appropriate images and understandings, but the very limitations of life itself are faced. It is a powerful sense of God's transcendence, the infinity in our bones, the impossibility of life, no matter what the human development, to finally and fully satisfy life's promise. The experience of God's love is a dark education for the soul.

In the light of that love, the soul's distance from the self, others, and God is manifest, and its essential powerlessness is accepted. In the depth of the night the human is finally weaned from life as nourishment and is deeply aware of the mystery of God as the only true nourishment, the One who finally and fully satisfies.

At this point Teresa of Avila found her mortal life a hindrance and source of suffering. She wanted to die and get it over with; get over the suffering she experienced in the knowledge of her sinfulness, and get over the distance between herself and God. John of the Cross complained that God's messengers were no substitute for the reality and he asked that the veil be torn.

But this condition was not final for them in this life. As John expressed in *The Living Flame of Love*, peace and joy return to the human in the experience of the night. Still alive, still within the human condition, the person now lives solely for God's will, and is free of particular desires to live or die.

Teresa wrote in the seventh dwelling place,

> You have already seen the trials and afflictions these souls have experienced in order to die so as to enjoy our Lord. What surprises me most of all now is that they have just as great a desire to serve Him and that through them He be praised and that they may benefit some soul if they can. For not only do they not desire to die but they desire to live very many years suffering the greatest trials if through these they can help that the Lord be praised, even though in something very small. . . . (The soul) has no more fear of death than it would of a gentle rapture. The fact is that He who gave those desires that were so excessive a torment now gives these others. May He be always blessed and praised.[44]

John wrote that those who die of love die differently. On the climb up the ladder of love, the night removes from us the burden of intention and motivation, and we simply love. The intention has passed into God, and we live God's intention for this world.

A Final Commentary

The dark night of the spirit we have been discussing is part of the lifelong pilgrimage John details in his commentaries. This night of the spirit is a prelude to the dawn of union with God, which John described in *The Living Flame of Love*.

The next, and final, chapter presents John's commentary *The Spiritual Canticle*. In this work the entire pilgrimage is once again described. It serves as a fitting overview of the preceding chapters.

THE SPIRITUAL CANTICLE

1. Where have You hidden,
Beloved, and left me moaning?
You fled like the stag
After wounding me;
I went out calling You, and You were gone.

2. Shepherds, you that go
Up through the sheepfolds to the hill,
If by chance you see
Him I love most,
Tell Him that I sicken, suffer, and die.

3. Seeking my Love
I will head for the mountains and for watersides,
I will not gather flowers,
Nor fear wild beasts;
I will go beyond strong men and frontiers.

4. O woods and thickets
Planted by the hand of my Beloved!
O green meadow,
Coated, bright, with flowers,
Tell me, has He passed by you?

5. Pouring out a thousand graces,
He passed these groves in haste;
And having looked at them,
With His image alone,
Clothed them in beauty.

6. Ah, who has the power to heal me?
Now wholly surrender Yourself!
Do not send me
Any more messengers,
They cannot tell me what I must hear.

7. All who are free
Tell me a thousand graceful things of You;
All wound me more
And leave me dying
Of, ah, I-don't-know-what behind their stammering.

8. How do you endure
O life, not living where you live?
And being brought near death
By the arrows you received
From that which you conceive of your Beloved.

9. Why, since You wounded
This heart, don't You heal it?
And why, since You stole it from me,
Do You leave it so,
And fail to carry off what You have stolen?

10. Extinguish these miseries,
Since no one else can stamp them out;
And may my eyes behold You,
Because You are their light,
And I would open them to You alone.

11. Reveal Your presence,
And may the vision of Your beauty be my death;
For the sickness of love
Is not cured
Except by Your very presence and image.

12. O spring like crystal!
If only, on your silvered-over face,
You would suddenly form
The eyes I have desired,
Which I bear sketched deep within my heart.

13. Withdraw them, Beloved,
I am taking flight!
(Bridegroom) Return, dove,
The wounded stag
Is in sight on the hill,
Cooled by the breeze of your flight.

14. (Bride) My beloved is the mountains,
And lonely wooded valleys,
Strange islands,
And resounding rivers,
The whistling of love-stirring breezes,

15. The tranquil night
At the time of the rising dawn,
Silent music,
Sounding solitude,
The supper that refreshes, and deepens love.

16. Catch us the foxes,
For our vineyard is now in flower,
While we fashion a cone of roses
Intricate as the pine's;
And let no one appear on the hill.

17. Be still, deadening north wind;
South wind come, you that waken love,
Breathe through my garden,
Let its fragrance flow,
And the Beloved will feed amid the flowers.

18. You girls of Judea,
While among flowers and roses
The amber spreads its perfume,
Stay away, there on the outskirts:
Do not so much as seek to touch our thresholds.

19. Hide Yourself, my Love;
Turn Your face toward the mountains,
And do not speak;
But look at those companions
Going with her through strange islands.

20. (Bridegroom) Swift-winged birds,
Lions, stags, and leaping roes,
Mountains, lowlands, and river banks,
Waters, winds, and ardors,
Watching fears of night:

21. By the pleasant lyres
And the siren's song, I conjure you
To cease your anger
And not touch the wall,
That the bride may sleep in deeper peace.

22. The bride has entered
The sweet garden of her desire,
And she rests in delight,
Laying her neck
On the gentle arms of her Beloved.

23. Beneath the apple tree:
There I took you for My own,
There I offered you My hand,
And restored you,
Where your mother was corrupted.

24. (Bride) Our bed is in flower,
Bound round with linking dens of lions,
Hung with purple,
Built up in peace,
And crowned with a thousand shields of gold.

25. Following Your footprints
Maidens run along the way;
The touch of a spark,
The spiced wine,
Cause flowings in them from the balsam of God.

26. In the inner wine cellar
I drank of my Beloved, and, when I went abroad
Through all this valley
I no longer knew anything,
And lost the herd which I was following.

27. There He gave me His breast;
There He taught me a sweet and living knowledge;
And I gave myself to Him,
Keeping nothing back;
There I promised to be His bride.

28. Now I occupy my soul
And all my energy in His service;
I no longer tend the herd,
Nor have I any other work
Now that my every act is love.

29. If, then, I am no longer
Seen or found on the common,
You will say that I am lost;
That, stricken by love,
I lost myself, and was found.

30. With flowers and emeralds
Chosen on cool mornings
We shall weave garlands
Flowering in Your love,
And bound with one hair of mine.

31. You considered
That one hair fluttering at my neck;
You gazed at it upon my neck
And it captivated You;
And one of my eyes wounded You.

32. When You looked at me
Your eyes imprinted Your grace in me;
For this You loved me ardently;
And thus my eyes deserved
To adore what they beheld in You.

33. Do not despise me;
For if, before, You found me dark,
Now truly You can look at me
Since You have looked
And left in me grace and beauty.

34. (Bridegroom) The small white dove
Has returned to the ark with an olive branch;
And now the turtledove
Has found its longed-for mate
By the green river banks.

35. She lived in solitude,
And now in solitude has built her nest;
And in solitude He guides her,
He alone, Who also bears
In solitude the wound of love.

36. (Bride) Let us rejoice, Beloved,
And let us go forth to behold ourselves in Your beauty,
To the mountain and to the hill,
To where the pure water flows,
And further, deep into the thicket.

37. And then we will go on
To the high caverns in the rock
Which so well concealed;
There we shall enter
And taste the fresh juice of the pomegranates.

38. There You will show me
What my soul has been seeking,
And then You will give me,
You, my Life, will give me there
What You gave me on that other day:

39. The breathing of the air,
The song of the sweet nightingale,
The grove and its living beauty
In the serene night,
With a flame that is consuming and painless.

40. No one looked at her,
Nor did Aminadab appear;
The siege was still;
And the cavalry,
At the sight of the waters, descended.

CHAPTER NINE

A Mystic's Story of Our Humanity

The Spiritual Canticle

The Spiritual Canticle is a poem which tells the story of a soul wounded with love seeking the beloved. The search takes place in a pastoral setting where the lover journeys to mountains and watersides. She meets the beloved in an ecstatic encounter, and together they rest in intimate solitude.

The poem uses images and narrative from the Song of Songs in the Old Testament. But John creatively shapes this ancient story in a new telling. The poem and its commentary may serve as a synthesis of John's teachings, and an overview of material discussed in the preceding chapters.

This chapter partially summarizes John's commentary on the poem. It also contains a reflection on themes in the commentary. Unlike the preceding chapters which separated summary and reflection into two parts, here summary and reflection are interwoven.

This approach was chosen because John comments on each stanza of the lengthy poem, and it is better to offer reflections when appropriate. Also, the interplay of summary and brief reflection has the effect of rehearsing some of the earlier material.

The reflections highlight John's creation of an inner landscape for the spiritual journey. The story he tells is a fundamental story of humanity, the story of the heart seeking fulfillment, and experiencing a graciousness which is in accord with its deepest desires. The discussion also considers the effects of divinization in a humanity transformed by God's love.

A SUMMARY OF *THE SPIRITUAL CANTICLE,* WITH REFLECTIONS

The Prologue

The Spiritual Canticle begins with a prologue in which John expressly points to his poetry as the more complete expression of his experiences of God. He writes that the mystical experience can only be described in "figures and similes," just as in scripture the Holy Spirit speaks in "strange figures and likenesses."[1]

John says that his commentary on the poetry will necessarily be inadequate. Consequently, no one is bound to his explanations.

He is writing for those "beyond the state of beginners" and particularly for Ana de Jesús who requested the writing, and whom the Lord has favored.

John is careful to explain that while he uses real experiences as a basis for his teachings, confirmation for the teachings comes from the scriptural passages he quotes and interprets. And all the material is submitted to the judgment of the church.

Reflections

Since John's time, his poetry has usually taken second place to his prose commentaries. In this prologue we clearly see John's estimation of the poetry. It is the fullest possible communication of his mystical experience. The images of his poetry are the primordial words of his depth experiences.

In our day Jung identified image as the first language of the psyche. By image he meant anything which related to a psychic state. His concern was that we have forgotten how to hear that language, and how to speak it. He urged that we learn to live the "symbolic life."

The process of John of the Cross in hearing and communicating his basically inexpressible experiences of God is instructive for us today. He moves from attentiveness in the dark of experience to a wording of that experience which initially takes the symbolic form of poetry. And note that this initial wording contains no overtly religious language. His symbols are elemental. Then, in his commentary, a further step, he begins to reflect on the symbols and relate his experience to the tradition.

John's process exemplifies Bernard Lonergan's description of the interior process of coming to consciousness and living responsibly. His psyche followed the transcendental precepts to be attentive (in prayerful listening), to be intelligent (through attempts to word his experience, first in symbolic form), to be reasonable (through discussion in his commentary), to be responsible (in urging the active nights and openness to the passive nights). This process revealed a gradual union with God in love, pointing to a final precept to be in love.

The Theme

John says that his theme in *The Spiritual Canticle* poem is the entire spiritual journey, from the beginning until the final state of the spiritual marriage. The stanzas refer to the traditional three stages of the journey: the purgative, the illuminative, and the unitive. When John speaks about people in these stages he often refers to them as beginners, proficients, and the perfect.

The poem consists of love songs exchanged between the bride (the soul) and the bridegroom (Christ).

Reflections

It is apparent that the poem could be read profitably without the commentary, and that the commentary may stand alone as well. But as one writer observed, when a poet bothers to offer an explanation of the poetry it makes sense to read both. Since the poem was the first expression of the mystic's experience, and draws on intuitive depths, a reader might do well approaching the poem first, without preconceived interpretations drawn from the commentary.

The poetry reveals a John of the Cross who is quite different, at times, from the person met in the prose commentaries. The poet is lively and sensual, speaking a language of desire. The commentator can be lyrical as well, but often is quite analytical and seemingly removed from the realm of feeling.

> 1. (Bride) Where have You hidden,
> Beloved, and left me moaning?
> You fled like the stag
> After Wounding me;
> I went out calling You, and You were gone.

Summary

The bride who speaks in the beginning of this poem is a mature person who is dissatisfied and anxious: life is short, the path narrow, the world is vain, everything comes to an end and fails, salvation is difficult; it is late, the day far spent, God is hidden, and the heart is touched with dread and sorrow. From within this condition she calls: "Where have You hidden, Beloved. . . ."

The Bridegroom's love has wounded her. But he is a hidden God and she suffers his absence. The hiding place of the Word of God is in the bosom of the Father. Neither sensible gratification nor dryness indicates greater presence or absence of God. The soul is not asking for sensible devotion, but for "the manifest presence and vision of His divine essence. . . . ,"[2] which is only fully possible in the next life. She wants to see this hidden God face to face. Since this God, Father, Son, and Spirit, is hidden in the center of the soul, John advises the soul to enter within itself in deep recollection.

John encourages the dark way of unknowing. "Never stop with loving and delighting in your understanding and experience of God, but love and delight in what is neither understandable nor perceptible of Him."[3] Faith and love are the true guides.

The soul burns with desire for God since God has visited the soul with "touches of love" which are like "fiery arrows."[4] These spiritual wounds of love heighten the sense of absence. No medicine can cure them, except that given by the Beloved.

This love of God causes the soul to go out in self-forgetfulness, and to turn away from "natural supports, manners, and inclinations, thus inducing her to call after God."[5] The soul lives in detachment.

The suffering from such desire is particularly intense for those nearing the state of union with God. "For an immense good is shown them, as through the fissure of a rock, but not granted them."[6]

Reflections

At first glance, *The Spiritual Canticle* appears to be about the soul's search for God. But it is actually the story of God's search for us. God initiates the human journey by wounding the heart with love, and throughout life this heart seeks fulfillment of that love. As Karl Rahner wrote, to be a human is to be a mystic. We are God-touched and God-targeted, and hidden within the activities of our lives is this search for God.

There are many ways to tell the story of humanity. John of the Cross tells a story of hope and meaning. At the core of our humanity is a gracious Presence who loves us. Far from being indifferent, this Presence pursues us. God's desire for us is experienced in the desires of our heart. When we read John, we read our own story.

God's love draws a soul away from centering a life on anything other than God. This detachment is liberation for a heart which is easily enslaved by idols. For John an attachment is not simply a relationship with the world, but it is an inappropriate relationship which asks the world to be ultimate, to be God. These attachments, the enslavements, fall away under the action of God's love. A rigorous asceticism alone is not capable of such freedom. The experience of God's love, mysticism, allows then for the response of asceticism.

Bernard Lonergan's designation of the human as "unrestricted eros" may be recognized in John's description of the soul suffering from wounds of love. It is this eros, this desire which impels humanity into consciousness and responsible living. The Holy Spirit drives the human spirit in an authentic self-transcendence.

> 2. Shepherds, you that go
> Up through the sheepfolds to the hill,
> If by chance you see
> Him I love most,
> Tell Him that I sicken, suffer, and die.

Summary

The soul sends its desires as messengers to the Beloved to tell him of her suffering. The shepherds are angels as well, who carry messages between us and God. Faithfulness in such prayer is the key. "Every soul should know that even though God does not answer its prayer immediately, He will not on that account fail to answer it at the opportune time if it does not become discouraged and give up its prayer."[7]

The bride sickens because she does not see God; she suffers because she does not possess God; and she dies because without the vision and possession of God her suffering is like death.

John notes that the soul is not asking for something specific, but only expressing a need. Mary pointed out a need for wine at Cana, and Lazarus' sisters pointed out his sick condition. Only the Lord in his compassion and wisdom knows the proper response. John writes that in expressing its needs the soul is saying, in effect, "Tell my Beloved, since

I sicken and He alone is my health, to give me health; and, since I suffer
and He alone is my joy, to give me joy; and, since I die and He alone is
my life, to give me life."[8]

Reflections

John's symbols are the result of a psychic process, as well as a
statement of a spiritual condition. Jungian analyst James Hillman writes
of the "pathologizing" process of the psyche. Imagination expresses the
suffering of the soul through images of wounding. These images allow
us to articulate our grief and to hold and enter into the experience.
"Paradoxically," Hillman writes, "we gain breadth of soul and wider
horizons through vertical descent, through the inwardness of the
image."[9] This pathologizing process of the psyche undermines the heroic ego and opens the person to archetypal depths where the otherness
of the self and of God are experienced.

The night which disorients and the flame which burns are among
the images of woundedness used by John. Through them the psyche says
all is not well with the soul. It begins to see its real condition through its
afflictions. Speaking of such suffering Hillman holds that it "moistens
the dry soul and dries the wet. It brings refuge, limitation, focus, gravity,
weight, and humble powerlessness."[10]

The Spiritual Canticle tells the story of the whole spiritual journey.
Often John is writing about the experiences of those souls close to the
final state of union, but at other levels these stanzas speak of the struggles of the beginner. The nights of spirit and sense find expression in
words of sickness, suffering, and death.

> 3. Seeking my Love
> I will head for the mountains and for watersides,
> I will not gather flowers,
> Nor fear wild beasts;
> I will go beyond strong men and frontiers.

Summary

Desires alone will not find God. The soul must search through
works as well. John writes of the soul that "she must practice the virtues
and engage in the spiritual exercises of both the active and the contem-

plative life."[11] She must not only pray but do what she can through her own efforts.

John says the mountains refer to virtues by which the soul leads a contemplative life. The watersides, down low, are penances and spiritual practices by which the soul lives both the contemplative and active life. Both virtue and mortification are necessary. The formula for searching for God is "to do good works for Him and mortify evil within oneself. . . ."[12]

The flowers are the temporal, sensory, and spiritual satisfactions which occupy the heart and make it unfree through attachment. The soul promises not to set her heart on such flowers as she journeys in search of God.

She will also not be stalled on her search by "wild beasts" (the world), "strong men" (the devil), and "frontiers" (the flesh).

John concludes: "The method, in sum, consists of steadfastness and courage in not stooping to gather flowers; of bravery in not fearing the wild beasts; of strength in passing by strong men and frontiers; and of the sole intention to head for the mountains and watersides of virtues, as we explained."[13]

Reflections

It is interesting to note that at this stage of the journey John speaks of the courage and determination necessary for life's pilgrimage. Prayer alone does not suffice; virtuous activity must accompany words. Teresa of Avila notes that these two must always be wed, even in the inner rooms of *The Interior Castle.*

This person is engaged in life, not removed. Yet, the heart remains free in its search for Whomever has wounded it and made it restless.

It may be disconcerting to a reader who has been moved by John's poetry to find him mechanically assigning meanings to his poetical images, such as: the mountains refer to virtues and the lowlands refer to penances. It is doubtful he had such meanings in mind when his imagination marshalled images in the creative process of writing poetry. But he does use his poetry, at times, as a basis for an orderly presentation of his thoughts, which he expresses in traditional categories.

Nonetheless, as he warns in his prologue, this poetical imagery is an attempt to speak of realities which cannot be contained by the usual categories. Even his didactic use of imagery has a cumulative effect which invites the reader into an atmosphere of infinite nuance and subtlety.

Here John's imagination establishes a heroic motif of scaling heights, descending into depths, and overcoming obstacles. The journey of the ego into the unknown depths of the unconscious, and the encounter with the polarities of the self may be one level of reading in John's images.

> 4. O woods and thickets
> Planted by the hand of my Beloved!
> O green meadow,
> Coated, bright, with flowers,
> Tell me, has He passed by you?

Summary

Here the soul meditates on God's creation. Through the creatures, the Creator is known. The soul addresses the animals and plants of the earth, the numberless fish of the waters, the variety of birds in the air, and the element of fire which, along with other elements, animates all these creatures. And John comments: "Only the hand of God, her Beloved, was able to create this diversity and grandeur."[14] The heavens, too, with their stars and planets, and the angels, saints, and departed souls who adorn the heavens all invite the soul to ask about God.

Reflections

John's spirituality does not disdain this world. Through self-knowledge and through engagement with this world we come to know the God who is present in this creation. The experience of God is an experience of the transcendent dimension present in ordinary human experience. An interpretation of John's spirituality which would find no place for this world and its wonders would be a misreading. John appreciated settings such as the location of the Carmelite house on the hill of the Alhambra overlooking Granada, and the house in Segovia with its view of a wide sky, hills, and the striking Alcazar. Reports tell of John spending long hours outside at night letting nature speak of God.

Contemporary psychology explains that the entrance to the unconscious is through symbol. Something symbolic is the best possible expression of something else which is basically mystery. Jung reported that the universe within the psyche was as vast as the universe outside. The inner universe has its own sun, moon, and stars. And this world expresses itself through the images of the outer world. Jung wrote that we meet our self in a thousand different disguises on the road of life. The images in John's poetry become a language for this wider life.

Contemplating nature, and living a symbolic life, appear to be the same religious process. For Jung, religion is obedience to awareness. The mystery of God and the mystery of the self are heard in such prayerful attentiveness.

Yet, while this world does speak of Mystery, John ultimately learned, and wrote in *The Living Flame of Love*, that "the soul knows creatures through God and not God through creatures."[15]

> 5. Pouring out a thousand graces,
> He passed these groves in haste;
> And having looked at them,
> With His image alone,
> Clothed them in beauty.

Summary

Creatures are "like a trace of God's passing."[16] God passed quickly by most creatures, pouring out graces, but with the Incarnation and the mysteries of faith God took more time. All things are elevated in the Incarnation and Resurrection of the Son of God; all are clothed "wholly in beauty and dignity."[17]

Reflections

Again, John affirms the goodness of creation and the graced nature of reality. Authentic human development, too, is a graced process. It is simultaneously psychological transformation and spiritual conversion.

One can read in these stanzas telling about the soul's encounter with the world, a story of ego's necessary engagement with life. Jung spoke of the outer journey in the first half of the individuation process as ego takes its place in the center of an emerging consciousness and interacts with the world around in the shaping of a persona.

John of the Cross, too, assumes this "day of development" as the heart's desires carry it into life with love, passion, commitment. The night only occurs where the heart has been lost. The language of detachment and the *nadas* is language for an adult spirituality, at least for those who have the spiritual maturity of the adult. Such language assumes human development which has engaged life, taken on an identity, and has given its heart so fully that it is in danger of worshipping at altars of false gods.

6. Ah, who has the power to heal me?
Now wholly surrender Yourself!
Do not send me
Any more messengers,
They cannot tell me what I must hear.

7. All who are free
Tell me a thousand graceful things of You;
All wound me more
And leave me dying
Of, ah, I-don't-know-what behind their stammering.

Summary

The soul will find its heart's fulfillment only in the vision and possession of God. All else that speaks of God wounds the soul more and appears to delay the final union. And so the soul cries out, "Now wholly surrender Yourself!"

Creatures cause a "wound"; knowledge of the Incarnation of the Word and of the mysteries of faith cause a "sore wound." And a third kind of suffering John describes as a "dying of love." He says that "She lives by dying until love, in killing her, makes her live the life of love, transforming her in love."[18]

John delicately speaks of a Presence in this life which has yet to be revealed. The world only stammers of this mystery. John says there is something "yet to be said, something unknown still to be spoken, and a sublime trace of God, as yet uninvestigated, revealed to the soul, a lofty understanding of God which cannot be put into words."[19]

Reflections

John, in the prologue, said that his poetry was a kind of stammering. He could not word his experience of God in a fully satisfying manner, and therefore used "figures and similes." It may be said that his imagination used archetypal images which gave expression to his depth experience. These symbols, bridges thrown out to the unseen shore of spirit, point to the "more" in his experience.

They form a narrative which becomes John's story, and hint at processes available to a reader to tell her story. In the telling of the story, through symbolic expression, the soul enters more fully into the mystery of the self and the mystery of God; both are part of the soul's story.

> 8. How do you endure
> O life, not living where you live?
> And being brought near death
> By the arrows you receive
> From that which you conceive of your Beloved.

Summary

The natural life is now like death since it thwarts the spiritual life. John writes: "To understand these lines it should be known that the soul lives where she loves more than in the body she animates. . . ."[20]

> 9. Why, since You wounded
> This heart, don't You heal it?
> And why, since You stole it from me,
> Do You leave it so,
> And fail to carry off what You have stolen?

Summary

John conjures up the image of a stag wounded by a poisoned arrow staggering in and out of waters searching for relief, until the poison reaches its heart and it dies. The soul asks the one who wounded her to finally slay her with the force of love.

How do we know if we love God purely, or love our own satisfaction? John gives two signs which indicate that a heart has been stolen by God: "If it has longings for God; or if it finds no satisfaction in anything but Him. . . ."[21] Like a servant longing for shade, or a worker awaiting the end of the day, the soul waits for the end of her work of love.

Reflections

Teresa of Avila, in the sixth dwelling place of her inner castle, the rooms of betrothal, writes that the nearness of God, and yet the distance between the soul and God, was so painful that she wanted to die and complete the union. In the seventh dwelling place, the rooms of the spiritual marriage, she was free even of that desire. It was replaced by a desire to continue living if her life would contribute to God's praise and the benefit of souls.[22] She had no fear of death, and likened it to a gentle rapture.

> 10. Extinguish these miseries,
> Since no one else can stamp them out;
> And may my eyes behold You,
> Because You are their light,
> And I would open them to You alone.

Summary

The soul in this condition of love is like a sick person who longs for health, has lost a taste for anything, and for whom everything is burdensome. John says, "A characteristic of the desires of love is that all deeds and words unconformed with what the will loves, weary, tire, annoy, and displease the soul as she beholds that her desire goes unfulfilled."[23]

Reflections

In *The Dark Night* John tells about the experiences of one whose desire is frustrated in her search for fulfillment: life and prayer lose meaning; the person wishes the situation were not so, but is unable to alter it; the soul suffers an inability to meditate. Such signs are the effect of God's love, and the beginning of contemplation. The soul then enters the way of proficients, and the condition described in this stanza 10, according to John.

> 11. Reveal Your presence,
> And may the vision of Your beauty be my death;
> For the sickness of love
> Is not cured
> Except by Your very presence and image.

Summary

John explains that God is present in three ways: by essence which sustains the life of all creatures; by grace in which God abides in the soul; and by spiritual affection, through which he refreshes the soul.

The soul's cry for the healing presence of God refers primarily to God's affective presence. "This presence is so sublime that the soul feels an immense hidden being is there from which God communicates to her some semi-clear glimpses of His divine beauty."[24] Moses experienced this type of divine presence on Mount Sinai.

The soul asks that this vision be its death. John reports that only two visions kill: the look of the Basilisk (a fabled African reptile), and the vision of God. For the soul that loves, death is thought of as the "friend and bridegroom."[25] It will be the cause of love's completeness.

The soul may be sick but it will have full health in the love of God. The sketch is then completed into an image.

John points out that the experience of this lack of love means that one does love and can recognize what is lacking. If one did not love at all, or were perfected in love, there would be no experience of a lack.

> 12. O spring like crystal!
> If only, on your silvered-over face,
> You would suddenly form
> The eyes I have desired,
> Which I bear sketched deep within my heart.

Summary

The silver of faith covers over the gold of God, the goal of the soul. In union the sketch of faith is drawn over by the sketch of love, "The eyes I have desired." The image of the Beloved is sketched in the will so that the ". . . Beloved lives in the lover and the lover in the Beloved."[26] Here is St. Paul's expression, "I live, now not I, but Christ lives in me. (Gal 2:20)"[27] The soul's life and Christ's life are one in the union of love.

The closer the object of the soul's desire, the more intense the longing and pain, because the union is not completed. John finds Job's words apt: "Before I eat, I sigh; and the roaring and bellowing of my soul is like overflowing waters (Jb 3:24) . . ."[28]

Reflections

In *The Dark Night* John elaborates on this condition. The intensity of this desire, and the transforming power of God's love may lead to a night of the spirit as a prelude to the dawn of union.

As the soul has the image of God sketched in it by faith and love, so the psyche has images of God, primordial words for the ultimate. John's imagination has expressed the mystery of God in a multitude of God-images, and the entire poem may be understood as psyche's expression of its experience of graciousness, as an image of God.

Some psychologists argue that Christianity, because it is monotheistic, cannot provide the variety of God-images the soul needs to read its depths. They argue that the Greek pantheon provides a better mirroring of the powers of the psyche.

John of the Cross does not return to the Greek pantheon for images of gods and goddesses, but uses elemental symbols and scriptural imagery to attempt to capture what is beyond image and word.

The Greeks domesticated their gods, presenting them as idealized persons with all too human foibles. These gods were the subjects of artists, sculptors, and poets. The Hebrews, on the other hand, found themselves in relationship with One Whom they could not visualize. Unable to be imaged, God became the "great I," bound to no form, place, or ritual.[29]

In the treasury of the scriptures, John found a myriad of images and stories which are so many windows to the transcendent, and powerful expressions of humanity's depths.

> 13. Withdraw them, Beloved,
> I am taking flight!
> (Bridegroom) Return, dove,
> The wounded stag
> Is in sight on the hill,
> Cooled by the breeze of your flight.

Summary

Drawing nearer to God, the soul has been experiencing the void of God. Now he visits her with expressions of love which cause her to leave her senses in rapture and ecstasy, and she asks that he turn his eyes because her body cannot endure the experience.

God, as a wounded stag, is wounded by her wounds. John explains: "Among lovers, the wound of one is a wound for both, and the two have but one feeling."[30] God comes to the soul in the "cool breeze" of its contemplation. The soul's love entices God's love. And to have this love the soul must follow St. Paul's teaching: "Charity is patient, is kind, is not envious, does no evil . . . (1 Cor 13:4–7)."[31]

Reflections

The explicitly mystical experience John describes is an experience of God which apparently reverberates through the psyche and even the body. Such a reaction probably depends, in part, upon the psychological makeup of the individual and the intensity of the religious experience.

God is present in our everyday activities, usually only implicitly experienced. This presence can be attended to explicitly, and one can be aware of a direct, though always mediated, experience of God. And, at times, whatever mediates the experience of God may fade and all that is left to the soul is an awareness of Presence.

Karl Rahner spoke of this mystical experience as an experience of one's orientation to God. Bernard Lonergan described mystical experience as an experience of our desire for God, when all the ways of expressing that desire become inadequate. The ecstatic experience John describes in this stanza is a moment when this experience of the transcendent powerfully affects psyche and even body.

Ecstatic experiences are not of the essence of contemplative prayer. Teresa of Avila had many such experiences, and they were integral to her journey. However, for the most part they ceased, as did dryness in prayer, when she entered the seventh dwelling place of the castle, the rooms of the mystical marriage. Conformity to God's will was the goal of her prayer, not extraordinary experiences. She writes: "So there are many holy persons who have never received one of these favors; and others who receive them but are not holy."[32]

14. (Bride) My Beloved is the mountains,
And lonely wooded valleys,
Strange islands,
And resounding rivers,
The whistling of love-stirring breezes,

15. The tranquil night
At the time of the rising dawn,
Silent music,
Sounding solitude,
The supper that refreshes, and deepens love.

Summary

Now, in her recollection, the soul sings the praises of her Beloved. While God gives to some souls more and to others less in this state of spiritual espousal, John says that in these stanzas he is recording "the most that God communicates to the soul at this time."[33]

God is all of these things for the soul, so John quotes St. Francis' prayer: "My God and my all." God is graceful as a mountain, pleasant as a valley, wonderful as a strange island, forceful and peaceful as a river; God is delightful as a breeze, restful and quiet as the night at the time of rising dawn. And God is the music, the solitude, the supper.

Not only is God all of these attributes for the soul, but each of these creatures and works of God is God for the soul. "So creatures will be for the soul a harmonious symphony of sublime music surpassing all concerts and melodies of the world."[34]

Still, since this state is one of espousal and not marriage, the soul may suffer the withdrawal of God and sensory disturbances. Stanza 22 describes the beginning of the spiritual marriage.

Reflections

John's imagery describes a terrain upon which the human spirit and God's spirit encounter one another. He creates an inner geography on which he maps the human experience of God. His images and poems become a language of interiority, a language for soul.

This story of God's pursuit of humanity has been going on since the beginning of humankind. At first, simple locomotion through the African landscapes hinted at a more fundamental journey. Over millennia, language and landscapes were interiorized and became expressive of a journey to the center of the soul, a pilgrimage of spirit.

The paradoxical nature of John's imagery, such as "silent music," gives symbolic evidence of a union of fundamental psychic polarities as the self emerges in the marriage of the human and divine.

> 16. Catch us the foxes,
> For our vineyard is now in flower,
> While we fashion a cone of roses
> Intricate as the pine's;
> And let no one appear on the hill.

> 17. Be still, deadening north wind;
> South wind come, you that waken love,
> Breathe through my garden,

Let its fragrance flow,
And the Beloved will feed amid the flowers.

18. You girls of Judea,
While among flowers and roses
The amber spreads its perfume,
Stay away, there on the outskirts:
Do not so much as seek to touch our thresholds.

19. Hide Yourself, my Love;
Turn Your face toward the mountains,
And do not speak;
But look at those companions
Going with her through strange islands.

20. (Bridegroom) Swift-winged birds,
Lions, stags, and leaping roes,
Mountains, lowlands and river banks,
Water, winds, and ardors,
Watching fears of night:

21. By the pleasant lyres
And the siren's song, I conjure you
To cease your anger
And not touch the wall,
That the bride may sleep in deeper peace.

Summary

These stanzas continue to attempt descriptions of the state of union with God which is spiritual espousal. The soul asks the angels to "catch us the foxes," the sensory parts of the soul which might disturb the flowering vineyard of union.[35] She asks the withering north wind of spiritual dryness to cease[36]; and she invites the refreshing south wind of the Holy Spirit to awaken love in the soul.[37]

The soul warns away the "girls of Judea," the images of imagination, fantasy, and memory which are derived from the exterior senses, and which move the appetites and attract the will.[38]

The Bridegroom, the Son of God, quiets the soul and transforms all of its movements with his love.[39] And so the birds, lions, mountains, winds, and all other elements of disorder are captivated by the "pleasant lyre" of this love. God completes the preparation for the spiritual marriage.

> 22. The bride has entered
> The sweet garden of her desires,
> And she rests in delight,
> Laying her neck
> On the gentle arms of her Beloved.

Summary

John comments that this stanza expresses the beginning of the spiritual marriage, which is "a total transformation in the Beloved in which each surrenders the entire possession of self to the other with a certain consummation of the union of love. The soul thereby becomes divine, becomes God through participation, insofar as is possible in this life."[40] And John says the intimacy of this union is expressed in the words of St. Paul: "I live, now not I, but Christ lives in me. (Gal 2:20)"[41]

Here John explains the relationship of the stanzas of the poem to the spiritual journey.

The purgative way of mortification and meditation is described from stanza 1 until stanza 5: "Pouring out a thousand graces. . . ."

The illuminative way, the beginning of contemplation, is described from stanza 6 up to, but not including, stanza 13, "Withdraw them, Beloved . . . ," which begins "spiritual espousals."

The unitive way is described from stanza 13 until the end, including stanza 22, "The bride has entered . . . ," which begins the "spiritual marriage."[42]

> 23. Beneath the apple tree:
> There I took you for My own,
> There I offered you My hand,
> And restored you,
> Where your mother was corrupted.

> 24. (Bride) Our bed is in flower,
> Bound round with linking dens of lions,
> Hung with purple,
> Built up in peace,
> And crowned with a thousand shields of gold.

25. Following Your footprints
Maidens run along the way;
The touch of a spark,
The spiced wine,
Cause flowings in them from the balsam of God.

26. In the inner wine cellar
I drank of my Beloved, and, when I went abroad
Through all this valley
I no longer knew anything,
And lost the herd which I was following.

27. There He gave me His breast;
There He taught me a sweet and living knowledge;
And I gave myself to Him,
Keeping nothing back;
There I promised to be His bride.

28. Now I occupy my soul
And all my energy in His service;
I no longer tend the herd,
Nor have I any other work
Now that my every act is love.

Summary

And, again, these stanzas draw upon The Song of Songs for images by which John attempts to communicate the reality of transformation.

This transforming love has its origins "beneath the apple tree," under the tree of the Cross.[43] Gradually that espousal led to a spiritual marriage. John quotes Ezekiel's touching words: "And your breasts grew and your hair increased, and you were naked and full of confusion. And I passed by you and looked at you and saw that your time was the time of lovers, and I held my mantle over you and covered your ignominy. (Ez 16:7-8)"[44]

The soul's bed is "crowned with a thousand shields of gold."[45] She drinks of God's love "In the inner wine cellar." He explains, "This wine cellar is the last and most intimate degree of love in which the soul can be placed in this life."[46] This drink gives divine wisdom to the soul. Beside this wisdom all other knowledge is ignorance. "For where God is unknown nothing is known."[47]

No human affection, not even a mother's love, is comparable to God's love for the soul. God is "as solicitous in favoring her as He would be if He were her slave and she His god."[48] In this divinization of the soul every activity of the soul, its affections, knowledge, care, work, and appetite, is inclined toward God, and not even the soul's "first movements" are contrary to God's will.[49] John says ". . . all her actions love."[50]

In this transformation the soul is not even necessarily aware that she is serving God.[51] She simply no longer "tends the herd" of her own pleasures and appetites.[52]

Reflections

John continues to develop his myth of humanity, the fundamental story of our lives. He testifies to a graciousness at the core of our being, a God who does not annihilate us, but enlivens us. This relationship, in John's experience, has seasons, rhythms, and so has its own developmental path. He reveals that human development is, ultimately, divinization.

This divinization effects such a transformation of humanity that the person cannot help but live in a loving manner. Whatever she does is "for God," but, as John writes, such an intention may not be explicitly in her awareness.

Teresa of Avila reported an intimate union with God in the seventh dwelling place, but it did not preoccupy her. "On the contrary," she wrote, "the soul is much more occupied than before with everything pertaining to the service of God, and once its duties are over it remains with that enjoyable company."[53]

> 29. If, then, I am no longer
> Seen or found on the common,
> You will say that I am lost;
> That, stricken by love,
> I lost myself, and was found.

Summary

Until reaching this state of union, John recommends that the soul live both an active and contemplative life.[54] But in this spiritual marriage he observes that the soul withdraws from an active life and concentrates on the one thing necessary: "attentiveness to God and continual love of

Him."[55] It would bring harm to the soul and to the church to demand that the individual become engaged in active works, even if important and lasting only a short while.[56]

John then has strong words for those who are active ministers: "Let those, then, who are singularly active, who think they can win the world with their preaching and exterior works, observe here that they would profit the church and please God much more, not to mention the good example they would give, were they to spend at least half of this time with God in prayer, even though they may not have reached a prayer as sublime as this. They would then certainly accomplish more, and with less labor, by one work than they otherwise would by a thousand. For through their prayer they would merit this result, and themselves be spiritually strengthened. Without prayer, they would do a great deal of hammering but accomplish little, and sometimes nothing, and even at times cause harm."[57]

Commenting on the line of poetry, "I lost myself and was found," John describes how the soul who walks in the love of God pays no attention to herself or to creatures. She concentrates on the Beloved, losing herself in God, and judges this loss to be gain.

Reflections

John is not setting up an opposition between contemplative prayer and ministry. He encourages living both contemplatively and actively until the time of the spiritual marriage. At that point the soul is so united to God that whatever way one lives is in accord with God's will. The experience may be such that one is powerfully called to an attentiveness in silence and solitude, an outcome John defends.

But it is also possible that the divinized soul continues to engage in ordinary activity and effective ministry because all her acts are love and she can only live in a way which cooperates with God's kingdom. Here there is no dichotomy between contemplation and ministry. Teresa's dynamic reform of the Carmelite Order continued while she lived in a contemplative union which she identified as the mystical marriage.

It is not a question of lifestyle for John. Whether one's human experience is rooted in a contemplative lifestyle or in an active lifestyle of ministry, an openness to God in the experience, and a willingness to be transformed, is essential. John's concern is that ministry, and any life, not rooted in this relationship to God serves false kingdoms.

30. With flowers and emeralds
Chosen on cool mornings

We shall weave garlands
Flowering in Your love,
And bound with one hair of mine.

31. You considered
That one hair fluttering at my neck;
You gazed at it upon my neck
And it captivated You;
And one of my eyes wounded You.

32. When You looked at me
Your eyes imprinted Your grace in me;
For this You loved me ardently;
And thus my eyes deserved
To adore what they beheld in You.

33. Do not despise me;
For if, before, You found me dark,
Now truly You can look at me
Since You have looked
And left in me grace and beauty.

34. (Bridegroom) The small white dove
Has returned to the ark with an olive branch;
And now the turtledove
Has found its longed-for mate
By the green river banks.

Summary

    John begins a series of stanzas which express the beauty of this intimate union with God. The gifts the soul receives from God are like a garland of flowers.[58] And the church, in its virgins, holy doctors, and martyrs weaves garlands for the head of Christ, its Bridegroom.[59] John likens the strength of the soul's love for God to the love between Jonathan and David. (1 Kgs 18:1)[60]

    Because God has gazed upon the soul, and made the soul desirable, the hair upon her neck captivates God.[61] And her eye with its single-vision wounds God with love.[62] In loving the soul, God brings the soul within himself, loving her "with the very love by which He loves Himself."[63]

Because God looked upon the soul when she was unsightly with sins and imperfections, she confidently asks God to continue to look at her now that she has grace and beauty. As God loves her more, she becomes more lovable, and now God loves her "not only on account of Himself but also on account of herself."[64]

In stanza 34 the Bridegroom compares the soul to the dove Noah released from the ark to find land.[65] The soul, a "small white dove," went forth from God and passed through the waters of sin and imperfection. She found no place of rest for her appetites. When God caused the waters of her imperfections to cease, she returned with an olive branch of victory to rest in God. With a similar image John says, "now the turtledove has found its longed-for mate by the green river banks."[66]

> 35. She lived in solitude,
> And now in solitude has built her nest;
> And in solitude He guides her,
> He alone, Who also bears
> In solitude the wound of love.

Summary

God grants the soul what he promised through Osee: "I shall lead her into solitude and there speak to her heart. (Os 2:14)"[67] Living apart from all created things, and in union with her Beloved, the soul now has liberty of spirit.

Previously, nothing comforted the soul, and all drove her into greater solitude. Resting in the Lord she now finds refreshment in this solitude. God elevates her intellect, moves her will, and fills her memory.[68]

Reflections

The silence and solitude to which the soul is drawn in contemplative prayer is basically an inner condition. The soul is learning to be a "watch in the night," in all its activities. But physical conditions also play a role in assisting the interior process. Teresa said that in the seventh dwelling place she wished to either be serving souls or be alone.

> 36. (Bride) Let us rejoice, Beloved,
> And let us go forth to behold ourselves in Your beauty,
> To the mountain and to the hill,
> To where the pure water flows,
> And further, deep into the thicket.

Summary

The soul rejoices in this love, both in the interior union with God, and in exterior works which serve God.[69]

The soul asks that she be transformed into God's beauty, and that they both see themselves in that divine beauty. John's description becomes a prayer:

> "That I be so transformed in Your beauty that we may be alike in beauty, and both behold ourselves in Your beauty, possessing now Your very beauty; this, in such a way that each looking at the other may see in the other his own beauty, since both are Your beauty alone, I being absorbed in Your beauty; hence, I shall see You in Your beauty, and You shall see me in Your beauty, and I shall see myself in You in Your beauty, and You will see Yourself in me in Your beauty; that I may resemble You in Your beauty, and You resemble me in Your beauty, and my beauty be Your beauty and Your beauty my beauty; wherefore I shall be You in Your beauty, and You will be me in Your beauty, because Your very beauty will be my beauty; and therefore we shall behold each other in Your beauty."[70]

And the soul asks to go "further, deep into the thicket." This thicket is the depth and immensity of God's wisdom, and it is also the suffering of the soul which itself is a guide into this wisdom through the "thicket of the cross."[71]

Reflections

John reminds the reader that this transforming union is not without cost, and always has over it the shadow of the cross. Paradoxically, in hiding in this thicket the soul encounters the world's suffering as well.

37. And then we will go on
To the high caverns in the rock
Which are so well concealed;
There we shall enter
And taste the fresh juice of the pomegranates.

Summary

The rock is Christ. The soul anticipates entering so deeply into the wisdom of God that it will know the "mysteries of the Incarnation, in which is contained the highest and most savory wisdom of all His works."[72] The soul is speaking of the profound mysteries involved in the union of the human and divine in Christ, and in the union of humanity and God.

John writes: "There is much to fathom in Christ, for He is like an abundant mine with many recesses of treasures, so that however deep men go they never reach the end or bottom, but rather in every recess find new veins with new riches everywhere."[73]

38. There You will show me
What my soul has been seeking,
And then You will give me,
You, my Life, will give me there
What You gave me on that other day:

Summary

The soul will not be satisfied until she loves God as God loves her. She is experiencing a true union with God now, but it cannot be as strong as the union with God in glory. Then, without destroying the soul's will, the soul's will and God's will become one will, God's will. And the soul then loves with God's love, with God's very strength. "As if He were to put an instrument in her hands and show her how it works by operating it jointly with her, He shows her how to love and gives her the ability to do so."[74]

In the poem the soul asks to be given "what You gave me on that other day." The day referred to, says John, is the day of God's eternity. What was given her on that day, she wishes to possess fully in glory.

John then enters into a discussion concerning the incomprehensibility of the "what" (*aquello*) God has given her. John refers to seven expressions or comparisons Christ used to explain the "what" to St. John in the Apocalypse, ending with the seventh expression: "To him that overcomes I will give to sit with me on my throne, as I also have conquered and sat with my Father on His throne. He who has ears to hear, let him hear. . . . (Apoc 3:21–22)"[75]

John concludes that the "what" God gives is undiscoverable, but he describes it as "the happiness toward which God predestined her."[76] He images it as drinking the juice of sweet pomegranates.

> 39. The breathing of the air,
> The song of the sweet nightingale,
> The grove and its living beauty
> In the serene night,
> With a flame that is consuming and painless.

Summary

In this stanza John continues to image the "what" God gives in this spiritual marriage: it is breathing of the air, the song of the nightingale, a grove and its beauty, a serene night, and a consuming flame. The soul asks for these gifts.

The image of breathing is an attempt to communicate the transformation of the soul. The Holy Spirit, in the Father and the Son, breathes out to the soul in order to transform her. She, in turn, "breathes out in God to God the very divine spiration which God—she being transformed in Him—breathes out in Himself to her."[77]

The song of the nightingale is like the voice of God calling the soul. The soul "feels a new spring, in spiritual freedom and breadth, and gladness."[78] The soul, in return, sings a new song in unison with God. As John writes, ". . . she loves God with God Himself. . . ."[79]

The grove and its beauty is God who nourishes the life of the soul. The soul asks for knowledge of the harmony of creation: ". . . she intends to beg for the grace, wisdom, and beauty which every earthly and heavenly creature not only has from God but also manifests in its wise, well-ordered, gracious, and harmonious relationship to other creatures."[80]

The serene night is contemplation. John also identifies contemplation as mystical theology and defines it as a "secret or hidden knowledge of God."[81] Without words or activity of any faculty, in silence, God teaches the soul. "Some spiritual persons call this contemplation knowing by unknowing."[82] It is a sublime night, but in comparison with the vision of God in heaven, it is a dark night.

The consuming flame is the Holy Spirit, who brings the love of the soul to perfection. In glory this flame is painless, whereas in this life it still brings the soul suffering. The soul asks for this consummation and perfect love.

Reflections

In this next to last stanza of his poem, John once again uses the images of night and flame, images which are central to his mystical poetry. Their use invites the reader to recall the poetry and teachings of *The Dark Night* and *The Living Flame of Love*.

> 40. No one looked at her,
> Nor did Aminadab appear;
> The siege was still;
> And the cavalry,
> At the sight of the waters, descended.

Summary

These lines express the condition of the transformed soul. The soul is withdrawn from all things and experiences a deep interior recollection. The devil, Aminadab, is defeated and cannot appear in this interior place. The passions are in order and the appetites mortified, so the siege is still. The inner and outer sensory faculties, the cavalry, are recollected and share in the overflow of God's spiritual gifts to the soul.

Reflections

Through these enigmatic images drawn from his Spanish heritage, John of the Cross attempts to convey the inwardness and stillness of a humanity transformed in love. His imagination is pressed into service one more time, to tell of its own subjugation to spirit. His final words are a prayer:

> "May the most sweet Jesus, Bridegroom of faithful souls, be pleased to bring all who invoke His name to this glorious marriage. To Him be honor and glory, together with the Father and the Holy Spirit, *in saecula saeculorum*. Amen."[83]

CONCLUSION

This study approached John of the Cross with a conviction that his spirituality is particularly appropriate for adult Christians. John does not offer a program, or even a method, nor does he emphasize doctrine or institution.

The spirituality of John of the Cross is no tougher than life itself. He expresses in poetry and prose experiences of the tragic which are part of every human life. He tells of being lost, alone, hurt. He writes of losing meaning, finding no strength within himself or support from outside. He feels, at times, that even God has turned away.

John's words and images give expression to the pain and confusion we all sometimes experience. We recognize ourselves in the mirror of his writing. Mature spirits will not look away, but will acknowledge the realities of which John speaks. He carries on a prophetic ministry of "articulated grief," announcing the action of God in toppling the idols of our lives.

John's words speak to adults who have become enmeshed in life, whose hearts are scattered about the landscape, and who ache for meaning and peace. His words address the shipwrecked, those who lose the way, as well as those who live in situations of injustice and violence. Hence, the previously noted observation of Segundo Galilea: "One arrives at the mystics; one doesn't begin with them."

In what seems to be an emphasis on the dark side of life, John surprisingly then points to the sparks of new life, the hidden turning points where the flame no longer only pains but begins to heal. He sees the healing before we do and is able to predict a positive outcome. Out of his own experience he counsels patience and trust.

John raises up for us the healing presence of God deep within our sorrows. He is a champion, not of the dark, but of the fundamental graciousness of life. John writes of night, flame, and abandonment, not because he is morbid but because in the experiences captured by these images, he learned of God's love and found his own life renewed.

John analyses the human heart and its search for fulfillment. He is convinced that our deepest desires express hungers for which only God is sufficient food. But in its yearning the heart gives itself away in slavery to what is not God.

In our relationships and through our possessions we seek a fulfillment which is not theirs to give. The mystic speaks of *attachments* when we ask someone or something to be God for us, to be our complete meaning, our full happiness, the fulfillment of our heart's desire. When life promises such fulfillment our heart gives itself away in slavery. The pilgrimage stops and we settle down with our gods.

Two deaths begin to occur. Whomever or whatever we are asking to be our god cannot bear such a burden. Nothing in life is ultimate, and when we ask it to be ultimate for us we expect too much and we begin to squeeze the life out of our loves.

And we ourselves begin to die in the process. A lesser god means a lesser self; we cannot grow past our god. Initially such a relationship brings life, but then a dying begins as the heart finds itself asking too much of its loves. It becomes enslaved to what is not God, and its desire is frustrated.

John is convinced that the human personality grows healthily only when centered on God. Any other center, or other gods, eventually distort our humanity.

John encourages a relaxed grasp on life. He advises a letting go of what we are hanging onto for dear life. He counsels detachment from the idols of our life. But he also knows that we cannot free our hearts from their slavery only through our own determined efforts. We cannot change simply through an ascetical regimen in our lives.

Only a more powerful love can invite us to move from our deteriorating situation. The heart becomes free, not by leaping into an affective vacuum, John learned, but by slowly accepting the invitation of a deeper love, a love which brought us to our other loves in the first place.

The presence of such a love begins to heal our distorted way of living. Attachments, which resisted our efforts to break free, now begin to fall away. Our many loves are now reordered by this one love.

Initially, this deeper love darkens the soul. It was John's experience that the person who has loved, cared, been compassionate and committed, now experiences a heart grown cold, a confused mind, and words that fail. Far from being an experience of ecstatic oneness, God's love seems to even negate the person.

John is a strength for us; he encourages an acceptance of the dark, a contemplative waiting and listening with patience and trust. It is not a time for words, he counsels. It may even be a time to put one's mouth in the dust.

Something is being done in the darkness. John teaches us not to be afraid of the dark, not to fear loss of meaning, and apparent failure. It is a time of attending to our life carefully and not giving up hope. In our contemplation we hear God who asks us to go by a way of unpossessing and unknowing, the way of *nada*.

Perhaps John's most powerful image for our human journey is that of night. Life is a pilgrimage through a dark night. It is always in faith with journey's end never clearly in sight; one's strength is often in doubt, and farewells are frequent.

John does not mean that we continually suffer, but that we always travel in mystery. We are supported by a Presence which, paradoxically, is most palpable when we have no resources left to continue the journey.

This night is not fundamentally dark, but light. It is actually a positive experience of a loving God who is renewing our lives. The night *is* God, who comes to us now as a "dark ray." John writes, "The brighter the light, the more the owl is blinded."

In the process the soul softens. God is met as Mystery; reverence replaces presumption. The soul conforms to the first commandment: "Have one God."

The otherness of the self is encountered as well. God's love supports a self-acceptance, and a willingness to acknowledge that it is all gift. With a relationship to the true center of its existence, the personality begins to heal and function harmoniously.

Other people are now not competitors nor extensions of ourselves, but are respected in their uniqueness. The soul slowly appreciates its place in a community of brothers and sisters. John's teaching is confirmed: this world is only truly known in God.

Not only do John's insights and reflections instruct us, but the process he used to communicate his experience of God is also instructive. He models a way of attending to our own depth experiences where we hear ourselves addressed by Mystery.

John found primordial words, images, to begin to capture his experience. At first he did not use overtly religious language, but began to word the experience with elemental images such as night, fire, mountains, islands. Through these images he created an inner geography, a land where the Spirit of God and the human spirit meet.

John's imagination calls us to attend to our own symbolic living. Our most basic hopes and our deepest desires are held for us by places, people, things, which make real and speak to us of mysteries within our lives. A special place, a piece of literature, loved ones, a particular memory, all shimmer with possibility and become windows opening to dimly perceived worlds. We are reminded of Jung's comment that symbols are "bridges thrown out towards an unseen shore." They become the words and images for the poem of our lives. Through them we can only stammer like John.

The reality of the self and the graciousness of God are caught in these images. They allow us to contemplate our lives. Images such as these speak of the paschal mystery, the dying and rising inbuilt in our human development. Our deaths are noted in these markers; and surprisingly they also announce our return to life with hope renewed and strength for the journey.

John teaches that our human development is ultimately a process of divinization; we begin to share in God's knowing and loving. The story of our lives is told in God's Word. Fasten your eyes on this Son of God, John urges.

Contemplation is an openness to the activity of God in our lives, however God approaches us. It is not a question of this or that lifestyle, but a sensitive listening to God's invitation from deep within our lives, no matter what the source of our human experience. Contemplation is a willing acceptance of being emptied of what is not God, and being filled with God; John wrote of it as a loving "inflow of God."

In the process our humanity is transformed. We begin to live from an interior place where our prayer is God's prayer, and our activity is God's activity. Such a transformed humanity sees the world clearly, possesses it in God, and works in a manner which is cooperative with God's Kingdom.

John of the Cross tells the human story as a love story, God's love pursuing us into life, freedom, and a loving union. It is a story of graciousness at the core of life.

The imagination of a contemporary Carmelite poet provides our final images. Jessica Powers (Sr. Miriam) conjures a landscape of mercy, capturing John's spirit and telling again his timeless story:

THE MERCY OF GOD

I am copying down in a book from my heart's archives the day that I
    ceased to fear God with a shadowy fear.
Would you name it the day that I measured my column of virtue
and sighted through windows of merit a crown that was near?
Ah, no, it was rather the day I began to see truly
that I came forth from nothing and ever toward nothingness tend,

that the works of my hands are a foolishness wrought in the presence
of the worthiest king in a kingdom that shall never end.
I rose up from the acres of self that I tended with passion and
    defended with flurries of pride;
I walked out of myself and went into the woods of God's mercy,
and here I abide.
There is greenness and calmness and coolness, a soft leafy covering
from the judgment of sun overhead,
and the hush of His peace, and the moss of His mercy to tread.
I have naught but my will seeking God; even love burning in me
is a fragment of infinite loving and never my own.
And I fear God no more; I go forward to wander forever in a
    wilderness made of His infinite mercy alone.[1]

NOTES

Chapter One

1. General sources for this chapter: Richard Hardy, *Search for Nothing: The Life of John of the Cross* (New York: Crossroad, 1982); *John of the Cross: Selected Writings*, ed. Kieran Kavanaugh, O.C.D. (New York: Paulist Press, 1987), pp. 7–39; Crisogono de Jesus, *The Life of St. John of the Cross*, trans. Kathleen Pond (London: Longmans, Green and Co., 1958); Joachim Smet, O. Carm., *The Carmelites*, 2 (Darien, Illinois: Carmelite Spiritual Center, 1976).

2. Sources used for information on *The Book of the First Monks* are: Smet, *The Carmelites*, 1, pp. 67–68, and notes from a lecture by Paul Chandler, O. Carm., at Whitefriars Park, Melbourne, 1988. For useful summaries of each chapter see Norman Werling, O. Carm., "The Book of St. John 44," in *The Sword*, 3 (1939), pp. 293–304. Werling also published an English translation in *The Sword*, 4 (1940), p. 20ff. For a recent translation see *The Book of the First Monks*, trans. Michael Edwards (Boars Hill, Oxford: Teresian Press, 1985).

3. Teresa of Avila, *The Foundations* in *The Collected Works of St. Teresa of Avila*, 3, trans. Kieran Kavanaugh, O.C.D. and Otilio Rodriguez, O.C.D. (Washington: ICS Publications, 1985), chap. 3, par. 17.

4. For a discussion of the first Carmelites see Carlo Cicconetti, O. Carm., *The Rule of Carmel*, trans. Gabriel Pausback, O. Carm., ed. and abridged by Paul Hoban, O. Carm. (Darien, Illinois, Carmelite Spiritual Center, 1984).

5. Smet, *The Carmelites*, 1, p. 67.

6. Information on persons and reform movements in Avila from Jodi Bilinkoff, "St. Teresa of Avila and the Avila of St. Teresa," in *Carmelite Studies*, 3 (Washington: ICS Publications, 1984), pp. 53–68.

7. The location inspired another famous writer. In the spring of 1829, Washington Irving visited Granada and lived in the Alhambra, which was in a state of neglect at that time. From its walls and windows he was able to look down on the daily life of the citizens of Granada. Living in the Alhambra itself were several families who traced their presence through past generations. From them Irving heard ancient legends of the Moors and Christians, often chivalrous and romantic love stories. He recounted these stories in his *Tales of the Alhambra*.

8. Gerald Brenan, *St. John of the Cross: His Life and Poetry* (Cambridge University Press, 1973).
9. Colin Thompson, *The Poet and the Mystic: A Study of the Cantico Espiritual of San Juan de la Cruz* (Oxford University Press, 1977).
10. Ibid., pp. 65–67.
11. Ibid., p. 75.
12. Joachim Smet says there is little evidence to show that Dorian had a vendetta against John of the Cross, or that John was particularly close to Gracián. And Smet wonders about the accuracy of a 17th-century account which says John offered to go to Mexico. Smet, *The Carmelites*, 2, pp. 127–130.
13. Two Carmelites who died in these concentration camps have recently been beatified by the church. Titus Brandsma, O. Carm. was killed in Dachau. Edith Stein, O.C.D. died in Auschwitz.

Chapter Two

1. C.G. Jung, *Psychology and Alchemy*, vol. 12 in *The Collected Works of C.G. Jung*, Bollingen Series 20 (Princeton University Press, 1968), par. 219.

    Further references to Jung's *Collected Works* will give the name of the volume, the volume number, and the paragraph number.
2. John of the Cross, *The Ascent of Mount Carmel*, Book 2, in *Collected Works of St. John of the Cross*, trans. Kieran Kavanaugh O.C.D. and Otilio Rodriguez O.C.D. (Washington, D.C.: Institute of Carmelite Studies, 1979), chap. 16, no. 4.

    In the present work references to the writings of John of the Cross will use the translation of Kavanaugh and Rodriguez, and will follow this format: A = *The Ascent of Mount Carmel*, which will be followed by the book number, chapter, and paragraph number; N = *The Dark Night*, followed by the book number, chapter, and paragraph number; C = *The Spiritual Canticle*, followed by the stanza number and paragraph number; F = *The Living Flame of Love*, followed by the stanza number and paragraph number.
3. Urban Holmes, *Ministry and Imagination* (New York: The Seabury Press, 1976), p. 88.
4. Ibid., pp. 97–98.
5. Philip Keane, *Christian Ethics and Imagination* (New York: Paulist Press, 1984), p. 81.
6. Andrew Greeley and Mary Greeley Durkin, *How To Save the Catholic Church* (New York: Viking Penguin, Inc., 1984), pp. 24–25.
7. C. Prologue, 1.
8. C.G. Jung, *The Spirit In Man, Art, and Literature*, 15, par. 115.
9. Ibid., par. 125.
10. Ibid., par. 130.
11. Ibid., par. 131.

12. James Hillman, *Re-Visioning Psychology* (New York: Harper and Row, 1975), p. 140.
13. David Tracy, *The Analogical Imagination* (New York: Crossroad, 1981), p. 165.
14. Ibid., p. 166.
15. C.G. Jung, *The Spirit In Man, Art, and Literature*, 15, par. 129.
16. Julian Jaynes, *The Origins of Consciousness in the Breakdown of the Bicameral Mind* (Boston: Houghton Mifflin Company, 1976), p. 256.
17. Robert Johnson, *Inner Work* (San Francisco: Harper and Row Publishers, 1986), pp. 51–134.
18. Ibid., p. 64.
19. Ibid., p. 66.
20. Ibid., p. 99.
21. Ibid., p. 102.
22. C. Prologue, 1.
23. F. 1, 5.
24. F. 1, 19.
25. F. 1, 5.
26. F. 1, 20.
27. F. 2, 2.
28. F. 1, 16.
29. F. 1, 21.
30. Walter Brueggemann, *The Prophetic Imagination* (Philadelphia: Fortress Press, 1978), p. 20.
31. Ibid., p. 53.
32. F. 1, 1.
33. F. 2, 17.
34. F. 1, 28.
35. Hillman, *Re-Visioning Psychology*, p. 142.
36. A. 3, 39, 2.
37. A. 3, 42, 1.
38. A. 3, 42, 3.
39. A. 3, 42, 5.
40. A. 3, 44, 4.

Chapter Three

1. Evelyn Underhill, *Mysticism* (New York: E.P. Dutton and Co., Inc., 1961), p. 414.
2. Ibid., p. 420.
3. A reminder that translations being used in this work are from John of the Cross, *Collected Works of St. John of the Cross*, trans. Kieran Kavanaugh O.C.D. and Otilio Rodriguez O.C.D. (Washington, D.C.: Institute of Carmelite Studies, 1979).
4. C.G. Jung, *C.G. Jung Speaking*, ed. William McGuire and R.F.C. Hull, Bollingen Series (Princeton University Press, 1977), p. 89.

5. Donald Johanson and Maitland Edey, *Lucy: The Beginnings of Humankind* (New York: Simon and Schuster, 1981), p. 24.
6. Quoted in Brian Fagan, *The Adventure of Archaeology* (Washington, D.C.: The National Geographic Society, 1985), p. 303.
7. Richard Leakey and Roger Lewin, *People of the Lake* (Garden City, New York: Anchor Press/Doubleday, 1978), p. 121.
8. Quoted in John Putman, "The Search for Modern Humans," *National Geographic* 174 (October, 1988), p. 477.
9. C.G. Jung, *Memories, Dreams, Reflections*, ed. Aniela Jaffe (New York: Vintage Books, 1965), pp. 255–256.
10. John Cobb, *The Structure of Christian Existence* (New York: Seabury Press, 1979); William Thompson, *Christ and Consciousness* (New York: Paulist Press, 1977).
11. Quoted in Thompson, *Christ and Consciousness*, p. 35.
12. Julian Jaynes, *The Origin of Consciousness in the Breakdown of the Bicameral Mind* (Boston: Houghton, Mifflin Company, 1976).
13. Ibid., p. 143.
14. Ibid., p. 75.
15. Ibid., p. 83.
16. Ibid., p. 276.
17. Ibid., p. 277.
18. Bernard Lonergan, *Method In Theology* (New York: Herder and Herder, 1972).
19. Ibid., p. 106.
20. Ibid., p. 29.
21. Vernon Gregson, *Lonergan, Spirituality, and the Meeting of Religions* (New York: University Press of America, 1985), p. 80.
22. Ibid., p. 81.
23. Walter Conn, *Christian Conversion* (New York: Paulist Press, 1986), p. 149.
24. Ibid., p. 150.

Chapter Four

1. F. Prologue, 2.
2. F. 1, 1.
3. F. 1, 3.
4. F. 1, 3.
5. F. 1, 4.
6. F. 1, 7.
7. F. 1, 8.
8. F. 1, 12.
9. F. 1, 15.
10. F. 1, 20.
11. F. 1, 23.
12. F. 1, 28.

13. F. 1, 29.
14. F. 1, 30.
15. F. 1, 32.
16. F. 1, 36.
17. F. 2, 2.
18. F. 2, 4.
19. F. 2, 7.
20. F. 2, 9.
21. F. 2, 10.
22. F. 2, 14.
23. F. 2, 21.
24. F. 2, 21.
25. F. 2, 34.
26. F. 2, 34.
27. F. 3, 8.
28. F. 3, 10.
29. F. 3, 14.
30. F. 3, 18.
31. F. 3, 23.
32. F. 3, 29.
33. F. 3, 29.
34. F. 3, 32.
35. F. 3, 32.
36. F. 3, 34.
37. F. 3, 34.
38. F. 3, 35.
39. F. 3, 39.
40. F. 3, 49.
41. F. 3, 49.
42. F. 3, 54.
43. F. 3, 57.
44. F. 3, 75.
45. F. 3, 80.
46. F. 3, 82.
47. F. 3, 83.
48. F. 3, 83.
49. F. 4, 5.
50. F. 4, 5.
51. F. 4, 17.
52. A. 2, 16, 2.
53. A. 2, 16, 4.
54. A. 3, 16, 6.
55. C.G. Jung, *Psychological Types*, 6, par. 797.
56. F. 1, 36.
57. F. 2, 1.
58. F. 1, 12.

59. F. 3, 8.
60. F. 1, 4.
61. F. 1, 9.
62. F. 3, 82. A shift in the locus of motivation is a concept developed by Hein Blommestijn, O. Carm., in an unpublished lecture at the Centro Internazionale S. Alberto, Rome, 1988.
63. F. 3, 80.
64. F. 2, 34.
65. F. 3, 8.
66. F. 2, 34.
67. A theme developed by Daniel A. Helminiak, *Spiritual Development: An Interdisciplinary Study* (Chicago: Loyola University Press, 1987), pp. 166–170.
68. Cf. William Thompson, *Christ and Consciousness* (New York: Paulist Press, 1977), pp. 48–84.
69. F. 3, 8.
70. F. 3, 23.
71. Bernard Lonergan, *Method in Theology* (New York: Herder and Herder, 1972), p. 29.
72. F. 3, 23.
73. F. 3, 49.

Chapter Five

1. A. Prologue, 2.
2. A. Prologue, 8.
3. A. 1, 1, 4.
4. A. 1, 2, 1.
5. A. 1, 2, 5.
6. A. 1, 3, 4.
7. A. 1, 4, 2.
8. A. 1, 4, 3.
9. A. 1, 4, 3–4.
10. A. 1, 4, 6.
11. A. 1, 4, 6.
12. A. 1, 5, 7.
13. A. 1, 6, 1.
14. A. 1, 6, 7.
15. A. 1, 10, 4.
16. A. 1, 11, 3.
17. A. 1, 11, 4.
18. A. 1, 11, 4.
19. A. 1, 12, 5.
20. A. 1, 13, 3.
21. A. 1, 13, 4.

22. A. 1, 13, 4.
23. A. 1, 13, 6.
24. A. 1, 13, 9.
25. A. 1, 13, 11.
26. A. 1, 14, 2.
27. A. 1, 14, 2.
28. A. 1, 14, 3.
29. A. 1, 6, 1.
30. A. 1, 7, 1.
31. A. 1, 4, 3.
32. Ann Ulanov, "The Self as Other" in *Carl Jung and Christian Spirituality,* ed. Robert L. Moore (New York: Paulist Press, 1988), p. 39.
33. C.G. Jung, *Psychology and Religion: East and West,* 11, 1969, par. 757.
34. C.G. Jung, *Psychology and Alchemy,* 12, 1968, par. 13.
35. Ibid., par. 14.
36. Ulanov, "The Self as Other," p. 57.
37. A. 1, 13, 9.
38. F. 3, 8.
39. A. 1, 13, 4.
40. A. 1, 3, 4.
41. A. 1, 13, 6.
42. Teresa of Avila, *Interior Castle,* trans. Kieran Kavanaugh, O.C.D. and Otilio Rodriguez, O.C.D. (New York: Paulist Press, 1979), Dwelling Place 7, chap. 3, no. 4.
43. A. 1, 13, 10.
44. A. 1, 4, 4.
45. C.G. Jung *Aion,* 9ii, 1968, par. 79.
46. A. 1, 2, 2.
47. William Thompson, *Fire and Light; The Saints and Theology* (New York: Paulist Press, 1987), p. 134.
48. Ibid., p. 135.
49. Segundo Galilea, *The Future of Our Past* (Notre Dame, Indiana: Ave Maria Press, 1985), p. 54.
50. A. 1, 14, 2.
51. A. 1, 14, 2.
52. Galilea, "The Future of Our Past," p. 34.
53. Erich Neumann, *The Origins and History of Consciousness* (Princeton University Press, Bollingen Series 42, 1970), p. 10.
54. Psychologists today believe the ego is present much earlier in the growth of consciousness: "Psychoanalysts and analytical psychologists now agree that an element of perceptual organisation is present at least from birth and that before the end of the first year of life a relatively sophisticated ego structure is in operation." Andrew Samuels, Bani Shorter and Fred Plaut, *A Critical Dictionary of Jungian Analysis* (New York: Routledge and Kegan Paul, 1986), p. 51.
55. Some Jungians dispute the helpfulness of viewing the psyche as arranged in polarities. They believe such a theory distorts our observation of the images of

the psyche. Nevertheless, the theory of polarities is an interpretive schema which has considerable explanatory power.

Chapter Six

1. N. 1, 1, 2.
2. N. 1, 1, 3.
3. N. 1, 1, 2.
4. N. 1, 2, 5.
5. N. 1, 2, 7.
6. N. 1, 3, 1.
7. N. 1, 3, 2.
8. N. 1, 3, 2.
9. N. 1, 3, 3.
10. N. 1, 4, 2.
11. N. 1, 4, 5.
12. N. 1, 4, 7.
13. N. 1, 5, 2.
14. N. 1, 5, 3.
15. N. 1, 6, 2.
16. N. 1, 6, 5.
17. N. 1, 6, 8.
18. N. 1, 7, 3.
19. N. 1, 8, 3.
20. N. 1, 9, 2.
21. N. 1, 9, 3.
22. N. 1, 9, 3.
23. N. 1, 9, 7.
24. N. 1, 9, 8.
25. N. 1, 9, 9.
26. N. 1, 10, 1.
27. N. 1, 10, 4.
28. N. 1, 10, 4.
29. N. 1, 10, 6.
30. N. 1, 11, 4.
31. N. 1, 12, 2.
32. N. 1, 12, 3.
33. N. 1, 12, 5.
34. N. 1, 12, 8.
35. N. 1, 12, 8.
36. N. 1, 12, 9.
37. N. 1, 13, 11.
38. N. 1, 14, 3.
39. N. 1, 14, 5.

40. N. 1, 14, 6.
41. N. 1, 1, 3.
42. Teresa of Avila, *Interior Castle,* Dwelling Place 3, chap. 1, no. 3.
43. N. 1, 9, 3.
44. Gerald May, *Care of Mind, Care of Spirit* (San Francisco: Harper and Row Publishers, 1982), pp. 90–91. May cautions that these observations are general and psychological, and are not meant to replace traditional methods of discernment.
45. N. 1, 10, 1.
46. C.G. Jung, *Two Essays in Analytical Psychology,* 7, 1966, par. 261.
47. Ibid.
48. Ibid., par. 262.
49. Ibid., par. 264.
50. Ibid., pars. 254–259.
51. N. 1, 10, 6.
52. Teresa of Avila, *Interior Castle,* Dwelling Place 6, chap. 7, no. 14.
53. Murray Stein, *Jung's Treatment of Christianity* (Wilmette, Illinois: Chiron Publications, 1985), p. 41. For example, it would be possible to interpret images in the poetry of John of the Cross in a Freudian manner, reductively, as images of repressed sexuality. These same images, however, when expressive of a mature spirit, may be interpreted prospectively, as symbols of a deep longing for, and experience of, wholeness and union.
54. Thompson, *Fire and Light,* pp. 125–127.
55. C.G. Jung, *Letters* 2, ed. Gerhard Adler, Bollingen Series 95 (Princeton University Press, 1975), p. 159.
56. In describing this plate, mythologist Joseph Campbell enjoyed commenting that the waters here are not like the pure and sweet waters flowing from Mother Nature's bosom; these waters are like water that backs up in the tub!
57. C.G. Jung, *The Practice of Psychotherapy,* 16, 1966, par. 456.
58. Ibid., par. 479.
59. C.G. Jung, *Letters* 2, 268.
60. Gerald May, *Care of Mind, Care of Spirit,* pp. 88, 89.

Chapter Seven

1. A. 2, 3, 1.
2. A. 2, 5, 7.
3. A. 2, 6, 2.
4. A. 2, 7, 8.
5. A. 2, 7, 8.
6. A. 2, 7, 10.
7. A. 2, 7, 11.
8. A. 2, 8, 6. Pseudo-Dionysius, a fifth-century Syrian monk, is credited with introducing the word "mystical" into the Christian tradition. In the work, *Mys-*

tical Theology, he wrote of a mystical contemplation beyond concepts and symbols. It was a knowledge of God by a way of unknowing. In the darkness the soul is transformed by God's love.

John Scotus Erigena translated *Mystical Theology* into Latin in the ninth century, and it had a major influence on Christian mysticism from the twelfth century onward. cf. John Welch, "Mysticism" in *The New Dictionary of Theology*, eds. Joseph A. Komonchak, et al. (Wilmington, Delaware: Michael Glazier, Inc., 1987), pp. 694–697.

9. A. 2, 11, 6.
10. A. 2, 12, 9.
11. A. 2, 13, 2.
12. A. 2, 13, 3.
13. A. 2, 13, 4.
14. A. 2, 15, 4.
15. A. 2, 15, 4.
16. A. 2, 16, 2.
17. A. 2, 16, 4.
18. A. 2, 16, 11.
19. A. 2, 17, 3.
20. A. 2, 17, 4.
21. A. 2, 18, 3.
22. A. 2, 22, 5.
23. A. 2, 22, 11.
24. A. 2, 22, 19.
25. A. 2, 24, 6.
26. A. 2, 26, 9.
27. A. 2, 27, 4.
28. A. 2, 31, 2.
29. A. 2, 32, 4.
30. A. 2, 32, 5.
31. A. 3, 2, 4.
32. A. 3, 2, 8.
33. A. 3, 2, 9.
34. A. 3, 2, 16.
35. A. 3, 5, 3.
36. A. 3, 7, 2.
37. A. 3, 15, 1.
38. A. 3, 15, 1.
39. A. 3, 15, 2.
40. A. 3, 16, 1.
41. A. 3, 16, 2.
42. A. 3, 18, 1.
43. A. 3, 18, 3.
44. A. 3, 19, 9.
45. A. 3, 21, 1.
46. A. 3, 22, 3.

47. A. 3, 22, 5.
48. A. 3, 27, 1.
49. A. 3, 28, 5.
50. A. 3, 30, 1.
51. A. 3, 33, 2.
52. A. 3, 35, 4.
53. A. 3, 35, 7.
54. A. 3, 36, 3.
55. A. 3, 37, 2.
56. A. 3, 38, 2.
57. A. 3, 41, 2.
58. A. 3, 41, 2.
59. A. 3, 42, 1.
60. A. 3, 42, 2.
61. A. 3, 42, 3.
62. A. 3, 42, 5.
63. A. 3, 43, 2.
64. A. 3, 44, 5.
65. A. 3, 45, 4.
66. A. 3, 45, 6.
67. A. 3, 45, 6.
68. James Fowler, *Becoming Adult, Becoming Christian* (San Francisco: Harper and Row Publishers, 1984), p. 50.
69. Ibid., pp. 50–51.
70. Ibid., pp. 51–52.
71. Ibid., p. 52.
72. Ibid., p. 53.
73. Ibid., p. 54.
74. Gabriel Moran, *Religious Education Development* (Minneapolis: Winston Press, Inc., 1983), p. 147.
75. Fowler, *Becoming Adult, Becoming Christian*, p. 55.
76. Ibid., p. 60.
77. Ibid., p. 64.
78. Ibid.
79. Ibid., p. 65.
80. Ibid., p. 68.
81. Ibid., p. 70.
82. Moran, *Religious Education Development*, p. 155.
83. Ibid., p. 182.
84. Ibid., p. 133.
85. F. 1, 12.
86. Moran, *Religious Education Development*, p. 136.
87. Ibid., p. 117.
88. Dermot Lane, *The Experience of God* (New York: Paulist Press, 1981), p. 9.
89. Moran, *Religious Education Development*, p. 137.
90. Ibid., pp. 137–138.

91. Hillman, *Re-Visioning Psychology*, p. xi.
92. Ibid., pp. 69–70.
93. Moran, *Religious Education Development*, p. 132.

Chapter Eight

1. N. 2, 1, 2.
2. N. 2, 3, 3.
3. N. 2, 5, 3.
4. N. 2, 5, 7.
5. N. 2, 5, 2.
6. N. 2, 5, 5.
7. N. 2, 7, 7.
8. N. 2, 8, 1.
9. N. 2, 9, 1.
10. N. 2, 10, 7.
11. N. 2, 11, 4.
12. N. 2, 11, 7.
13. N. 2, 12, 7.
14. N. 2, 13, 2.
15. N. 2, 13, 8.
16. N. 2, 13, 9.
17. N. 2, 13, 11.
18. N. 2, 17, 2.
19. N. 2, 17, 6.
20. N. 2, 19, 1.
21. N. 2, 19, 2.
22. N. 2, 19, 4.
23. N. 2, 19, 5.
24. N. 2, 20, 1.
25. N. 2, 20, 2.
26. N. 2, 20, 3.
27. N. 2, 20, 4.
28. N. 2, 20, 5.
29. N. 2, 21, 11.
30. N. 2, 23, 11.
31. Thérèse of Lisieux, *Autobiography*, trans. Ronald Knox (New York: P.J. Kenedy and Sons, 1958), pp. 255–256.
32. Gerald May, *Care of Mind, Care of Spirit* (San Francisco: Harper and Row, Publishers, 1982), p. 88.
33. Ibid., p. 89.
34. N. 2, 5, 5.
35. N. 2, 7, 1.
36. C.G. Jung, *Psychology and Religion: East and West*, 11, 1969, par. 581.

37. Murray Stein, *Jung's Treatment of Christianity* (Wilmette, Illinois: Chiron Publications, 1985), p. 165.
38. Ibid., p. 169.
39. Robert Doran, "Jungian Psychology and Christian Spirituality: I, II, III" in *Carl Jung and Christian Spirituality*, ed. Robert Moore (Mahwah, New Jersey: Paulist Press, 1988), p. 104.
40. Gustavo Gutierrez, *We Drink From Our Own Wells*, trans. Matthew J. O'Connell (Maryknoll, New York: Orbis Books, 1984), p. 129.
41. Doran, "Jungian Psychology and Christian Spirituality," p. 107.
42. William Thompson, *Fire and Light: The Saints and Theology* (New York/Mahwah: Paulist Press, 1987), pp. 91–92.
43. Jung, *Psychology and Religion: East and West*, par. 148.
44. Teresa of Avila, *Interior Castle*, Dwelling Place 7, chap. 6, no. 7.

Chapter Nine

1. C. Prologue, 1. The version being used is *Canticle B* or the second redaction of the poem and commentary. Compared with *Canticle A* this redaction has an additional stanza (11), some stanzas are reorganized, and the commentary is more detailed.
2. C. 1, 4.
3. C. 1, 12.
4. C. 1, 17.
5. C. 1, 20.
6. C. 1, 22.
7. C. 2, 4.
8. C. 2, 8.
9. Hillman, *Re-Visioning Psychology*, p. 94.
10. Ibid., p. 98.
11. C. 3, 1.
12. C. 3, 4.
13. C. 3, 10.
14. C. 4, 3.
15. F. 4, 5.
16. C. 5, 3.
17. C. 5, 4.
18. C. 7, 4.
19. C. 7, 9.
20. C. 8, 3.
21. C. 9, 6.
22. Teresa of Avila, *Interior Castle*, Dwelling Place 7, chap. 3, no. 6.
23. C. 10, 5.
24. C. 11, 4.
25. C. 11, 10.

26. C. 12, 6.
27. C. 12, 8.
28. C. 12, 9.
29. John Cobb discusses the differences between the Greek development of consciousness and the development experienced by the Hebrews. The Greeks and Hebrews moved into axial consciousness about the same time. Greeks projected unconscious powers into Olympian gods and goddesses. It was an aesthetic projection in that the images were subordinated to rational consciousness.

    An aesthetic objectification took place; the numinosity of unconscious emotions and passions was distanced. Dionysianism and the Greek tragedy were attempts to keep these elements in the ordered, rationally controlled Homeric world.

    Hebrew critical and reflective activity was directed toward rationalizing and understanding their *relationship* to the deity. The prophetic movement of the 8th and 7th centuries was bearer of axial consciousness, although beginnings of reflective consciousness occur in writings at least as early as the time of David. The prophets and the Deuteronomic code marked a decisive breakthrough into new structures of existence.

    For the Greeks, god was either reason or a lingering myth. The Hebrews, on the other hand, existed as a community by their relationship to Yahweh. For them the essential task of reflection was to understand this relationship. Divine initiative was the key; covenant followed election. cf. Cobb, *The Structure of Christian Existence*, pp. 94–106.
30. C. 13, 9.
31. C. 13, 12.
32. Teresa of Avila, *Interior Castle*, Dwelling Place 6, chap. 9, no. 16.
33. C. 14–15, 2.
34. C. 14–15, 25.
35. C. 16, 4.
36. C. 17, 3.
37. C. 17, 4.
38. C. 18, 4.
39. C. 20–21, 4.
40. C. 22, 3.
41. C. 22, 5.
42. C. 22, 3.
43. C. 23, 3.
44. C. 23, 6.
45. C. 24, 9.
46. C. 26, 3.
47. C. 26, 13.
48. C. 27, 1.
49. C. 27, 7.
50. C. 27, 8.
51. C. 28, 5.

52. C. 28, 6.
53. Teresa of Avila, *Interior Castle*, Dwelling Place 7, chap. 1, no. 8.
54. C. 29, 2.
55. C. 29, 1.
56. C. 29, 3.
57. C. 29, 3.
58. C. 30, 6.
59. C. 30, 7.
60. C. 31, 2.
61. C. 31, 8.
62. C. 31, 9.
63. C. 32, 6.
64. C. 33, 7.
65. C. 34, 4.
66. C. 34, 6.
67. C. 35, 1.
68. C. 35, 5.
69. C. 36, 4.
70. C. 36, 5.
71. C. 36, 13.
72. C. 37, 2.
73. C. 37, 4.
74. C. 38, 4.
75. C. 38, 8.
76. C. 38, 9.
77. C. 39, 3.
78. C. 39, 8.
79. C. 39, 9.
80. C. 39, 11.
81. C. 39, 12.
82. C. 39, 12.
83. C. 40, 7.

Conclusion

1. Jessica Powers, "The Mercy of God," in *Selected Poetry of Jessica Powers*, eds. Regina Siegfried and Robert Morneau (Kansas City, Missouri: Sheed and Ward, 1989), p. 3.

SELECTED BIBLIOGRAPHY

Works

San Juan de la Cruz; Obras Completas. Edited with textual revision, introductions, and notes to the text by José Vicente Rodríguez. With doctrinal introductions and notes by Federico Ruiz Salvador. 2nd ed. Madrid: Editorial de Espiritualidad, 1980.

The Complete Works of Saint John of the Cross. Translated and edited by E. Allison Peers, from the critical edition of Silverio de Santa Teresa. New ed., ref. 3 vols. Westminster, Md.: Newman Press, 1953. Reprinted by Sheed and Ward, 1 vol., 1978.

The Collected Works of St. John of the Cross. Translated by Kieran Kavanaugh and Otilio Rodriguez. With introductions by Kieran Kavanaugh. 2d ed. © 1979 by Washington Province of Discalced Carmelites. I.C.S. Publications, 2131 Lincoln Road, N.E., Washington, D.C. 20002.

John of the Cross: Selected Writings. Edited with an introduction by Kieran Kavanaugh and preface by Ernest Larkin. New York/Mahwah: Paulist Press, 1987.

Biographies

Bruno de Jésus-Marie. *Saint John of the Cross.* Edited by Benedict Zimmerman. New York: Sheed and Ward, 1932.

Crisógono de Jesús Sacramentado. *The Life of St. John of the Cross.* Translated by Kathleen Pond. London: Longmans, Green and Co., 1958.

Hardy, Richard. *Search for Nothing: The Life of John of the Cross.* New York: Crossroad, 1982.

Studies

Arraj, James. *St. John of the Cross and Dr. C.G. Jung.* Chiloquin, OR: Tools for Inner Growth, 1986.

Brenan, Gerald. *St. John of the Cross: His Life and Poetry.* With a translation of his poetry by Lynda Nicholson. Cambridge: Cambridge University Press, 1973.

Buckley, Michael J. "Atheism and Contemplation." *Theological Studies* 40 (1979): 680–99.

Culligan, Kevin. "Toward a Contemporary Model of Spiritual Direction: A Comparative Study of St. John of the Cross and Carl Rogers." *Ephemerides Carmeliticae* 31 (1980): 29–90. Reprinted in *Carmelite Studies* 2 (1982): 95–166.

Edward, Denis. "Experience of God and Explicit Faith; A Comparison of John of the Cross and Karl Rahner." *Thomist* 46 (1982): 33–74.

Egan, Harvey. *Christian Mysticism.* New York: Pueblo Publishing Co., 1984.

FitzGerald, Constance. "Impasse and Dark Night." *Living with Apocalypse.* Edited by Tilden H. Edwards. San Francisco: Harper and Row Publishers, 1984.

Galilea, Segundo. *The Future of Our Past: The Spanish Mystics Speak to Contemporary Spirituality.* Notre Dame, Ind.: Ave Maria Press, 1985.

May, Gerald. *Addiction and Grace.* San Francisco: Harper and Row Publishers, 1988. (Not a study of John of the Cross, but a contemporary work related in spirit to John.)

Pacho, Eulogio. *San Juan de la Cruz y sus escritos.* Madrid: Ediciones Cristianidad, 1969.

Peers, E. Allison. *Spirit of Flame: A Study of St. John of the Cross.* Wilton, Conn.: Morehouse-Barlow Co., 1979. Reprint edition.

Ruiz Salvador, Federico. *Introduccion a San Juan de la Cruz: El hombre, los escritos, el sistema.* Madrid: Biblioteca de Autores Cristianos, 1968.

Thompson, Colin. *The Poet and the Mystic: A Study of the Cantico Espiritual of San Juan de la Cruz.* Oxford: Oxford University Press, 1977.

Thompson, William. *Fire and Light: The Saints and Theology.* New York/Mahwah: Paulist Press, 1987.

INDEX

Albert of Jerusalem, 7
Alvarez, Catalina, 3
Ana de Jesús, 11, 176
Ana de Peñalosa, 11, 12
Anger, 93, 94
Answer to Job, 162
Anthropology, of John of the
   Cross, 55–57
Appetites, 56
Archetypes, 59
The Ascent of Mount Carmel,
   summary of Book One, 71–78;
   summary of Books Two and
   Three, 118–135
Attachments, 72–75
Avarice, 91, 91

Beginners, Imperfections of,
   90–95
Boniface VIII, 8
The Book of the First Monks, 4
Brandsma, Titus, 208
Brenan, Gerald, 12
Brueggemann, Walter, 25

Calvario, El, 10, 11
Carmelites, 6–8
Christ and the church, 125, 126
Cobb, John, 34
Conjunctive faith, 140, 141

Conn, Walter, and affective
   conversion, 42, 43
Consciousness, pre-conventional,
   34; language and, 35, 36;
   conventional, 36, 37; axial,
   37–39; historical, 39, 40;
   Greek and Hebrew
   development of, 220
Contemplation, signs of, 96, 97,
   121, 122; and individuation,
   114–117; as mystical theology,
   155, 200
Conversion, 42, 43, 65, 66
Córdoba, Sebastián de, 12
Creation, 182

Dark night, image of, 72; signs of,
   96, 97; recommendations
   concerning, 97, 98; benefits of,
   98, 99; not solely
   psychological, 103, 104;
   societal, 164, 165
The Dark Night, poem, 68, 69;
   summary of the commentary,
   Book One, 90–100; summary
   of the commentary, Book Two,
   150–157
Daza, Gaspar, 9
Devotions, 134, 135
Díaz, Mari, 9
Divinization, effects of, 62, 63;

and human development,
63–66, 194
Doran, Robert, 164, 165
Doria, Nicholás, 13
Dreams, innerwork with, 22, 23
Duruelo, 6

Ecstatic experiences, 189
Ego, 58, 213
Ego-transcendence, 160
Elijah, 4
Envy, 94, 95

Faith development, stages of,
137–143; and John of the
Cross, 143, 144
Fernández, Pedro, 8
Fontiveros, 3
Fowler, James, and faith
development, 136–143
Freud, Sigmund, and images of
God, 137
Friendship, 93

Galilea, Segundo, 85
Garcilaso de la Vega, 12
Gluttony, spiritual, 94
God-image, 61, 62
Gods die, when, 112, 113
Gracián, Jerónimo, 11, 13
Granada, 11
Gregson, Vernon, and psychic
conversion, 42
Guttierez, Gustavo, 85, 164

Hillman, James, 18, 147, 148, 180
Human development, "day" of,
86–88
Humans, the earliest, 31–33;
modern, 33

Ignatius of Loyola, 9
Iliad, 38, 39

Imagination, 15–17; as faculty, 16
Imitation of Christ, 75, 81, 82
Individuating-reflexive faith, 139,
140
Individuation, and contemplation,
114–117
Inflation, 105, 106
Innerwork of John of the Cross,
22–28
Innocent IV, 7
Intellect, 56; active night of,
118–128
Intuitive-projective faith, 138

Jaynes, Julian, 21, 37, 38
Job, 162, 163
Johanson, Donald, 31, 32
John of Avila, 9
Johnson, Robert, 22
Jung, Carl, 17, 20, 34; model of
the psyche, 57–59; passion of
the ego, 84; journey into
consciousness, 87, 88; shift to
inner orientation, 103; and
John of the Cross, 114, 115
Justice, and asceticism, 85

Knowledge, John's theory of, 124.

Lane, Dermot, 144
Lascaux Cave, 33
Leakey, Mary, 32
Leakey, Richard, 33
Levinson, Daniel, 100
The Living Flame of Love, poem,
44; summary of commentary,
46–55
Lonergan, Bernard, and
transcendental precepts, 40, 41,
177; and conversion, 42, 65, 66

"Lucy," 31
Lust, spiritual, 92, 93

May, Gerald, 161
Medina del Campo, 3
Memory, 56; active night of,
    128–130
Moran, Gabriel, 138, 140, 142,
    143, 146
Mount Carmel, 4, 6
Mystical experience, 189
Mystical theology, as
    contemplation, 155, 200
Mythic-literal faith, 138, 139

Neumann, Erich, 87
Nicholas the Frenchman, 7

Odyssey, 38, 39
Ormaneto, Nicholás, 10

Passions, 56, 57
Persona, 88; a religious, 101, 102;
    regressive restoration of, 106,
    107
Perverted self, 84, 85
Philip II, 8, 10
Pilgrimage, 133
Pius V, 8
Places of prayer, 133, 134
Preachers, 135
Pride, 91
Primal faith, 137, 138
Projections, 158
Pseudo-Dionysius, 151, 215, 216
Psyche, poetry and, 17, 18; and
    conversion, 42, 43; definition
    of, 58; and image, 147, 148

Rahner, Karl, 178
Religious experience, 144–146

Ribot, Philip, 4
Rossi, John Baptist, 5
Rule of Carmel, 4, 7

Scripture, as archetypal
    amplification, 23, 24
Self, otherness of, 79, 80
Self-transcendence, 160
Senses, 55, 56; active night of,
    70–78; passive night of, 90–100
Shadow, 110, 111; night and, 111,
    112
Sloth, 95
Song of Songs, 175
Soul, 55–57; sensory part, 55;
    spiritual part, 56
Spirit, active night of, 118–135;
    passive night of, 150–157
The Spiritual Canticle, poem,
    169–174; summary of the
    commentary, 176–201
Spiritual director, 51–53, 66, 125
Spirituality, and psychology,
    115–117
Spiritual marriage, 192
Statues, 132
Stein, Edith, 208
Supernatural experiences,
    120–127
Symbol, 109; and religious
    experience, 146, 147
Symbolic living, 108, 109, 182,
    183
Synthetic-conventional faith, 139

Teresa of Avila, 5, 6, 10, 109,
    110, 167, 185, 186, 194
Thérèse of Lisieux, and dark
    night, 159, 160, 165
Thompson, Colin, 12
Thompson, William, 34, 84, 85,
    112

Tracy, David, 20
Transcendental precepts, 40, 41

Ubeda, 13
Ulanov, Ann, 79, 80
Unconscious, personal and
  collective, 58
Underhill, Evelyn, 19, 30

Universalizing faith, 141–143
Uroboric state, 87

Vargas, Francisco, 8
Visions, discernment of, 123, 124

Will, 56; active night of, 130–132

Yepes, Gonzalo de, 3